To Don —
memories of Walpole, N. H.
From
Sid
Christmas 1964

# A
## Vanishing America

# A
# Vanishing America

—

## THE LIFE AND TIMES OF

## *The Small Town*

—

### TWELVE REGIONAL TOWNS BY

Hodding Carter, Thomas D. Clark, William O. Douglas,

James Gray, A. B. Guthrie, Jr., David Lavender,

W. Storrs Lee, Oscar Lewis, Conrad Richter,

Winfield Townley Scott, John Edward Weems,

William E. Wilson

———

### INTRODUCTION BY WALLACE STEGNER

Edited by Thomas C. Wheeler

*Illustrated with photographs and drawings*

———

HOLT, RINEHART AND WINSTON

NEW YORK · CHICAGO

SAN FRANCISCO

First Edition

Designer: Ernst Reichl

88112–1314

Printed in the United States of America

# Editor's Note

—

THIS IS a book about the vanishing phenomenon of small-town life. It asserts that small-town values are a continuing heritage, important to an age of bigness that has swept aside many of these towns and swallowed up small communities. Some of the towns in this book were primitive and adventuresome, others remarkably cultivated in the midst of expanding economies. All were notable expressions of individual vision, examples of private responsibilities fully exercised, instances of a common concern for the look of a place and for its natural bounty. Rather than smug or self-satisfied, sectional in concept or suspect of outsiders, the towns were microcosms of a growing nation testing its strength and expanding its outlook. The towns composed a national scene through the nineteenth century and into the early years of the twentieth. They are prototypes of the countless towns from which much of the continent was developed.

The book appears because its contributors believe that the community patterns developed in the small-town past are worth remembering and worth saving. The achievements of the towns in the face of adversity suggest solutions to modern crises even if their special coherence has long since vanished. The towns were episodes in innovation that met needs which continue and which untended have become social blights and dull ills. Such a seemingly quaint custom as community "bees" that helped build a New England town and a Minnesota village is worth thinking about hard as a way of transforming urban slums. The local theatrical groups that held the stage of the opera houses for more than half a century have their suburban counterparts today with quite possibly better plays and with added enrichment to many lives. The close relationship between the town scene and a man's work, as in Pine Grove, Pennsylvania, is not an impossible standard for decentralized industry, moving out of congested areas into a countryside it need not spoil. The towns are an example of a life in which commerce and education, work and pastime were in unity. An age that is split-leveled in its general arrangements of living and single-minded in many of its goals is not too far removed from the versatility of the small town to tap its values. The new opportunity for increased leisure stands in grave need of the old interests if it is not to become a national waste of time. The protest in this book is a collective cry for the exercise of personal interests, an appeal for the care of a countryside once cherished and now blighted by tourists' refuse and local exploitation. As the towns cropped up in strange places, the spirit that was mobile in the first place now has new domains to contest.

Grateful acknowledgments for help in the preparation of this book are made to Professor Arthur K. D. Healy, President of the Sheldon Art Museum and Chairman of the Art Department, Middlebury College, for his invaluable assistance in collecting pictures of Middlebury; to Mrs. Hubert McAlexander of the Holly Springs Garden Club for pictures of an old South and Mr. Bern Keating for photographs of the present; to Mr. Don Blair of New Harmony, Indiana, and to the American Philosophical Society for illustrations of New Harmony; to the Minnesota Historical Society for pictures of Marine on St. Croix; to Mildred Wyatt and Elizabeth Tucker of the Stephen F. Austin State Library in Nacogdoches, Texas for their kind assistance; to Mr. Todd Webb for his pictures of Chimayo, New Mexico; to Mr. Homer E. Reid of Telluride, Colorado, for his excellent old photographs and to Mrs. Alys Freeze of the Denver Public Library for her help; to Mr. Larry Banks of Choteau, Montana; to Mr. Bert Kellogg of Port Angeles, Washington, for his remarkable pictures of Forks. And to those in Pine Grove, Pennsylvania, Harrodsburg, Kentucky, and Red Bluff, California, who generously helped the authors in their search for pictures.

Appreciative thanks are due to Mr. Ernst Reichl for designing the book and Miss Lynda Armani for her help. And to the staff of Holt, Rinehart and Winston profound thanks for making this book a reality.

T C W

# Contents

—

# Introduction

---

## BY WALLACE STEGNER

A book entitled *A Vanishing America: The Life and Times of the Small Town,* is an unabashed invitation to nostalgia. No editor could conceive and no author contribute to such a volume without acknowledging the homesickness that encloses local history as bark encloses a tree. And homesickness not simply personal, but tribal; and not simply for a place, but for a time, a tempo, a way of thinking and working and being, a way of associating with other people and with the natural world. These twelve essays are as various as the geography and history of America, but they are all the product of love: this is not a place to read about the revolt from the village.

The nostalgia here is personal and local in its terms, but it reflects a tendency at least as old as the republic. In the oldest colonies, the homesick harked back to the old country, but once the renewed surge of expansionism began during the years of the Revolutionary War, it was American towns that served as bases and jumping-off points for adventure into the West, and because that adventure is one of our few real traditions, both the towns it founded and the towns it left behind became something more than towns—became something in the mind and memory and affections. A country which as a condition of its settlement and consolidation had to repudiate the past and renounce memory could not indefinitely escape a double reaction. On the one hand the old home reasserted itself in some-times-sentimental recollection, and on the other the new one began to demand the recording of its free and innocent beginnings. American nostalgia may often reach back through several generations, several moves across successive frontiers, as a barbershop's opposing mirrors show a fascinated boy his own shorn skull and exposed ears receding in multiple images.

But a good part of our affection for the past is the other side of an angry repudiation of the life that industrial urbanism has shaped for us. Addicted though we probably are to the products of technology, we may find spiritual satisfactions harder to come by than they used to be; we concede to natural activities, honest materials, and simple pleasures a poetic possibility that we do not find in mechanized entertainment and mass-produced gadgets. "The chief product of life, which modern planners mistakenly consider ease, is really joy," says Conrad Richter in his love letter to Pine Grove, Pennsylvania; and it is joy whose presence in old Pine Grove he celebrates, and whose disappearance from new Pine Grove he laments. He would agree—and so would every writer in this book, probably—with Faulkner's character Darl Bundren in *As I Lay Dying:*

When I was a boy I first learned how much better water tastes when it has set a while in a cedar bucket. Warmish-cool, with a faint taste like the hot July wind in cedar trees smells. It has to set at least six hours, and be drunk from a gourd. Water should never be drunk from metal.

And at night it is better still. I used to lie on the pallet in the hall, waiting until I could hear them all asleep, so I could get up and go back to the bucket. It would be black, the shelf black, the still surface of the water a round orifice in nothingness, where before I stirred it awake with the dipper I could see maybe a star or two in the bucket, and maybe in the dipper a star or two before I drank.

It is possible that human beings, an extraordinarily adaptable species, may in the far future feel nostalgia for today's chlorine-smelling glass foaming with ineradicable detergents; but I do not think it likely. And the difference between Darl Bundren's dark fragrant drink and the reconditioned sewage that we draw from our city taps explains why some of us remember and regret the small town. Whatever the statistics say about life expectancy and the GNP under modern conditions, and whatever the dangers of sentimentalizing the past, we may see more poetry, more hope of a really personal relationship with earth and natural things, in an old oaken (or cedarn) bucket than in a stainless-steel sink. And we can hardly be human without hating the megalopolitan sprawl that has overrun our authentic towns, or feeling a twist in the soul at the way a haunted anonymity, a faceless television flicker, more and more replaces the features that made us identities.

A young writer of my acquaintance, fully modern but not necessarily reconciled, and with just enough money to indulge his inclinations, is moving out into the redwoods of the Coast Range, into a place awkward and difficult for his family, with termites in its foundations and much fog in its air and few of the amenities that we are supposed to think indispensable and often do. He says he likes what he is moving to because it gives him what he hardly gets anywhere else—the feeling that it is a *place*. Too many other places have become Everywhere, have melted into the standardized streets and suburbs, flower beds and facilities, service stations and shopping centers for the indistinguishable ciphers we hate to admit we have become.

For there is no question about what we have become, or that the small town as we have historically and perhaps personally known it is a part of archaeology. In 1790 the urban population of the United States—urban being defined as any place of more than 2,500 population—was 5.1 per cent of the total. By 1850 it had become 15.3 per cent, by 1880 28.2 per cent. By 1910 it was teetering on the edge of a significant change, with 45.7 per cent, and 1920 had taken it over the edge to 51.2 per cent. Through the depression years of the 1930's our urban population increased hardly at all—it is hard to starve in a small town or on a farm, and furthermore, those homely places illustrate Robert Frost's remark that home is

> ... where, when you have to go there,
> They have to take you in. ...

But the war changed all that, and the cities began to explode again: 64.0 per cent in 1950, 69.9 per cent in 1960, and continuingly upward from there. Down the east coast from Bangor to Miami, down the west coast from Santa Rosa to San Diego, and outward from every metropolitan and industrial center, both the small towns and the countryside have been overrun. We no longer need the words "town" and "country"; we can call ourselves conurbia, suburbia, or exurbia. In what a few years ago were orchards and cabbage fields and crossroads settlements, citizens resistant to Progress pack the meetings of their supervisors and selectmen, come forward to take their lickings and retire to lick their wounds. Or they hunt for places to live that are less exposed to the forces creating Megalopolis, and in hunting them expand the forces that they hope to escape.

Hence the nostalgia of those who knew the towns before they ceased to be places, and hence the yearning of many who did not. But linked with nostalgia and yearning is a historical impulse that is the expression of just as real and personal a need. Aware as many of us are that we have grown up almost without history, we become hungry to restore it or even to create it by remembering. An elaborate program within the National Park Service conserves battlefields, ruins, buildings, as National Battlefields, National Historical Parks, or Historical Landmarks. Local, county, and state historical societies sift the attics and the archives. Publishers conceive and carry out series on the regions of America and the trails and waterways by which they were opened. The present book, besides being a hymn to lost simplicity, is one of those attempts to fix and comprehend time and change, and by discovering what we have been, to define what we are. From the graded and sterile parking lot of the present, the view back is both saddening and heartening, for in revealing how much we have given up, it reveals that something is still left; and if that something persists mainly in what Hodding Carter calls the "suspended places," then it is all the more important to commemorate them as evidence, in the midst of our uniformity, of how great our national variety once was.

Twelve other writers might have selected twelve other towns that would have reflected quite as well the variety of geography, climate, history, ethnology, resources, products, architecture, and way of life still apparent in America. But these will do. Geographically, they demonstrate upper New England, the Middle Atlantic region, the Border South, the Deep South, the short-grass plains, the Rockies, the Sierra foothills, the Northwestern rain forests, the semidesert Southwest, and the watery height-of-land among the entangled sources of the Mississippi. In age they run all the way from Chimayo, founded just after 1600, and nearly a generation before Plymouth Rock, to Forks, Telluride, and Choteau, all well under a century old. Most were settled by Anglo-Americans, but Spaniards planted two of them, and Germans one. Most are pins on the map of the American westering, which means that they can look back to, and sometimes persons in them can remember, a time when nothing covered their sites but woods or grass, and nothing marked them but scars of Indian campgrounds that would hardly survive a hard rain. However far they look back, they still look back on diversity: the falls on Otter Creek where Middlebury came into existence in 1773 never did, even as wilderness, much resemble the high bowl in the San Juan range that became the site of Telluride about a hundred years later; and neither was at all like the parkland in northern Mississippi in which would be built Holly Springs, or the hot and aromatic hills where Red Bluff was settled in the early years of the Gold Rush.

Many kinds of resources have enlisted human energy in these towns, either as the lures that drew men in or as the expedients they developed in order to stick. There is no oil town on the list, but soil, coal, timber, minerals, grass, and water power have played important parts in the history of one or another community; and even geographical location would have to be called a valuable resource of at least two: strategic position on the border between two empires brought Nacogdoches into being, and isolation from the contaminations of the civilized world was the essential condition in the founding of New Harmony. For a few, the original resource remains the only one, and so Choteau is still cattle and Chimayo is still beans and corn and chilis watered from the *acequia*. Some of the towns owe their sleepy preservation to the depletion of the resources that brought them to life; but some, like Middlebury, have shuffled with Yankee ingenuity from waning resource to waning resource, running through farming and manufacturing and sheep and dairy cattle, and bringing up finally against tourism, skiing, and the perennial spending power of a college or of summer and winter visitors. Others, like Holly Springs, have been rescued by TVA and soil conservation sponsored by the Federal Government, and still others have taken half or whole steps toward "modernizing," principally through the encouragement of factories or through tourism. At least one, New Harmony, has become a museum.

Resigned or energetic, lively, moribund, or dead, existing in their own right or as playgrounds for people from elsewhere, these are all towns that have a history, a character, and a local pride, and they illustrate most of the motivations that settled the continent. Middlebury was the nearly singlehanded creation of one energetic man, Gamaliel Painter. New Harmony was founded as an idealistic and utopian colony, Chimayo as part of a group settlement, Nacogdoches as a fort, Choteau as an Indian agency. Most of the rest were casual agglomerations of families settling where accident or opportunity dropped them, and applying to the geography and climate of the new country whatever traditions they happened to have brought along.

In nothing else is the variety of adaptation so apparent as in architecture. For, while some of these towns, especially poorer and newer ones like Choteau or Forks, have never got much beyond the impermanent shacks that marked their earliest stage, others have had a more complex architectural history. In Telluride, big money erected occasional structures of elegance amid the flimsy and temporary. In Chimayo, as in New Mexico generally, Spanish adaptations of Pueblo building practices produced an indigenous and valid architecture. The core of New Harmony was constructed in durable stone, at the very beginning, by the German disciples of Father Rapp, with the re-

sult that from its first years it presented to the Indiana wilderness a transplanted Old World face. With some modifications wrought by time, it still does. And in certain of these towns of New England, the middle Atlantic states, and the South—such towns as Middlebury, Pine Grove, Harrodsburg, Holly Springs, and Nacogdoches—an authentic and sophisticated style seeped across time and distance and in new circumstances had its effect in formalizing men's taste. The seeping worked sometimes through trained architects, sometimes through visual imitation, sometimes through such informal vendors of tradition as *The Country Builder's Assistant* and *The American Builder's Companion*. Trained architects and visual imitation account for the pillared porticos and Georgian windows of the plantation houses of Holly Springs; the builders' manuals created Middlebury churches that reveal the hand of Sir Christopher Wren, and Vermont farmhouses whose rightness of proportion makes you wonder where farmers and barn builders got so discriminating an eye.

Readers of this volume will find an astonishing amount of the nation's history scattered through it, plus a great deal more about the murders, trials, power struggles, catastrophes, and eccentric characters that constitute the more intimate lore of any locality. What might be engraved on the bronze plaque at the foot of the statue in Court House Square, the names that might be painted on the tank whose treads are embedded in the courthouse lawn to the left of the stacked Revolutionary War cannon balls— these are things that none of these twelve writers has been able to leave out, the sort of material that is both expected and legitimate. The details vary, the content and tone remain those of local antiquarianism, and all of this will be of abiding interest to those who want to check on the history of specific communities. Furthermore, though nostalgia and local piety do soften the outlines of most of these places, their authors do not commonly stoop to whitewash. James Gray is not altogether indulgent with the provincial snobbishness and xenophobia of Marine on the St. Croix; Justice Douglas does not pretend that Forks has invariably conducted itself by the Good Book; A. B. Guthrie, Jr., and David Lavender acknowledge the frontier rawness of their home towns.

But what is most noticeable about all these essays, something as pervasive as local lore and delight in local eccentricity, and more pervasive than acknowledgment of the narrow provincialism which is the other side of village peace, is a distaste for the present that amounts to a confession of national cultural failure.

The American Dream—which was by no means as idealistic in fact as it sometimes sounds in history books, but which *was* a dream, with both a material and an ideal side —may have been closer to realization in the settled small towns of preindustrial America than it will ever be again.

I do not mean the towns on the frontier, characteristically brawling and violent, or the towns of the South, where grace and amenity, though often highly developed, were distributed primarily to one color and class. I mean the Eastern, Midwestern, and Western towns in the second, third, or fourth generation after settlement; the sort of one-class society that William Dean Howells remembered in *A Boy's Town*, the sort that by judicious idealization Mark Twain transformed into enduring myth as the St. Petersburg of *Tom Sawyer*, the sort of elm-lined village that fed its sons into the furnace of the Civil War or sent them into the open adventure of the West, the sort that Sherwood Anderson loved for the way it enlisted the senses and employed the hands.

One of its qualities was quiet—and that observation makes us remember that high-level noise is a neural poison, with definite physiological effects. There are strains of laboratory mice that will die of a loud noise, and we are not so unlike mice; we suffer from noise pollution as surely as we suffer from the polluted air of our cities. Another of its qualities was naturalness, a closeness to earth and animals, an intimacy with wood, stone, leather, horn, and the other natural materials. It had, characteristically, a handicraft economy based on those materials shaped by simple hand tools. Sherwood Anderson, more passionately than any other, has recorded the ruin of that sort of quiet, natural, one-class handicraft town by industrialism, and his *Poor White*, though a somewhat flawed novel, is an important document. If we are sick in the soul, as it seems we are, the sickness may indeed have come in where Anderson said it did.

For human warmth was more perceptible in those places where one risked its corollary, nosiness; and the pleasures of growing up, the sense of confident belonging, were stronger in places where work and play and learning were all entangled as Conrad Richter describes them; where the making of shoes or harnesses or wagons, the preparation of flour and meal, the shoeing of horses, the forging of a gate hinge, even the slaughter of animals, were carried on in the sight of all, and could be learned from. As one who never saw a playground until he was grown up, but who spent hundreds of good hours playing in lumberyards,

dump grounds, stables, wagon sheds, icehouses, and grain elevators, I can join Mr. Richter and these others in feeling that play is most fun when it is not self-consciously play, but can imitate work and make use of work's implements. For all its gadgetry, modern life has not given us a fair equivalent for what, in destroying the towns, it took away.

In those towns, whatever their historical limitations, we were a reasonably natural species, in balance with the natural earth. Industrialism has made us a weed species, expanding at the expense of every other living thing. Having committed ourselves to a high-energy technology and the absolute manipulation of the environment, we have no choice but to go further forward into a termite life, eradicating whole ecologies in our course and struggling always to keep from smothering in our multiplying wastes.

And we hate it. What really shines out of this cluster of essays is an abiding, ineradicable hatred of the "improved," sanitized, pre-shrunk, prefabricated, machine-tooled life that the industrial and the electronic and the other revolutions have made for us. As we become more and more dependent on the products, we suffer more and more from the consequences, both physical, in the way of the manifold pollutions, and spiritual, in the way of the mind's and heart's peace. Pine Grove's mud-filled water system, the inevitable consequence of Pine Grove's greedy rape of its own forested watershed, is a paradigm of what happens to us when we forget that life should aim at joy.

It may be that the human race likes what it knows, and that generations never having known peace or naturalness will not miss the towns as they once were, and will approve of them as the museums or tourist traps or industrial suburbs the survivors may become. It may be that generations having no natural contact with earth, and acquiring no traditional handicraft skills, will get equal satisfaction from the feelies or the home color-organ sunsets or whatever the future substitutes for nature. It may be that after a generation more there will be no one to question, as Conrad Richter questions here, a Progress that leads deeper and deeper into a metallic, neon-lighted maze called Everywhere.

But I hope not. And until time determines these matters for us, I am profoundly grateful that a few of the old towns remain. We may need them for seed.

# A
## Vanishing America

*The stores and factories beside the falls of this late nineteenth-century painting (opposite) were the result of a town father's spirited plan a century earlier. But the original pattern in which industry, agriculture, and education were neatly balanced was already in the town's past and its self-sufficiency was on the wane. Middlebury was becoming a supplier of cities with its farm produce, a refuge for the citified, and a college town with national ties.*

# The Vision of a Yankee

—

## *Middlebury, Vermont*

—

### BY W. STORRS LEE

Saturday was market day in Middlebury—as close an imitation of the old European market in a cathedral square as Yankees could contrive. The whole periphery of Painter's Park from the Congregational Church to Merchants Row was crowded with hawkers' stands, artless displays of fruit, vegetables, drinkables, poultry and home-cured pork, islands of heterogeneous secondhand goods and chattels, delivery wagons stacked with discount wares, Connecticut peddlers' carts, farm rigs backed off the street so that tailboards could serve as counters, all besieged by a milling, chattering throng of old and young from the four corners of the county.

Merchants Row on the south flank of the Park was a chaos of jostling buckboards, oxcarts, and mill lorries vying for right of way; and Main Street was worse, choked with slow-moving teams, sedate carriages drawn by sleek spans, giant freight vans waiting in line to cross the narrow bridge over the Falls, and a stagecoach or two weaving recklessly through the snarl.

With all the conveyances, flocks, herds, and commercial vehicles converging on Main Street any day of a week during the early decades of the 1800's, Middlebury had a traffic problem that should have given a civic-minded selectman or inspector of highways the shudders. Instead, officials and their electorate alike were proud of their problem. To them the traffic symbolized prosperity—complainers be hanged. Middlebury, they confidently believed, was destined to become the largest, finest, and richest city in the state of Vermont, and only a lot of traffic would make it that. The more traders and transients that could be induced to use Main Street, the better.

There was evidence that the dream of Middleburians regarding their destiny wasn't too farfetched. The town had become an important stopover in the stage routes between Boston and Montreal or between New York and Montreal; it boasted a thirty-six-hour coach connection with Troy or Albany, New York; though Lake Champlain and its network of canals was fourteen miles away, the town was a major outlet for the wharves on that great body of water; Middlebury was the western terminal for the strategic Center Turnpike that cut over a minor sag in the backbone of the Green Mountains, bisecting Vermont north and south; and it was the focal point for half a dozen other turnpikes that crisscrossed Champlain Valley.

By the 1820's Middlebury was already a third larger than the lake city of Burlington, thirty miles to the north, twice the size of Saint Johnsbury, close behind booming metropolises like Bennington and Rutland, and easily holding its own with progressive centers of Vermont commerce like Tunbridge, Manchester, Brandon, and Castleton. In 1800 the population had been a mere 1,200, but since then it increased at the rate of almost 100 a year.

It was the shire town of sprawling Addison County and until 1808 had been a runner-up in the competition as site for the state capital. It was a mill town, a college town, a newspaper town, a farm town and trading center, a strait-laced churchy town with the largest Congregational Society in the state.

Yet despite all these boastworthy tags, it was an unimposing, untidy place, predominantly gray. To be sure, the handsome Congregational church at the head of Main Street, the courthouse and a few pretentious homes gave it a certain air of distinction, as did the county grammar school and the new college buildings to the west; the backdrop of Green Mountains across the valley and Mount Nebo—Chipman Hill—rising abruptly above Washington Street, provided a pleasant setting.

But everything was haphazard. There had been no planning in the street layout; lanes angled off in all directions; dismal alleyways separated stately brick residences from ramshackle shops and manufactories; and though it was a relatively youthful village, the rough seasons, the dust from the street, and the smoke from a dozen belching factory chimneys had given it a weathered look. It hadn't yet acquired the appearance of solid permanence. It was cramped and crowded, as if every proprietor of a store or mill had considered it essential that his establishment be planted on the steep banks of Otter Creek within a hundred yards of the roaring falls.

In addition to the other singularities, Middlebury was also a one-man town—Gamaliel Painter's town. Frequently in those early years people overlooked the chartered title and called it Painter's Falls or Painter's Mills. And with good reason. To him alone could be attributed the plan and placement of the courthouse on the upper edge of the park. The park or village green itself was one of his gifts. The Congregational church was the product of his mediation and, in large measure, his philanthropy.

He had promoted the founding of the Addison County Grammar School and the college. The spacious frame residence adjacent to the courthouse—the finest home in town—was his. In fact, the whole industrial complex at the Falls had to be credited to Painter; the factories and stores were built on land he once owned; not only the type of town it had become, but its location was due to his personal pleadings and machinations.

Painter died in 1819, but the community continued to thrive on what he had given it. The story of early Middlebury was Painter's story, though he could hardly be blamed for the tardiness in its settlement. Compared to other Vermont villages with which Middlebury was competing for industrial and intellectual prowess in the 1820's, '30's and '40's, it had been a very slow starter. More than twenty years elapsed between the 1761 date of its royal charter and the period when it began to show signs of permanent development.

Middlebury had been one of those abortive "Grant" towns sold by Governor Benning Wentworth of New Hampshire, Harvard 1715, Surveyor of His Majesty's Woods in North America, and the most colossal swindler in the British colonies. Not content with a domain of 9,000 square miles that he had wheedled from Massachusetts to convert into a province called New Hampshire, nor yet content with all the boodle he acquired as Surveyor of His Majesty's Woods, Wentworth surreptitiously extended his realty claims westward to include another 9,000 square miles, for which he hadn't the slightest legal or seignorial title.

Specifically the Connecticut River was the western boundary of New Hampshire. Wentworth jumped the river, moved his border a hundred miles into New York, dubbed the usurped territory "The New Hampshire Grants" and proceeded to sell off whole plots of it to gullible Connecticut Yankees on a come-and-take-it basis. Sixty-three restless adventurers and speculators from around Salisbury, Connecticut, gained title to the Middlebury Grant on November 2, 1761, and then carelessly overlooked the clause in the charter which decreed that every grantee, by 1766, was obliged to clear, plant, and cultivate five acres for every fifty he owned.

For years the proprietors held regular Middlebury town meetings—not in Middlebury, but at John Everts' Tavern in Salisbury, Connecticut, where over the well-filled cups they laid plans for moving to northern New England. But it was all talk; none of them moved. Wentworth's swindle

*The legacy of farmers and tradesmen, Middlebury's Congregational Church was
inspired by the architecture of Sir Christopher Wren and by New England pride.
It was built between 1805 and 1809 with community-wide labor and support.*

meantime was uncovered in London. He was summarily removed from office and the Grant lands restored to New York.

No one called a Yankee liked being taken in. The proprietors resolutely maintained that they had paid good cash for territory in New Hampshire, and, by cracky, they were going to hold on to it—in New Hampshire. Grantees in scores of other towns in the disputed area were likeminded. Under the leadership of a fellow Salisburian, the impulsive Ethan Allen, "Committees of Safety" were set up to protect the Grants from grasping Yorkers, who insisted that the towns would all have to be repurchased and rechartered in Albany, New York. A pot-shot frontier war between settlers who should have been good neighbors was soon in progress.

Middlebury was situated vulnerably along the front line of the conflict. It was this quarrel and the uncertainty of the title that delayed the settlement as much as anything. Gamaliel Painter's brother-in-law, John Chipman, crack

ORIGINAL SETTLEMENTS
IN THE
TOWN
OF
MIDDLEBURY
VT

*Drawn from deeds and surveys by Cyra Brainerd*

Scale

MAX PETERSEN

*The river, because it was a power source, became the lifestream of the early factory town. The farmland along its lower banks was favored at first over the hillside at the falls (upper middle).*

woodsman and obstreperous gun-toter, was packed off one summer to look over the land, cut a clearing, and do what he could to make the town look occupied. He returned starry-eyed and excited to report that the town had fabulous possibilities: the soil was powerful rich, would grow anything; the timber was magnificent; the streams alive with trout; the woods full of game; Otter Creek Falls, in the heart of the Grant, mighty enough to supply power to all the grist- and sawmills they could construct in a lifetime. Even the mountain scenery was spectacular.

It wasn't until the spring of 1773, more than a decade after the first town meeting, that Chipman himself was ready to make a return trip. By that time he had a bride to take along and an eager recruit in Gamaliel Painter; and Gamaliel had a wife and two young sons. Together the two families made the long trek into Champlain valley, established communal housekeeping on the southern tip of the Grant, and set an example for more reluctant Connecticut emigrants. Before the end of summer a dozen other Salisburians had been shamed into claiming their property and were working on neighboring clearings. And of prior importance to all, Mrs. Chipman's father, Abisha Washburn, had a sawmill in operation at the Falls.

From the start Painter assumed casual leadership over the little settlement—not meddlesomely, not conspicuously, not autocratically. The conscientious member of a black-sheep family, Painter was a modest man, a sober country fellow. Painfully faltering in speech, untainted by erudition, he was as ingenious a jack-of-all-trades as ever bore the title. It was the ingenuity in him that made people look up to him. Back in Salisbury, farming, of course, had been his line—in an era when any seasoned tiller of the soil was also an adequate carpenter, mason, blacksmith, woodsman, dairyman, horse breeder, and general handy man. Painter fulfilled all these qualifications and more, for on the side he had acquired good experience in such diversified fields as surveying, wagon building, tanning, and cobbling. Given the time and materials, he could fashion just about anything a household needed, and frequently seemed able to do without the prescribed materials. He had the makings of a model pioneer.

Under his left-handed guidance, Middlebury flourished for a few seasons, despite frequent skirmishes with the Yorkers. Then came Lexington, Concord, and the Revolution. The settlement, less than fifteen miles from strategic Fort Ticonderoga, stood directly on the long British lifeline extending down the Richelieu River, through Lake Champlain and Lake George to the Hudson and New York. Painter, Chipman, and a considerable delegation of their neighbors were close behind Ethan Allen and Benedict Arnold when those two warriors stormed past the dazed sentry just before dawn on May 10, 1775, to demand the surrender of Ticonderoga "in the name of the Great Jehovah and the Continental Congress."

MAX PETERSEN

*Gamaliel Painter, shown in a contemporary portrait, made Middle-
bury a model of versatility and know-how, commerce and piety through
his gifted leadership.*

After that there was no hope for peace along the borders of Lake Champlain. Middlebury was the prey of British scouts, Indians, and Tories, and the route along Otter Creek became an open thoroughfare for army looters. The settlement had to be evacuated.

Except for two or three hardy hermits, it remained abandoned for the next six years. The men went off to war; their families took refuge in Connecticut. But interest in Champlain Valley was not entirely dissipated. Delegates in uniform appeared at Westminster in January, 1777, to participate in the convention that declared the New Hampshire Grants "forever hereafter to be considered as a free and independent jurisdiction or state . . . known and distinguished by the name of New Connecticut, alias Vermont." And Painter himself, then one of General Washington's most reliable artificers, turned up at Windsor, New Connecticut, six months later to help draft a constitution for the new republic.

The war was a grim setback for other Vermont towns, but few were wiped out as completely as Middlebury. The settlers along Otter Creek had to begin all over again in 1782. In the entire Middlebury region there were but four buildings left standing. Where the Painters, the Chandlers, the Evertses, the Bentleys and their neighbors had lived

there were now only ugly remnants—a crumbling cellar hole here, a lone lilac bush there, a broken sleigh, a split-rail fence enclosing nothing but briars and fireweed. And the saddest relic of all was the tottering foundation of Washburn's sawmill at the Falls. Burgoyne's raiders had missed the cabins of the Hydes, the Torrances, and the Thayers, and had given up trying to demolish John Chipman's barn. It had been built of such stout green timber that the impatient British pillagers could neither fell nor burn it. It stood erect and trim at the south end of town, a weathered sentinel of a ghost community.

The war also took a heavy toll among the first Middlebury families, left widows and orphans, broken homes and broken spirits, but it had at least broadened the trails leading to Vermont. Hardly had the news of Yorktown been posted before settlers were streaming back over them to the new republic. They returned driving herds of cattle, sheep, and porkers, maneuvering over the rutted roads ox-carts and clumsy wagons stacked high with kettles and cribs, hens and highboys, fiddles and family rockers, plows and portraits, books and breadstuff. And Connecticut neighbors came with them.

There was no time for despair or brooding over the devastation they found. "Forget the past," they kept remind-

*Pillars of the settlement, Barnabas J. and Millie Russell Myrick were typical in
dress and probity of Middlebury's founders. The painting was done in 1790.*

ing each other. They were building for the long future.
That spirit produced something close to a miracle.

In 1782 Middlebury was a war-ravaged waste; five years
later it was a thriving community, as animated as the Connecticut villages whence the people had come.

"Woods make people love one another, and kind and
obliging and good-natured," concluded the transient missionary, Nathan Perkins, after stopping off at Middlebury
during that period. The woods may have helped, but the
character, the persistence, and the industry of the townsfolk did much more. Despite the hardships, they ushered
in a kind of Arcadian existence with all its traditional rustic
contentment, simplicity, and self-reliance.

Washburn's sawmill was back in operation at the Falls
soon after the war, and a gristmill too. But aside from the
lumber and meal they furnished, the fields, forests, and
farm kitchen supplied just about everything. From the
fields came flax for linen, as well as rye, buckwheat, oats,
and corn. From the sheep pasture came wool for blankets
and greatcoats, as well as mutton for the table. From the
cattle herd came shoes and saddles, as well as steaks,
cheeses, and butter. And along with building materials
and fuel from the wood lot came maple sugar and butter-
nuts, barrel staves, chunks to be turned into breakfast
bowls, and choice seasoned oak for bedsteads and bureaus.

Colonel Chipman and Captain Painter returned from
the wars more optimistic than ever about the future of their
town. Although Painter was outranked in military title, in
civilian status he was unquestionably the squire. Chipman
immediately set out to build himself a fine brick house in
keeping with his rank, and a few rods down the frontier
highway his brother-in-law modestly started construction
with logs, then changed his mind and framed the main
part of the house in good spruce timber. In architectural
dignity Chipman had certainly outclassed him.

But Painter had reasons for not going whole hog in residential refinement. Though, like many of the early farm-
minded settlers, he had elected to locate in the southern
end of town, three miles from the Falls, the squire had
reservations about that location. The rolling valley floor
was ideal for agriculture, but the war had cultivated in him
interests larger than farming. At heart he was a Connecticut
tinkerer and tradesman—always the artificer.

He wasn't at all sure that the real center of Middlebury
wouldn't eventually be at the Falls, rather than in the open
valley. That had been the theory Abisha Washburn had
argued all along: commercial traffic would eventually make
the detour to the Falls. Gamaliel, never one to jump to any
conclusion, was almost convinced.

Then occurred a strange and unexpected event that
forced him to act. A cold-hearted surveyor general, in
checking the lay of the New Hampshire town grants, suddenly discovered that an error had been made in the original survey. The whole southern strip of the town, an eighth
of a mile wide, had been miscalculated and belonged to

Salisbury instead of Middlebury. By a squiggle of the pen the squire of Middlebury became a squatter in the town of Salisbury.

The Salisburians graciously invited Painter to keep the farm and become their fellow townsman. Horrified at the possibility of losing their first citizen, the Middlebury proprietors countered with an offer of two hundred acres anywhere within the town limits. At an anxious town meeting Painter stunned his bidders. He announced, or rather drawled, that he would "take fifty acres at the Falls," the mill lot.

Chairman and balloters alike were incredulous. The mill lot was the most undesirable piece of property in the town, utterly unsuitable for farming, half of it in a swampy quagmire and the rest on a limestone ledge, all of it on a downhill slant and much of it an impenetrable tangle of hemlock, fallen tree trunks and prickly ash. Overlooking the 50-foot waterfall, it was a gloomy, unsightly, almost terrorizing place.

The only persons who deigned to live in the vicinity were Asa Blodgett and "Hop" Johnson. Asa maintained a simple log hostelry for creek travelers on the west side; "Hop" a similar establishment on the east. Both stocked a good supply of poor liquor, which they sold cheaply to an undistinguished clientele, and "Hop", when he was sober and felt so inclined, operated a raft ferry for foot passengers. Washburn, of course, had his mill there, but certainly not a home.

Not until Painter, buying out Washburn, had erected one of the biggest combination saw and gristmills in Vermont; had cleared the area, subdivided the fifty acres and was selling land to prospective merchants at fancy prices; not until a toll bridge was built over the creek; not until 1787 when he had completed an elegant mansion on the highest point above the creek bank and invited the whole town to a grand housewarming, did his fellow citizens begin to comprehend what he was aiming at.

That housewarming party—the outdoor games, the banquet, the flow of liquor, the grand ball—was the talk of Champlain valley for a generation, immortalized by the county poet Samuel Bartholemew after he sobered up the next morning:

> This place called Middlebury Falls
> Is like a castle without walls.
> Surrounded 'tis by hemlock trees
> Which shut out all its enemies.
> The pow-wow now on Christmas day,
> Which much resembled Indian play,
> I think will never be forgotten
> Till all the hemlock trees are rotten.

Middlebury—the village—was off to a propitious start, and during the rest of Painter's seventy-six years it grew phenomenally. Every dream he created for it seemed to materialize. His idea of a successful village, blessed with water power, was the Connecticut idea—a factory town and trading center. And that was exactly what it became.

One of the first deeds of the subdivided mill lot went to Jabez Rogers, who quickly opened a general store less than a hundred yards from the mill. "Try getting your supplies shipped in by the Lake route, from New York, instead of overland from Boston," counseled Painter. "Water is the only cheap kind of transportation."

Jabez took the tip and in a few weeks had vanloads of stock coming in from Larrabee's Point on Lake Champlain: dry goods, hardware, sugar, flour, rum. Customers cleared his shelves and storeroom almost as fast as they could be filled. But there was more barter than cash trade. Jabez hated to see the vans go back to the docks empty. He needed a light, marketable product that would bring in cash at the Lake landings. "Try potash," advised Painter.

Rogers purchased an adjacent strip of land and opened a potash plant. Everyone loved him for it. Now farmers short of cash could bring in cartloads of ashes from the forests they were ravaging and Rogers' works converted the waste into concentrated potash which could easily be shipped out to help fill the demand at the industrial centers in England and New England.

That was only a start for Rogers. He was bothered by high transportation costs, particularly of the hogsheads of liquor his customers consumed. So he purchased another patch of Painter land and erected a distillery, "We had a quiet township of people," sighed a censorious spinster, "until Rogers built his stillhouse."

On the opposite side of the Creek, Daniel Foote, frontier capitalist and biggest landowner in town, was virtually duplicating what Painter and Rogers were doing on the east side. Gamaliel wrote him off as "a high-tempered, boastful man, conceited, vulgar, and highly inelegant in ye house," but he had to admire him and his big boisterous family for their enterprise. Competition was the first demand of a healthy, thriving village.

In promoting at least one industry the Foote syndicate got the jump on Painter. There on the riverbank just below the bridge, Eben Judd discovered the first Vermont marble—a treasure quarry of it: white marble, black marble, "elegantly variegated marble of a finer texture than any other in the United States." Within two years Eben and his son-in-law, Lebbeus Harris, had a 999-year lease on the quarry and a two-story mill in operation.

If people complained about the disturbance created by Jabez Rogers' distillery, they had far more reason to complain about the noise coming directly from Judd's marble mill. It was a massive structure that amplified the clamor of sixty saws swinging from gawky overhead arms as they ate into the chunks of marble. Day and night for thirty years, except on the Sabbath, the din of that mill never ceased.

BENJAMIN A. ROGERS

*Early nineteenth-century parlors looked like this restored room with period furnishings in the local museum. The girl in the portrait is Painter's daughter.*

Middlebury needed professional men as well as industrialists. Samuel Miller had just completed a law apprenticeship in Rutland. Painter coaxed him into opening an office at the Falls, and incidentally into buying a half-acre lot. Doctor Darius Matthews, twenty-three, didn't have a medical degree, but he had served a short and satisfactory apprenticeship in Tinmouth and was developing the right bedside manner. Painter buttonholed him and soon had the satisfaction of seeing his shingle displayed in the lot next to Miller's.

An up-and-coming town needed a good cabinetmaker and furniture designer, and a likely candidate was found in William Young of Burlington. Painter parted with the small lot beyond the doctor's and set Young up in business. To John Deming, experienced Connecticut blacksmith, went a full ten acres with the hope that John would bring his way the horseshoeing and forging trade. The blacksmith did better than Painter anticipated. He not only set up a smithy and stable, but on the side opened Deming's Tavern with a capacity of twenty-four guests.

One of the great inducements to southern New Englanders to migrate to a town like Middlebury was its new political status. In 1791 the Green Mountain Boys, equipped with the wisdom of approaching middle age, gave up the autonomy of their independent republic for statehood—the fourteenth state. It was all for the good in establishing confidence among outsiders.

The squire himself figured he had done so well on fifty local acres that he could afford a gamble at higher stakes in northern Vermont. If he were going to speculate, he would speculate in a big way—in thousands, in tens of thousands of acres. He purchased vast areas throughout the state, sometimes through fellow speculators in New York and Burlington. One acquisition was so great that it was bounded by towns rather than private holdings: "South on Orange, West on Montpelier, North on Marshfield, containing ten thousand acres."

What he bought in terms of hundreds of dollars, he sold in small parcels for thousands. And eventually all the wealth accumulated in the transactions was poured back into Middlebury. His ultimate concern was in the town he was fostering, not in acquiring personal wealth. While negotiating sales or purchases involving half his capital, he never lost track of the shilling's worth of corn ground at his mill or the board feet of lumber sawed there. Trade and production at the Falls was what mattered.

"In April 1793," alleged Jabez Rogers, "I counted every building at Middlebury Falls and found the number to be 62." About thirty years later Frederick Hall, precise mathematician and college professor, made another count and came up with a total of 604, including 33 "manufactories"—woolen mills, cotton mills, a trip-hammer shop, an iron foundry, a printing plant, producing a steady trickle of books and a weekly newspaper, a potter's works, two gristmills, two sawmills and that cacophonous marble mill with 65 saws.

This was the Middlebury, with its impressive traffic tangle and its chaotic Saturday markets, that visiting downstaters marveled at during the early decades of the 1800's. The principle of the self-supporting family had been carried a step further on the economic scale to make the town a self-supporting entity.

At his gun factory, Elias Hall turned out any kind of weapon from a ceremonial sword to a custom-built fowling piece. There was a clock and watchmaker; a saddler producing bridles and boots, saddles and satchels; a gold and silversmith shop where Orrin Stowell fashioned every conceivable variety of trinket from "treble-gilt watch chains" to silver toothpicks. A cooper's shop filled all local requirements for beer kegs, buckets, and hogsheads; and Brewster the potter modeled for thirteen cents many a pickle jug that would be resold years later as an ornamental lamp base for thirteen dollars.

At the looking-glass manufactory "just east of the Creek" could be purchased scroll-framed mirrors for the parlor or front hall, showy frames for family portraits, or any kind of "wall furniture of recent and approved patterns." Hastings Warren ground plaster on demand. John Dike built "pumps of all lengths and sizes;" and Will Andrus, the baker, supplied an assortment of cookies, gingerbread, lemon cakes, rusks, pies, and custards for bachelors and families who could afford not to do their own cooking.

Few of the Main Street merchants made any pretense of limiting their line of wares to the kind of store they nominally operated. The butcher actually sold meat, along with such by-products as tallow, "calf-bags," candles, and soap. And at the music store tunesters could purchase music— "Songs for Glees, Duetts and Trios, new and beautiful Marches, Quick Steps, Waltzes, Galopades," as well as "American, German, French and English musical instruments," but shop names meant little elsewhere. One went to the leather store to find a lace tassel; to the barber to get confectionery or salt mackerel; to the bookstore for gun powder or a pair of "Ladie's Morroco shoes;" to the apothecary for house paint; to the grocer's for rum; to the dry goods stores for snuff, pigtail tobacco, or harness buckles; to the bookbinder's for shaving soap and lead pencils; to the printing office for patent medicines. Most

MAX PETERSEN

*A kitchen of the early 1800's, restored in the museum, was an all-purpose family room, including even a cradle. An anonymous "Portrait of a Lady" hangs over the mantel.*

of the storekeepers displayed behind their counters a line of merchandise as varied as that of Ben Franklin's more famous printing establishment in Philadelphia. It was the heyday of the general store and emporium.

One reason for the variety in wares was the system of barter. In all the commerce little money ever changed hands. Currency was in short supply. Trade was literally *trade*. Customers merely swapped something they had raised, fashioned, or gathered, something they could do without, for something they needed. A book could be exchanged for a quantity of old rags or sheep pelts; a few bushels of wheat and a tub of butter paid for a new suit; a barrel of potash and a pair of neat cattle could purchase a fine silver-service set; a cord of wood was the swapping price for a year's subscription to the newspaper; a bag of flax seed could be switched for a keg of raisins and a few fleeces of sheep's wool for a new anvil. The merchant in turn had to dispose of all the goods he had taken in.

The secret of success in town industry was the home industry that fed it. Everybody worked. They worked from dawn to dark—often long before dawn and long after sunset. Even four-year-olds had their assigned chores; boys in their early teens were expected to do a man's work, put in a full twelve-hour day; girls and young women did double duty, toiling in the fields shoulder to shoulder with the men as kitchen responsibilities allowed; grandfathers and senile grandmothers worked themselves into their graves. Family labor was the cheapest element in the home economic system. It didn't cost anything.

The family was a sort of corporation, every member working without benefit of salary; business and household employment were inextricably interwoven. Father might be a bookbinder by profession, but that didn't free him from planting his field of oats for horse fodder, pasturing cattle, trapping foxes in season, or cultivating an orchard of plums and pippins. And in one way or another all the family industry centered around the home kitchen. It was buttery, butchery, brewery, chandlery, laundry, scullery, nursery, refectory, sitting room, chapel, and office—the biggest, busiest room in the house.

Around the cavernous fireplace—and later the flat-topped wood stove—where the meals were prepared, quilt making, pickle canning, apple paring, candle dipping, butter churning, sausage stuffing, sugaring off, spinning, and weaving took place according to the season. Amid all these family enterprises the man of the house might be executing a business or political deal with a couple of stubborn clients around a corner table.

The accumulation of scents that worked into the pine floor and furnishings was a tantalizing index of what went on in the kitchen. Essences of brine and curdled cream, fish and maple syrup, damp leather and baking bread mingled and mellowed. But the one scent that always predominated was of the dairy. The floor absorbed and preserved the perennial milk spillings, lending to the surface an even stain and to the air the pungence of ripe cheese. Year in and year out, the kitchen had its thorough Saturday scrubbing, but it could never remove the barnyard odor.

The schoolmaster, serving one-week hitches as boarder in home after home, was obliged to share the corporation climate.

"I find it pleases people most to have me sociable," confided one roving pedagogue, who must have been experiencing almost as much difficulty with his elementary spelling classes in school as he was in finding a place to concentrate at his host's. "I have a chance to see a little of everything. Last night in the room where I was, their was one of the family cutting sausage meat, one a-churning, one pairing apples with a pairing machine, with two or three great baskets around him, and two cutting up the

MIDDLEBURY COLLEGE NEWS BUREAU

*Middlebury College, part of the initial plan for a well-balanced town, had been flourishing more than half a century when this drawing was made in 1865.*

apples and boiling apple sauce. All this business was going on in one room, and you can judge how well I could study. In fact, I did not try. I put the best face on the matter and took hold and cut sassage meat all evening. And now I sit writing in one corner, and they are stuffing sassage meat and quartering apples with noise enough to deafen a saw-mill."

There had to be an occasional breather in the work schedule, and when it came, the skylarking was likely to be as excessive as the labor itself. Fourth of July brought the most boisterous diversion of the year. On that day nothing was spared. Hilarity was unconfined. Old uniforms were resurrected and let out at the seat; silk skirts and straw bonnets were refurbished; the hard cider came out of the cellar; unnumbered beer kegs littered Painter's Park; orators whetted their most fluent elocution and every gun barrel was kept warm.

The muskets came into play at dawn of the Fourth, pounding echoes into the mountains. The boom of cannon from surrounding villages resounded like a secondary echo. By midmorning the parade was under way, led by that old war hero, Colonel Chipman. The veterans wheeled through town, followed by a band, processions of dignitaries, college students, and flag-waving youngsters, and then broke up for prayers, a sermon, hymn singing, and a solemn reading of the Declaration of Independence.

For the noon "collation" wives and husbands separated, the women and children going off for a quiet picnic on the creek bank, the men gathering under a "green bower" in the park for a more expansive feast, livened by toasts to independence, the Constitution, George Washington, John Adams, Congress, the Army, the Navy—and on down the political and social scale to the town clerk, the clergy, and the orator of the day.

Each libation was accentuated with cheering and musket discharges, so that by the middle of the afternoon enough gun powder had been expended to fight a minor engagement, and enough liquor consumed to give the entire male population a sense of irresponsibility. On one occasion a statistical-minded participant counted the toasts, came up with a total of 55, and complained next morning that the concussions of the guns had broken the windows of his house on the east side of the park.

The college commencement program in late August was on the order of the Fourth of July to-do—parade, band, oratory, toasts, and picnics for the ladies, but no fireworks and a little less of the carnival spirit. The emphasis was on oratory, with every senior and most of the upperclassmen given an opportunity to demonstrate their elocutionary par in a "dialogue," colloquy, dispute, or special harangue in English, Latin, or Greek. The feast of erudition went on for two days and nights, and even the college president was astonished at the way farmers and their families flocked into town to sit in rapt attention, making believe they understood the flow of classic wit.

No pretense, however, was necessary to appreciate the Fair put on by the County Agricultural Society in the fall. Folks of all ages could have a part in this. Grandma brought her prize pickles to display; Aunt Sally, her latest quilt creation; fifteen-year-old daughters, the fancy straw hats they had woven. Fathers brought their bulls, oxen, and boars; and sons their yearlings, calves, shotes, sheep, roosters, geese, ducks, two-foot parsnips, out-sized cabbages, odds and ends of craftwork. Industrial establishments entered into the spirit of the occasion by exhibiting imaginative creations in gravestones, yard goods, clocks, pottery, and wrought iron. Practically everyone took home a ribbon or at least an honorable mention.

But the feature of the Fair to which the country folk most looked forward was the parade. Each community tried to outdo its neighbor in the construction of a symbolic float or some pantomime on wheels. The hit of all time was made in 1821 when a good showman conceived the idea of rounding up all the oxen in Addison County and attaching them to a float. More oxen responded than the most optimistic exhibitionist had calculated on. The morning of October 9 saw a grand total of 540 bovines, 270 yoke, gee-hawed into line. The procession was three-quarters of a mile long, stretching from one end of the village to the other. With no place to parade to, the master of ceremonies took charge and led the promenade on a circuitous route down side streets and alleys, frequently passing another part of the parade going in an opposite direction.

Bobbing along incongruously at the tail end of the ox train came a single cart "surmounted by a military flag and a sheaf of wheat, upon which might be seen the weaver operating his shuttle, the tailor with his needle, the shoemaker with his last, the saddler with his awl, and the clothier with his shearing machine, the card maker with his tooth cutter, together with the wheelwright with his saw, and the carpenter with his square and compass, and surrounded with many of the products of their various employments."

No other holidays had anything like the flair of Fair days, Commencement, and July Fourth. Christmas was still a religious festival, though some of the more liberal-minded Congregationalists were beginning to decorate their houses, give parties, and exchange presents. Two Thanksgivings—one in April and the other in December—were week-day Sabbaths dedicated to "public humiliation and prayer." Transient showmen, often coming to town unheralded, offered occasional gala diversions.

The forerunner of the circus came as early as 1807, in the form of a single 400-pound African lion, which was displayed to awed audiences in the lobby of the Vermont Hotel. Hundreds paid the 12½-cent admission fee to see the yawning beast. After that, in the course of years, came camels, llamas, ichneumons, anteaters, "Belona organs,"

*A bountiful day of hunting was celebrated by a group of residents that included
a chef ready to prepare the game, in October, 1865, at a local hostelry.*

and finally in 1830 a full-rigged Big Top with 27 wagons drawn by 80 horses, "the largest elephant ever offered to the American public" (12,000 pounds), a menagerie ranging from antelope to zebra, and a company of "Flying Phenomenons" that gave an unforgettable performance in the ring and high on the ropes.

Theatrical barnstormers made an early appearance and put on shows with a spiritual lift like "The Noble Shepherd," or with wholesome slapstick humor like "The Village Lawyer." But there was no question about it, plays ultimately had to be considered "the works of the devil." They were accordingly panned by the press and banned by the pulpit. After the first teasers, theater was ruled out by the town fathers for almost half a century. In the end, the homemade fun, the parlor sings, the Agricultural Society exhibits, the college oratorical contests, and the Fourth of July outbursts furnished all the amusement with which Middlebury's Puritanical conscience could cope.

Town meetings, with their long duration and occasional shortcomings, were treated with the profoundest solemnity. Middleburnians evolved the new role of participating in government. Every tax-paying, church-going male adult was entitled to a hearing as well as a vote. Superheated kitchens, unheated barns, and hotel barrooms were the accepted meeting places for early gatherings, and none of them was conducive to parliamentary order or expedition. The election of a moderator, a clerk, the selectmen, a constable, a treasurer, and a dozen other officers was a good afternoon's beginning.

Listers had to be selected, a collector of town rates, a leather sealer and a sealer of weights and measures, three grand jurymen, six "pettit jurors," and nine surveyors of highways. There had to be a poundkeeper, two tithing men, three fence viewers, and special investigative committees on all manner of contingencies from bridge building and roadside brush cutting to schoolteaching and political skulduggery.

Here democracy functioned in painfully slow motion, yet there was not a voter in the gathering who wasn't proud of the procedure. The offices had to be spread out among as many citizens as possible, given equitable geographical distribution, and the qualifications of each candidate weighed with embarrassing frankness.

The poundkeeper, for example, had to be centrally located, so that his pound was readily accessible to anyone who picked up a stray animal. His integrity had to be inviolable, for in every community there were scoundrels capable of turning a neighbor's cow loose in order to collect the fee for its return. The poundkeeper had to be appropriately suspicious, but above suspicion himself.

Fence viewers likewise had to be men of judicial acumen. Periodically they were obliged to go the rounds of barriers to make sure that stumps and rails were secure. And, of course, the political job calling for the most astute knowledge of law, order and human nature was the town clerkship. The town clerk was counselor and confident on all affairs, a scribe and a recorder. He had to assist in preparing a complicated title deed or to help a neglected husband satisfy the law in phrasing separation notice for the newspapers, *videlicet:*

The serpent has beguiled my Eve. She hath taken forbidden fruit and fled from the garden, and quitted my bed and board, without provocation or known cause.—This is to forbid all persons harboring or trusting Dolly Lewis on my account, as I will pay no debt of her contracting after this date.

The character, endurance, and impartiality of nominees for the office of church beadle had to be given long and weighty consideration. Even these Sabbath police might be tempted to overlook the naps of friends during service or permit an illegal Sunday-morning gossip session. And there were qualifications no less demanding to be applied to the sealers, the selectmen, the constable, the treasurer, and all the committeemen.

Election of these officers was taken in dead, unhurried earnestness. The meetings, often adjourned to evening sessions, also drafted ordinances covering such matters as permitting sheep to run at large along highways, authorizing doctors to inoculate for the smallpox, laying taxes for milestones and guideposts, and increasing the salary for the underpaid minister of the gospel.

Cantankerous exchanges developed in these meetings over vested interests and regional droit, but usually some sort of comfortable compromise would be worked out after heads had knocked together long enough. In its normal state the town was like one big happy squabbling family, in which adversaries of one day could be allies the next. And when causes involving the long-range welfare of the community came up, the townsfolk could work together as harmoniously as a fife-and-drum corps on parade.

Doing things together—even the most arduous, the dullest drudgery—could be turned into sport off the home premises. They called it a bee. There were men's bees for raising the rafters of a neighbor's barn or shingling it, women's bees for making quilts and carpets for newlyweds, mixed bees for husking corn, planting potatoes, or harvesting wheat. And then the principle of the bee was carried into civic improvements.

THE SHELDON ART MUSEUM

*With a favorite professor and two velocipedes, a class of Middlebury College students posed for a portrait on the college steps in the early years of this century.*

The beginnings of Middlebury College were actually a product of the bee idea. Addison County Grammar School came first. As the answer to inferior secondary schooling, academies were springing up in progressive communities everywhere in New England. Middlebury needed one. Gamaliel Painter did the spade work with the Legislature in getting a charter for the academy; then everyone pitched in, contributing labor, lumber, nails, hardware, cabinet work, doors, windows, and, those who could afford it, a little hard cash.

They built "Old East," as it was later called, themselves, and it was not a bad-looking building—three stories of it, with classrooms and a chapel on the lower floors, student dormitories on the third, all crowned characteristically with a quaint belfry on the roof. Within a year after the great building bee started, the grammar school was in operation, dormitories filled to capacity, and Jeremiah Atwater, a twenty-four-year-old Yale graduate, serving contentedly as principal and instructor.

It was such an immediate success that Gamaliel Painter was sent back to the Legislature to sound out that body on the proposition of expanding the school into a college. Again and again he was turned down; the lawmakers had already made provision for a seminary at Burlington—the University of Vermont—and its trustees were having a hard time raising funds; politically, the legislators couldn't afford to undercut the Burlington project by authorizing the establishment of a college thirty miles away.

But Painter with his blunt, persistent, homely parlance continued his intervention behind scenes. When Yale's peripatetic president, Timothy Dwight, unexpectedly showed up at Middlebury on a good-will tour, the case was put to him. Dwight surveyed the town, talked to some of his alumni, inspected the grammar school and concluded: "The local situation at Middlebury, the sober and religious character of the inhabitants, their manners and various other circumstances render it a very desirable seat for a college."

With an endorsement like that from New England's foremost educator, Painter had something to work with. Once more he went before the legislators with his drawling address, as though he were broaching the subject for the first time. Partly out of weariness they gave in. At least he wore down the resistance of enough of them to push his bill through.

The college was granted a charter on Saturday, November 1, 1800. A meeting of the trustees was immediately called, Principal Atwater was promoted to the presidency, candidates for admission were examined, and on Wednesday, five days after the issuance of the charter, seven undergraduates attended their first college recitations.

The opening of Middlebury College brought on another succession of fund-raising bees and building bees. There wasn't room in the grammar school for both academy and college students. Lawyer Seth Storrs started the ball rolling by deeding over a generous section of his farm west of the grammar school, and after that everyone chipped in. The small contributions of material and the large contributions in labor built West College—Painter Hall—and a few years later an impressive classroom and assembly hall called the chapel.

However, not every community project was favored with the wholehearted support given to education. Ironically, the God-fearing, puritanical citizens haggled for more than thirty years before they could get together on building a church. Not that anyone objected to having a house of worship; they fervently wanted it, but they all wanted it within walking distance of their front doors, or at least where they could hear the bell on a Sunday morning. And since the population was spread out over an area of some 25,000 acres, not even a respectable minority could agree on where it should be located.

For years committees were appointed and reappointed to choose sites and "stick stakes" for the church. Some of them broke up in discord before there was any stake sticking at all; more often stakes were stuck and reports made only to have the action disapproved in town meeting. Services meantime were held in Daniel Foote's barn, in Stephen Goodrich's house at the north end of town, in Will Thayer's at the south end, and in Ebenezer Sumner's barn in between. For a time they rotated among the taverns and then moved into the courthouse.

In the early years town and church society were one, under a state statute which specified that all legal voters of a parish should accept the faith of the majority, attend and support the church of the majority. The majority, of course, were Connecticut Congregationalists by birth. But by 1801 so much criticism had been leveled at this apparent violation of the Bill of Rights that the law was relaxed, and within two months some fifty members had withdrawn from "The Religious Society Consisting of the Town of Middlebury."

The withdrawal and a new statute agitated the situation still more and seriously affected church finances, for tithes could no longer be levied in town meetings. The committees and the stake setters worked resolutely and fruitlessly for another four years. It was Painter who at last broke the deadlock. At a meeting in 1805 he proposed removing the old tavern at the north end of Main Street, locating the church there—where he had privately maintained all along it should be—and defraying construction costs through the sale of pews rather than through taxation. The plan was the self-evident solution that the town had been awaiting for a generation. Dissension dissolved. People were not only ready to purchase pews, but eager to lend a hand in getting the building under way.

Country churches were usually planned and engineered by local carpenters or artisans who had established reputa-

*Two patriarchs with snow-white beards had seen a small town rise, fall, and revive by the time they rode with Henry Sheldon, the town's first local historian, in a 1904 celebration. One—Rev. Mr. Bidwell (right)—was born in 1808.*

tions as good barn builders. But after all the years of squabbling, no ordinary builder of barns was going to be entrusted with the Middlebury church. As chairman of the "Committee on Drawing a Plan for the Meeting House and Exposing Pews for Sale," Gamaliel Painter rode down to Bennington to look over a new meetinghouse there and meet its architect, Lavius Fillmore, who was beginning to be recognized as one of the most skillful designers in New England.

Like every successful American draftsman, Fillmore was familiar with the standard texts, *Country Builder's Assistant* and *The American Builder's Companion,* by Asher Benjamin, who had freely borrowed ideas from other architects, including Sir Christopher Wren. Painter—the artificer—and Fillmore—the architect—found that they had much in common. Fillmore had become a staunch admirer of the Wren tradition. He was shortly persuaded to leave his home in Bennington, move to Middlebury, and take on the church job where he could once more present in wood his interpretation of the great British architect's style.

The construction took four years. Again it was a question of everyone's contributing his share of nails, glass, hardware, lumber and labor—as well as buying a pew—but under the direction of an artist like Fillmore, the result surpassed anything that had previously been erected in town. On May 31, 1809, the Middlebury Congregationalists dedicated their first meetinghouse. Even in that day people were awed by the sheer beauty of the building, its exquisite detail, the massive white façade, the majestic interior bathed in a luxury of white and the graceful spire, faintly reminiscent of one of Wren's London masterworks, St. Martin's-in-the-Fields. It was an eloquent invitation to worship. No matter how one looked at it, the building had to be regarded as another Painter triumph.

Painter had given wealth in abundance to Middlebury, but his most enduring legacy was ideological rather than material. He was one of the examplars in a far-reaching social movement dedicated to rural democracy, to frugality, to industry, to self-determination. Pioneers of his ilk seasoned the character of Vermont and all New England.

*A nineteenth-century institution, the annual fair, continued into the first decades of the twentieth century with trotting races, agricultural exhibits, and cattle contests.*

Painter and his contemporaries fixed the course for the future of Middlebury. The legatees broadened it in the next century and a half. The college was originally established to promote liberal education among males—ministers and missionaries in particular. Pulpits in every part of America, especially the South, were occupied by early graduates, and missionaries with Middlebury degrees carried the New England gospel to the far corners of the earth—to Egypt, India, Siam, the Sandwich Islands, Turkey, Ceylon, Caesarea, Japan, Syria, the Marshall Islands, South Africa. But as with other colleges, the emphasis on theology soon lapsed in favor of the liberal arts. The institution had its ups and downs; occasionally in years of depression considered merging with the University of Vermont, which opened its doors shortly after Middlebury was chartered; occasionally changed emphasis by fostering a medical school, developing an engineering department, or going into vocationalized pedagogy; and in 1883 broke with precedent and admitted women.

In one respect Painter and his compatriots were sadly let down by posterity. Gamaliel saw Middlebury as a factory town and commercial center and established it as such. But never again in the history of the village was an auditor able to count as many as thirty-three "manufactories," as did Professor Hall in the 1820's or anything like the number of specialized stores. Merchants merged, demanded cash instead of country produce, and closed for good when they couldn't make ends meet. The cluster of mills at the Falls slowly disintegrated. One by one they moved nearer to the market or nearer the sources of raw material. Even the railroad that roared into town in 1849 to a din of clanging church bells, booming cannon, brass bands, and the cheers of inebriated citizens, couldn't stay the industrial exodus.

The woolen mills closed. The cotton mills closed. The saw mills moved back toward the mountains. Marble saws continued in motion for decades and didn't begin to slow down until the late 1920's; then they ceased altogether and Middlebury was factoryless until a modest, modern plastics plant found refuge there.

For two decades in the middle 1800's Middlebury ranked as a sheep-breeding center of the nation and both town and county flourished on the wealth. Merinos, smuggled out of Spain, had found their way to Addison County, where they prospered, and the farmers prospered with them. A single ram could bring an income of $6,000 a year. Breeding ewes sold for $500, $800, $1,200 a head. Middlebury Merinos were proudly exhibited in Boston, New York, Chicago, San Francisco, and well-heeled owners became world travelers as escorts of their precious flocks—to Ohio one year, to Nebraska or Colorado the next, and then on to South America, to Africa, and Australia. Addison County was famed around the globe for its sheep.

During those mid-century years the greatest entertainment luxury the town could brag of was its steamboat, *The Valley Queen*, a flat-bottomed ferry with side paddles, that splashed its way very slowly and very sedately on excursions twelve miles up Otter Creek. Gala events those were in spring and summer for Middlebury's social elect, for the Chi Psi's and D.U.'s at the college, and for distinguished visitors.

"Steamer Ahoy!" vociferated the local weekly. *"The Valley Queen* made several very successful trips last week and gave perfect satisfaction to all on board. Last Saturday the College faculty and several members of the Corporation, with a number of visitors from New York, went up twelve miles and held a picnic on the banks of the Creek. Farr's Band discoursed fine music during the supper and on the way up."

The opening of the Far West and the local packs of wild canines, that developed an appetite for mutton, broke the Merino monopoly in Middlebury. But enough had been made on sheep to tide over agricultural interests and keep the immense Victorian farmhouses in paint for decades—until the huge dairy farms emerged that helped supply Albany and Boston and New York with milk.

Perhaps the strongest ebb in Middlebury's fortunes came as a result of the Civil War—not because of any overwhelming number of casualties, but because country lads on military maneuvers saw broader horizons: taller grain than they could grow in Addison County, more energetic water power than could be generated at the Falls, cities displaying more enticing wares than those in the windows of Merchants Row.

The exodus wasn't hurried, but veterans couldn't forget what they had seen. Middlebury lost some of its best blood to the call of the cities and the call of the West. Farms changed hands; shops changed hands, and often the new owner had a French-Canadian or foreign name rather than a Yankee one. The balance of political power had always been equitably shared by farmers, the Main Street merchants and professional men, and it continued that way, but more of the politicking was done on the outside, and town meetings were sometimes perfunctory compared to what they had been for less heterogeneous assemblages.

Here and there near the turn of the century a fine old run-down farm on the outskirts of town fell into the hands of a new kind of settler that would have been an anathema to Gamaliel Painter—the gentleman farmer, a city-schooled fellow with money and a hankering to get back to the soil of his ancestors. Joseph Battell answered the description. He returned to the home town of his forebears for his health and moved into the Parker place as a guest, with the homely notion of turning wood chopper and farm hand to tone his muscles.

The Parker place was magnificently located under the shadow of Bread Loaf Mountain, a two-hour carriage drive into the hills east of Middlebury. Its piazzas commanded a glorious view of the Green Mountains in any season of the year.

Battell gave up wood chopping when the first nest of blisters formed on his hands. He bought out his host. Three years later he rechristened the farm "Bread Loaf" and opened a hotel on his own. Both his table and his entertainment were a critical success from the very first season. As far as making money on the establishment was concerned, that was his last worry. The dividends from the kind of inheritance he had would last twice his life expectancy.

He enlarged his dining room and partitioned off luxurious bedroom suites over it, constructed a music hall, a greenhouse, a library, a workshop, a bowling alley for his guests. When the labyrinth of passageways connecting old and new parlors, dens, reading rooms, verandas, and exercise rooms began to confound even the owner, he started building separate cottages.

One morning he heard a neighbor chopping in a nearby wood lot. It dawned on him that the loss of those trees could spoil his view. Immediately he dashed across the field to the woods and ordered the man to stop. He bought the wood lot on the spot. That gave him an idea. Wealthy friends of his were paying as much as $10,000 for paintings to hang on their walls. Why not buy the view rather than the picture? He could purchase a whole mountain for $10,000.

Battell did just that, and didn't stop with the possession of a single peak. Mountain after mountain he purchased at fifty cents per acre, twenty-five cents, even ten, until he owned practically all the land he could see from his Bread Loaf porches, and a great deal beyond. Later, people called him an imaginative conservationist, years ahead of his time.

On the side, the gentleman farmer bred Morgan horses at another Middlebury estate; he bought and published the weekly newspaper; he erected a block-long business building on Merchants Row to replace some of the sagging structures that dated back to Painter's day; as town philanthropist he took over where Gamaliel had left off. But it was as innkeeper that Battell was most appreciated. To Bread Loaf the townsfolk went for their soirees, their oyster suppers, their sleigh rides and weekend house parties, and to Bread Loaf flocked the first modern summer tourists.

Like Painter before him, Battell eventually willed most of his vast estate, including a collection of mountains, to the College on the Hill, but of greater value to the community was his promotion of Middlebury as a Vermont tourist center. He colorfully dramatized the fact that the college town was an ideal place to settle down for a long vacation or for retirement.

The tracks of the Rutland Railroad, over which rode the first generation of tourists, still snake up through Champlain valley, but passenger service has been discontinued for more than a decade. And, alas, that symbol of stirring economy, cultural prestige and progress, the rural railroad

*The church of the settlers nestled amid the mountain scenery, Middlebury continues much of its past diversity but in a less cohesive pattern. The college has a summer campus on Bread Loaf Mountain in the background. The farmland lies down the valley to the right.*

station, suffered until recently the indignity of being used as a liquor store.

The outlying farms are still prosperous, though there are more French-Canadian names on the R.F.D. mailboxes than names of old Middlebury settlers; very few farms have remained in the same family through the generations. The plastics factory is busy. The marble mill is converted into a warehouse and showroom for farm machinery and household appliances. The *Addison County Independent* has proven itself one of the newsiest, most literate and profitable weekly journals in New England—the energetic voice of an energetic town.

The college, renowned across the nation for its liberal arts indoctrination, its language schools and its skiing, has inducted into office its twelfth president, and has a distinguished future in store. Like every other American town of consequence, Middlebury has a shopping center to compete with the long-established emporia of groceries, hardware, and haberdashery. There are banks, parks, a theater, a town library, a golf course, a ski bowl, a hospital, a celebrated inn, and a great many tourist homes and motels. It took more than a hundred years for the town to regain the population it boasted in the 1830's and 40's, but at last count it had soared over the 5,000 mark.

Out-of-staters swarm into the town by car—in summer for the mountain scenery and the atmosphere, in winter for the skiing and the atmosphere. Next to homogenized milk and homogenized education, the visitors are now the major source of income. They are all escapists, most of them looking for something which their great grandfathers and great grandmothers possessed, but which they have lost and have an overpowering urge to regain—though they hate to admit it.

On the campus and around Painter's Falls they are pleased to find reminders of Gamaliel and his age, of Jabez Rogers, Daniel Foote, Jeremiah Atwater and Lavius Fillmore. Then they turn into the village reliquary—the Sheldon Museum. There the past is tidied up for display. On exhibition are countless tokens collected years ago when granddaughters of the frontiersmen were cleaning out their attics, getting rid of the unfashionable Windsor chairs, replacing run-down clocks, quaint tables, and ancient desks with a chic oak product from Grand Rapids, Michigan.

There is the great kitchen of the pioneers with the utilitarian fireplace, surrounded by butter churns and boot racks, looms and flintlocks; the dining-room table is set with woodenware and pewter; the parlor, used in grandmother's time only for funerals and holiday get-togethers; bedrooms; nursery; business office; even an adjoining country store and blacksmith shop. On display are the books the village fathers read, wrote, and published; the chairs they sat in; the musical instruments they played; the gadgets they invented. The place looks as though one of the ancestors had just stepped out to fetch the cow from the pasture, and would be back in a minute.

Out of this assemblage of souvenirs from the long past there seems to issue more than a hint of the real character of the forefathers. They all but live again and have their being. An old pioneer town like Middlebury needs such a museum to keep us properly haunted.

*Trees such as these on Tulpehocken Street in 1910 made the town verdant and shady. But these and others have been cut down in favor of concrete and modernity.*

# Individualists under the Shade Trees

—

## *Pine Grove, Pennsylvania*

—

### BY CONRAD RICHTER

This is the tale of a town I love, a glimpse of its life under early so-called backward conditions and under what is known today as enlightenment and progress. It is the town where I was born and now live, if only for a few months of the year.

Its birth and youth were romantic enough. Its name derived from a grove of virgin pines, the loftiest and most magnificent that early travelers, including Bartram, the botanist, left word they had ever seen and which I would give a great deal to walk under today. The early village or *schtetl,* as it was known by the founding Pennsylvania German settlers, lay on the historic Tulpehocken Trail used by the Six Nations and other Northern Indians journeying to William Penn and the provincial government authorities

in Philadelphia; also by officials and celebrated travelers setting out into the wilderness. Conrad Weiser tramped it on his missions to the Long House of the Six Nations at Onondaga. George Washington was said to have followed it to Fort Augusta. Indeed, the story was told me by older members of my family that the brass bell now on the table beside me as I write had called the father of his country to dinner at my great-grandfather's Mansion House still standing here. The only difficulty is that my great-grandfather did not come to Pine Grove until shortly after 1800 and George Washington died in 1799. The town is fairly old, however, as towns go in America. There was a Pine Grove township in 1771 while Pennsylvania was still a colony of Great Britain. It furnished companies of soldiers

34

for both the Revolution and the War of 1812. A powder mill delivered its product to the Continental cause. Iron furnaces and forges flourished in the surrounding forest and when coal was discovered, the settlement became the busy terminus of the Union Canal.

My own personal knowledge of and affection for the town came too late to hear the boatman's plaintive horn or see the flotilla of canalboats tied up in the upper and lower basins. But much of the early and original scene still remained. Tulpehocken Street was a great green shady tunnel under magnificent trees—elm, maple, horse chestnut, and especially ash, which flourishes mightily in our native soil. Even today I get letters from readers who passed through in their youth and remember the beauty of the street and charm of the town. There were in those days an ancient graveyard on the main street; two stone churches, one of them quite old; four covered bridges across Swatara Creek; and both basins of the canal still filled with water. As a small child, the latter seemed almost maritime to me, the Ed Christ family who lived and worked on its bank, seafaring folk who ferried cargoes from foreign lands. City people from Philadelphia came to Pine Grove to spend their summers at the Filbert House. An artist found her way here to paint and stayed to teach a class of which I was one.

Now, looking back, I'm aware how bountiful and artistic was the unseen hand of God or happenstance compared to the later schemes and contriving of man. A simple unaffectedness held all in a kind of natural relationship. Hard work and long hours were unresented then and the word exploitation unknown. Had you asked you would have been told there was little or no poverty. Jobs were to be had if a man wanted to work. There were two tanneries, a brick works, extensive hard-coal mines, and the railroad. Two lines crossed at Pine Grove. Nearly a score of passenger trains stopped daily, except Sunday, at the yellow and brown depot, often to a little crowd of onlookers. The chief product of life, which modern planners mistakenly consider ease, is really joy, and these trains gave joy, a sense of adventure. One generally stood before or behind the station steaming up to pull out to far places. The rails ran without interruption to palm trees and deep snows, to mountains and deserts, to eastern and western seaboards, and out on docks where liners left for alien shores. There was to most of us something beautiful about an engine bathed in the energy of its own white clouds of steam. A motor bus is an object inert and prosaic beside it. There was always activity generated or its expectation. The constant sound of steel wheels was reassurance that all was well. The going and coming of trains were the hands of the town clock, and engine whistles, the striking of the hours.

There's the two-twenty going down the cut, we thought, or: That's the seven-thirty with the mail whistling for Loser's Crossing.

Many of the railroaders lived in our town. Conductors, brakemen, engineers were our friends, affectionately known by their first names. Packages were often handed the conductor or baggageman to be delivered to someone who would call at a certain station, this rather than to the expressman for charges. Often trains stopped at crossings far downtown or uptown to let off some sick or crippled passenger nearer his home. I recall that the early morning flyer to Lebanon once halted at the Wood Street crossing to take on Ez Hawk, a salesman, who had overslept, had been missed and looked out for by the conductor. On another occasion the Harrisburg train waited at Rausch Gap, a mining town, for my Grandfather Henry to baptize a child and get back on the train.

Today no passenger train passes through the town and very little rail freight. He who wishes to travel must take his chances with the coal and carrier trucks that clog our highways. Train whistles are silent as the vanished boathorn. The lower canal basin has been ignominiously filled up, the other in part, the ancient water level lowered close to the muddy bottom to make easier the drainage of a modern swimming pool where the citizenry enter for pay to lie about on towels at ease, after the manner of celebrities reclining at their Hollywood pools. The same magnificent ring of hills and mountains still surrounds the town, but almost no one tramps them any more except in the commercialized hunting season and then no farther from his car than he has to. No daily Henner Kendall sets forth like Rip Van Winkle to roam the mountain till evening and none returns on foot any more with a catamount dragging the ground from his shoulder.

Our workmen's labor has been reduced, but so in many cases have dignity and manhood. Women on sewing machines practically support the town in five or six garment factories. For men, only the dye works are left and a few small independent mines known locally as bootleg holes. Most of the males who want to work must travel long distances daily to their jobs. And when they enter the industrial gate, it clangs behind them. The public is usually excluded. Employees Only is the word.

It was not so in the old days. Our stores provided benches and chairs for men to loaf and talk and observe the goings on of trade and commerce. Others passed the time within sound of the telegraph instrument at the depot or sat with one of the watchmen at the several railroad crossings. Freedom and fellowship in business were recognized. As a boy I could wander through the brickyard and tannery yard, watch the hide dressers at work and the moving of the waters in the dark mysterious vats where dogs and sometimes men, it was hinted, drowned. Our high-school graduating class did not go to Washington on a bus for our outing but boarded one of the miners' trains, boys and girls alike, to be dropped to the fifth or sixth level of a large

*This high-school portrait with the prettiness, innocence, and flair of its youthful figures, in high buttoned shoes and vests, conveys the turn-of-the- century composure.*

Reading Company mine, then unelectrified. We rode in darkness down the steep slope in uncleaned mine cars, were shepherded by amused fatherly miners along endless gangways and into inky stopes and headings, an educational treat that would be viewed with horror today by mine officials and parents alike. We boys hopped freights and were taken aboard cabooses.

Looking back, I feel today's separation of public and industry a loss to life and living. Fifty years ago on one small corner in Pine Grove, that of Maple and Carbon streets, stood a blacksmith shop, a wheelwright shop, and a paintshop for wagons and buggies, all open to the public and liberally patronized by audiences of all ages. Children swarmed the vicinity. They played nips, ball, and hide-and-go-seek in the street, watched sparks fly from the forge and hammer, pumped the bellows or switched flies from horses with an old horsetail. Small fry sat in a row in the wheelwright shop where they had to keep mighty quiet on a bench if they wanted to see the lovely shavings curl from the plane or a wheel take shape or turn red under the stubby hand of the kindly owner known as Uncle Ike. Under paintshop and blacksmith shop, which stood on stilts above the canal level, little ones played house in the stacked lumber. News that a kicking or killer horse was to be put in the stocks to be shod spread like wildfire over the neighborhood and spectators appeared like locusts out of the ground. Today all is gone; a planned playground on the schoolyard failed significantly for lack of interest. Man tries to play God, forgetting that God's ways are not man's.

Two other institutions have almost vanished from our town. They are front-porch sitting and the art of walking. Warm evenings and late afternoons people used to "repair" to their porches, sitting in comfort, greeting the passer-by who often stopped to exchange talk and feed the eternal loneliness in man's breast. Today almost no one walks. Men and women drive to the store and post office only a block or two away. Their eager efforts toward conversation with the checker or postal clerk reveal the unfed hunger for live companionship that the canned faces and voices of television and radio can never satisfy.

Thoreau wrote that the people in his time lived lives of quiet desperation. If that was true in my town, my youth kept me from seeing it. What I did observe widely was a strength, independence, or insensibility—call it what you may—an acceptance of the problems of life, that enabled a man or woman to go through deep waters that reduce present-day people to fears, anxieties, and running to the doctor. The population of our town and countryside, about five thousand, has increased little since I was a boy, but the sick and complaining that crowd our three doctors' waiting rooms have multiplied out of all proportion as have those fleeing to die in the county-seat hospitals. And yet despite the tidings of the new miracle age, our town men and women do not grow any older than the seventies, eighties, and nineties of past generations recorded on the stones of our cemetery. Life was met with a stouter heart. Coal mining, one of the most dangerous of occupations, was still more so in my youth. Moreover, it was carried on in dripping darknens, lighted only by the small lamp on a miner's cap. And yet a friend in a nearby mining patch tells me that as a girl she commonly heard the miners singing as they tramped to work at five and six o'clock in the morning. I never heard that, but on many an afternoon I saw them energetically drop in droves off the several miners' trains before they reached the station. Almost none walked and it was a common sight to see these black-face men, who had just labored ten or twelve hours underground, jog down the street like a football squad.

This unrestricted use of our town legs grew up with us. We thought nothing of walking a mile to the Sweety to swim or to climb up on one of the arches of the old red bridge to lie there hugging timber while a train roared through, deafening and shaking us on our wooden bolsters, filling our eyes and lungs with sulphur and smoke. That was what we had waited for. The favorite game of the older boys was Deer, and we younger ones looked up to it with longing, for only the elite in fleetness, endurance, and cunning were eligible. The deer herd would take off, leaving a trail of occasionally dropped scraps of paper, from which the hound pack would try to track them, following over

hill and cliff, through this hollow and that, through cornfields and wheat, across creeks and even up on the Blue Mountain. At night instead of paper the deer left a trail of occasional wild Indian cries, pattings of the lips. As a boy I have lain in bed listening to those distant sounds of chase and pleasure through the dark hemlock woods and over moonlit hills, feeling admiration for those who played it who would have looked with pity at some lonely track runner today plodding silently and dully through the town in white shorts, trying to achieve what the earlier generations of the youth in his town did with such savage joy and wild companionship.

I am well aware of the improvement in living ease and that neither boys nor men will ever go back. But I bear malice toward the sophisticated look of amusement on the faces of those today at what they consider the crudeness of early times, unaware that they, rather than early man, may be the ones to be pitied. Smug feelings of superiority were prevalent when I was a boy as now, but not over past generations. Had I smiled patronizingly at some older school picture of boys in outgrown short pants, girls in ancient

MISS MARY BOYER

*Picnickers in 1899 adjourned from their depleted hampers for a photograph on a bridge.*
*The gentleman astride the rails asserted his authority over the female gathering.*

capes and the principal in whiskers, my Aunt Lizzie would soon have sharply informed me what certain of those quaintly dressed boys had become, including the first vice president of the Pennsylvania Railroad, and that the man behind the whiskers was George Washington Channel, who had fought through the Civil War and who kept discipline in high school without raising his voice or a finger.

Our elders seemed to be impressed not so much by the image as the reality. Genuine was a word much used along with truth. "And that's the truth," they would say. People meant what they said. When I was promised a licking, I got it. People were rated not so much by what they professed to be, but by what they actually were. "He sneaks into her house to spend the night and then he wants to be so much," they would say. Modern social writers love to call this malicious gossip and jealousy. Fiction writers go to great lengths to show how such "libel" destroys the lives of the pure and innocent. My Aunt Lizzie and her kind believed, on the contrary, that knowledge of truth, fact, and reality was healthy. It exerted an influence for good rather than evil. You'd better go straight or most everybody in town would know it. However, if you wanted to sin—and many did—it was more admirable to do it openly.

For example, in those days town drinking by and large was unconcealed. No one shielded us boys from enjoying and learning from the antics of the drunken. In my youth there were almost nightly figures staggering down the street or lying in the gutter. More than once on a cold night a drunk was taken indoors and kept from freezing to death by the man whose gutter he had bedded in. Now our town drunks—and there are many more today including women —liquidate themselves at home in secret or drive home from legion, barroom or firehall in their cars, endangering unsuspecting traffic. Moreover, they contribute little to the enlightenment and enjoyment of the town. Their amusing orations, monologues, dialogues with nonpresent characters are unheard and their wisdom lost to the world, such as that of Seranus Kramer who told his pastor, "You say a lot about my great drinking, but you don't say anything about my great thirst." I remember the golden hour when as a boy my cousin woke me up at midnight to hear my favorite uncle, an imbiber, singing "Star of the Evening" outside the nearby firehall. And one of the pleasantest memories of the twenty-five years we lived in New Mexico is lying in my bed in the small hours in Taos listening to the *paisanos* wend their way home on foot from the cantinas, their Spanish ballads growing fainter and fainter with distance on the clear desert air.

So far I have said little about the real riches of our town. When I was a boy, Pine Grove was known as one of the wealthiest towns per capita in Pennsylvania. That meant little to me then and not much more now. The real riches,

although I did not fully appreciate them until much later, were in the individuality of our men and women, who thought their own thoughts, expressed their own philosophies, and went their own ways. We knew scarcely two alike. Uniformity—to be, talk, think, or act like somebody else—would have been degrading, to lose one's identity.

We had our Squire Filbert in a flowing beard, quite deaf, who walked benignly through the town with his walking stick held redoubtably behind his shoulders. He liked to ride his mare, Gypsy, down the middle of the railroad track, which was the shortest way to his farm, all oblivious of the whistles of the train that had to crawl behind him. The engineer, who knew the Squire only too well, had to send the fireman ahead by foot to notify the rider he was obstructing progress whereupon the Squire would say regretfully, "Gypsy, we'll have to give precedence to quantity over quality," turn the mare on the side path, and salute the apoplectic engineer equably as the locomotive went by.

The Squire had a brother, Sam, who also walked a good deal, carrying a huge brown umbrella. When proprietor of the Filbert House, he would decline to get up and serve a single customer at the bar, waiting until there were two to make it worth while. Two other members of this family, to which I was distantly related by marriage, were Peter Augustus, who went through the Civil War as captain and major, and Bill, who went through it as a private. Bill was the black sheep, a great inventive raconteur. My mother used to tell how when she and my Aunt Lizzie were children and had to go to bed, Bill would climb a tree in his yard outside their bedroom window and regale them with stories. His doings were sometimes *sub rosa* and the woman he lived with unacceptable to his brothers and sister, but Mother Filbert insisted on giving him a wedding equal to that of the others and that all be present to do their brother honor. Bill contributed much enjoyment to the town. His house on back street was a mecca for older boys. He would let them count his store of gold pieces and read his honorable discharge papers while he told them wild tales. He wore boots and a Western hat, would strike poses like figures by Frederic Remington, but his joy was his collection of watches. He carried one in every pocket, claimed he took them on the battlefield from dead Rebels to whom they were no good anyhow. When you asked him the time, he would pull a watch from one pocket, then one from another, and so on, telling you the time on each and often its history besides, a ritual hugely enjoyed by all.

My Grandfather Henry, a tall Abraham Lincolnesque figure, living next door to the Filbert homestead, had literally scores of anecdotes told about him, and my Great Aunt Esther was a familiar town figure, taking her troop of kindergarten children out to instruct them as they went. Nelse Knapp was a horse doctor who chopped off the finger that annoyed him. Banker Werntz straightened nails to save

*The surrounding scenery touched the back yards and was visible from the streets in 1915. But the natural atmosphere of the town has been heedlessly destroyed.*

them, was said to smoke the tobacco he chewed and dried, using the ashes for tooth powder. Sadie Fegley sat up at her front window most of the night so she could tell you who came home late and when. Mrs. Kitzmiller, a retired milliner, lived alone in her stone mansion, the rooms of which were piled with hatboxes to the ceiling so that only cowpaths were left between. And Billy Schultz, the lumberman, drove his fast horse at breakneck speed through the town and then handed Tom Hughes, the one-eyed constable, a ten-dollar bill, five of which was his fine for exceeding the speed limit in one direction and five for coming back.

I could go on endlessly and futilely. What impresses me living among a more monotonous humanity today is the originality and nonconformity of these earlier people. They would have disdained to take their opinions from anyone else, would have resisted him like the devil. Their flavor came from the grass roots and this was the inimitable ingredient that nourished and refreshed us as we heard or even saw them on the street. Their political convictions remained invincible. Among the town characters were Ed Christ, who ran the coal-and-lumber yard, and William Haldeman, known as Billy, the town jeweler and variety merchant. They were friends and spent regular evenings together arguing politics. At the start, Ed Christ was a Republican, Billy Haldeman a Democrat, and after fifty years of debate and persuasion, Ed Christ was still a Republican and Billy Haldeman a Democrat. Their arguments were often heated but at the conclusion, Ed would say, "Good night, William," and Billy would say courteously, "Good night, Edward."

This brings up the peculiar sweetness in many of the old-time figures. They had withering sarcasm for their enemies and for those they thought despicable, and deep loyalty for their friends. There would be a warm hand laid on your knee or shoulder and a voice and face of such confiding friendship and mutual esteem that the day's tensions melted, and hearer and speaker entered into a communion of heart-to-heart relaxation almost unknown today. Anyone looking at the stern pictures of these old-time men would never guess the light that could come into their faces. As a result, seldom is this quality to be found among today's actors portraying old-time roles. Men are shown as either tough and hard or inanely naïve and friendly. It was not so in real life. In the late 20's and early 30's I found the same simple, warm affection among rough men of the Southwest who had gone through the turbulence of the 80's and 90's, seen scalpings, murders and hangings, indeed, participated in some of them.

There is at this writing an old-timer still living in Pine Grove who never saw scalpings, but who personifies this old-time warmth, an eighty-odd-year-old storekeeper affectionately known as Billy. When he sits out on the bench of what used to be his store porch, under the one remaining wooden awning in town, passers-by are drawn to stop and talk to him. I can never listen to him without being reminded of my own father.

Not that I would want you to believe that these men suited their opinions and convictions to expediency or to politeness. On one occasion Major Filbert attended a military encampment. Coming back, halfway over Broad Mountain he overtook his enemy, Private Zimmerman. Both were Civil War veterans. The major, a kind considerate man, was alone in a buggy, driving his own spanking team. Private Zimmerman was also alone and on foot. Although each would defend the other's bravery, there was a feud between them and each man stayed true to his code. The major passed him by and there was no recognition between them.

*Boating on the canal basin was a popular pastime throughout the first decades of the century before a town dump, now on the lower banks, poisoned the air and water.*

"What would you have done if he'd stopped to pick you up?" friends asked Zimmerman.

"He never would," Zimmerman said. "He knew I'd never get in anyway."

This breed, so adamant in some ways, loved to entertain and amuse you. To be trite, dull, and conventional would have dried up the inward springs. Moreover in those times they had time to think up fresh things to say. Just yesterday I went uptown and found Otis Rehrer—pronounced Ottis in Pine Grove—an eighty-odd-year-old man energetically sweeping the sidewalk, not only his own but well onto those of his immediate neighbors. Otis has a son Mervin, a judge in Highlands County in Florida.

I said, "Are you going south this winter?"

"I guess so." He grinned, his accent on the so. "I wrote Mervin my long underwear's wore out."

In Helene Morley's amusing journal of her life as a girl in a Brazilian town, she says, "A town would be dull without lunatics." She didn't mean the violent and insane but the eccentric and curious-minded who often enjoy life more than we. Older Pine Grove was blessed with these who in the days of liberty were left undisturbed in their native habitat to live the life they and their families wanted. There was Mr. Clayton from England who could play any instrument in the band and who could be found in his later years in his red underwear sitting on a tombstone in the cemetery. In my day we had, among others, Eddie Barr, who never missed a funeral. He seldom lacked interests, had business at the coming of the trains, poked over every express package and then marched over town to inform merchants they had something for them at the station. But he refused to deliver telegrams. "I don't want anything on my mind," he said. His sayings were famous through the town. Once when men tried to rally him, he said, "You fellows aren't so bright. You work." He and George Wade, a contemporary, loved to lead the band. When Eddie marched ahead waving his hand George would shake his head. "He's a poor soul," he'd say. And when George took his turn, Eddie would do the same. "You have to pity him," he'd tell us.

Eddie had pride, felt himself somebody, did not treat everyone as his equal. His aunt was the mother of a successful novelist, and he used to greet me almost with affection, as was fitting between men connected to a noble profession. For a long time after his mother died, Eddie refused to get in an automobile for fear they would take him to imprisonment in a state institution. Some were sorry to see him finally a victim of human enlightenment, exiled from the town he loved.

Some of us have been sorry, too, to see the passing of the leading town families, the aristocrats as some called them, or the robber barons, if you prefer. It is the fashion today to make dens of evil out of the big houses of a community and monsters out of the men and women who lived in them, sin and shock being more useful to the novelist, dramatist, and sensational biographer than minor faults and common decencies. Our prominent families had their imperfections. One of our richest men, a coal operator, built his own Methodist church out of donations deducted arbitrarily from his miners' pay, so that many of them when passing the church would shake their fists at it and others point to bricks or stained-glass windows they claimed they had paid for. The coal operator had other failings. My mother and Aunt Lizzie, as girls, were warned at home never to enter his large house except in two's and three's. He fathered several children that did not bear his name.

But his children were unreproachable and his son left a foundation that has helped educate more than a hundred boys and girls from the town. Another of our big houses sent dinner out daily to a destitute old lady. For more than twenty years one of the daughters would go down the street carrying a basket packed with hot dishes covered with linen. And one who had been cook in another of the big houses told me that in the seventeen years she spent there she didn't "remember a day when something didn't go out of that house."

Not that these things are the basis of my regret to see the big old homes go. My feelings are less noble. To enter or even pass these houses in their heyday was a matter of personal pleasure to me: the lighted windows; the knowledge that lively dinner parties were going on inside; the glimpses we had of New York, Philadelphia or foreign guests in the yard, on the porches, or going out in carriage or car. The first ladies in our town to smoke cigarettes lived in several of these houses and boys used to sneak to the windows to see and confirm such scandalous doings. Those same boys saw some of the old women of town smoking pipes and Mandy Christ, who had a candy store, smoke her cigars, and they thought nothing of it. My chief admiration for the big houses came from something else. Four of them, perhaps five, had their own libraries. I don't mean a bookcase or two but an entire room known as the library and stacked from floor to ceiling along the walls with books. I'll never forget my feeling as a young boy being ushered for the first time into one of these caves of Ali Baba stored with glittering riches and told to pick out and take home to read any books I might like. The leading men of our town today are friendly democratic fellows, but to have a room they called the library might embarrass them. I'm sure they would prefer their television sets. Our millionaire, who died recently, had few books to his name and left little to local charity, although his expensive motor car was loaded with glittering symbols of county, state, and national AAA clubs of which he was an official.

Democracy has brought other changes. When I was a boy, the more or less cultured taste of the leading families was looked up to and followed. The trees that shaded their big homes found their counterparts over other houses. Today new and more democratic owners are chopping down the trees around the large houses and other citizens through the town do the same with their own. "They make dirt," they explain, meaning the leaves which have to be raked in the fall, as if this were a grave fault and unbearable tribulation unknown by former generations. Only a few partially shaded blocks are left on our once-beautiful mile-long Tulpehocken Street. Even a leading citizen who showed great interest in the charm of the town had the three large trees felled in front of his house, only one of which showed evidence of decay. The other two stumps were as solid under my hand as a rock.

This, I suspect, would hardly have happened in earlier days. The unspoken influence of the prominent families would have worked against it, or one of the strong-minded, outspoken daughters of the big houses might have taken it on herself to inform the prospective tree cutter of the contemplated injury to town, street, and his own property.

Life without shade trees is only one of the signs of our democratic evolution. Our town water from spring-fed mountain streams was once equal to the best in the state. Most municipalities guard their watersheds, planting them with evergreens to let the ground absorb rain, keep the

ALVIN C. SCHWALM

*Today, when the basin freezes over, its upper reaches invite a new generation to an old-time sport. Skaters play shinny and bonfires light the banks at night.*

springs flowing, and avoid muddying the reservoir. Our town several years ago sold its watershed timber to be cut without restriction or supervision. A sawmill was installed, the forest felled indiscriminately, timber dragged through runs and stream. I hasten to point out that this was done not by robber barons but by a duly and democratically elected borough council. Erosion naturally followed. Since then, after a hard rain or the flushing of a fireplug, our water has often been unfit for bathing or laundry. For our drinking water many of us go regularly to a mountain spring several miles above town where cars often must wait their turn to fill the gallon jugs in their trunks. The irony is that the borough has had to spend most of its timber money vainly trying to clean the pipes mud-coated by its blunder. Since then, forewarned by the timber-sale fiasco, town citizens have vigorously protested proposed strip mining on the watershed, so that council rejected a mining-company offer.

But other cancers of the times remain. Serious pollution runs through the town in streams where once I played as a child. The lower canal basin in which we boys used to fish has long been made into the town dump from which the reek of garbage, rot, rats, and dump smoke drifts into town houses, some of them only a stone's throw away. Citizens complain, but as a rule only in private to each other. The town paper tries patriotically to avoid presentation of evil. Angry women who write faultfinding letters, duly printed in the paper, are regarded as fussy, sometimes as cranks. Praise for our town is the watchword. The critic and would-be reformer is considered a kind of traitor to the town's good name and so to the people themselves. "Why do you tell the bad and not the good done by our Rotary and Lions Clubs and our big Halloween parade?" people will ask me, no doubt with justification. Our townspeople are generous and public-spirited in many ways. The strip-mining rebellion testifies that they can act when aroused. But at this writing the town dump still reeks, our polluted streams still run, and shade trees are still being felled from our streets.

One town tradition that survives is the personal observance of Decoration Day or what is known here as "The Thirtieth." For days our chief cemetery is a scene of activity. Private lawn mowers are heard from the hill. The day before and the morning of "The Thirtieth" the street is clogged with cars bringing flowers to the dead. Later a parade winds up into the cemetery, the band plays, a patriotic speech is made and rifles are fired over the graves, followed by a general visiting between friends and acquaintances, many of whom drive great distances and who may never see each other except here.

Another surviving tradition of rude earlier times comes at the inverse time of the year. We have days in winter, especially at the onset of cold weather, when ice skating flourishes on what is left of the upper canal. Be that through the want of a modern ice-skating rink, or as it may, for a brief time the ancient canal comes back into its own. Afternoons the reaches of ice are a scene of animation and color. Cries and laughter ring out. Boys play shinny, the local name for hockey, usually with homemade sticks and a battered tin can for a puck. Nights, particularly moonlit nights, fires glow again on the ancient towpath and modern youth can feel some of the sensations we once knew. Perhaps today there is a dearth of grown-up skaters, older men and women whom I was surprised as a boy to see on skates, but whose grace forward or backward soon won my respect. Perhaps, too, there is not quite the old-time daring. When I was young some of the larger boys would band together and skate over the dangerous stretches at the upper end of the canal where flowing springs in those days kept the ice thin. It would bend deeply under them as they passed and sooner or later one or more would break through and have to be fished out. If it was bitter cold, the old-time clamp skates would instantly freeze to his shoes and he would be obliged to melt them loose at the fire or manage to clop home as best he could on the steel runners.

But these are only a few remaining vestiges of the old-time life. Most of that life is gone, extinct as the dodo bird. We no longer tramp out to the mountain to cut our Christmas tree and bring it home on our father's back while we carry baskets of moss and ground pine for scenes under the tree. No more do we stand at the curb in front of our houses and light our own firecrackers, Roman candles, and sky rockets. Instead, we watch the studied show of fireworks put on by a local service-station owner and no doubt deducted as legitimate business expense from his income tax. And few outbuildings still stand in our town for the young ones to play house in, as Heinrich Heine relates in his poem, *Wir Waren Kinder:*

> My child, we were two children,
>   Small, merry by childhood's law;
> We used to creep in the henhouse
>   And hide ourselves in the straw.
> We crowed like cocks, and whenever
>   The passers-by near us drew—
> "Cock-a-doodle," they thought
>   'Twas a real cock that crew.

Perhaps when we lighted a firecracker with punk, held it while the fuse sputtered, and then threw it out to explode in mid-air—perhaps we were children like Heinrich Heine and it's the sophisticated child of today who is wise and mature. But some of us think it's the other way around, that man is not so much the ungrateful biped, as Dostoevsky called him, as the horse with blinders driven by progress with a small p. Charley Boyer, one of the last survivors of our big houses with libraries, said to his sister, Anna, "We lived in the best time."

*The trim fortress in a Harrodsburg park is a replica of the compound in which the settlers huddled to defend themselves against Indian raids inspired by the British.*

# The First Pioneers
# Blazed a Resort

—

## *Harrodsburg, Kentucky*

—

### BY THOMAS D. CLARK

The road leading southward from the Kentucky River climbs up the steep limestone face of the palisades. Far below the stream flows lazily around a great bend, changing its course to the northwest as it pushes off through the mighty limestone barrier toward the Ohio. For centuries this rugged little river in its spring rages has gnawed furiously at the great stone block which underlies the Kentucky Bluegrass. At the top of the long winding hill, the deeply imbedded road comes up for air and a sweeping view of the outer rim of the Bluegrass. Fields towering with stalks of oily green burley tobacco, great waves of golden ripening wheat, and rows of corn marching up and down hills give an air of prosperity to the landscape. Lush pas-

tures, dotted with fat cattle and round fleecy sheep, flank the rest of the way to Harrodsburg, eight miles away.

Studding the outer limits of the county town are the big rambling houses, monuments to a productive soil. Some of these reflect an architectural taste of the dreamy ante-bellum days when Sir Walter Scott's gothic romances were in vogue; others the grandeurs of the 1880's and 1890's. Occasionally a new house reflects the nostalgia of its owner for another age when Kentuckians of affluence forted themselves behind the embattlements of Greek-revival columns.

On the map, Harrodsburg is as near the center of the awkward geometrical shape of Kentucky as any spot can be. The town, however, shrinks away from being a part of

43

*This pre-Civil War mansion in the 1880's was the seat of a prosperous farm. The border town, unharmed in the war, had adjusted from a slave to a farm economy.*

the less promising knobs, or even from falling solely under the influence of the Salt River and its gnarly valley lying to the west.

Harrodsburg is self-satisfied, provincial, sleepy Bluegrass. Seldom is its collective mind disturbed over anything more ominous than the never-ending process of politics and recurring elections. It takes fresh heart in saying to itself that it, next to Lexington, is the best farmer's town in the Bluegrass. Maybe the drowsiness best applies to the past; Harrodsburg has become industrially awakened in the last few years, and to a considerable extent the old agrarian spell has been broken.

Main Street clambers up a hill, and then wanders off in several directions. It really splatters itself against a fire station and loses its identity in its branches. Tradition has it that business got out of hand before the town surveyors were ready to locate a principal thoroughfare. Today side streets are tree-lined, and along many of them comfortable middle-class and modest homes shelter a population that is proud of the past, hopeful for the future, and for the most part about as willing to accept perceptive change as the sun is to remain in total eclipse.

Near the top of the hill on Main Street the courthouse sits as complacently in its tiny island as do the whittlers along its public benches. Political placards stuck up on every wall and post reflect one of the main concerns of the occupants of this bastion of justice and public affairs. The hallways of the stained old building buzz with the talk of politicians, lawyers, and farmers who hardly feel they have been to town unless they gather in the gossip floating around the courthouse.

Occasionally the people of Harrodsburg recall the past almost as a sense of obligation for living in this ancient cradle of Kentucky civilization. They fill store windows with antique relics, ranging from flax wheels of frontier vintage to derby hats from the good old days of the early part of this century. Harrodsburg does owe a special debt to frontier American history, which, if it ever forgets, the place will be robbed of much of its charm and spirit. This debt dates from the opening of the trans-Appalachian frontier.

No doubt Daniel Boone, a definite visitor at a later date, walked this way in his lonely wanderings in Kentucky, from 1769 to 1771. Certainly two Virginia valley land scouts, Robert and James McAfee, braved the hardships of unbroken wilderness to come out to the Kentucky country to lay claim to numerous 400-acre plots of land. Land fever coursed the veins of Virginia and Pennsylvania backwoodsmen in this decade. Thomas Bullitt was at the Falls of the Ohio, taking possession of Kentucky's most likely spot for a city. Hancock Taylor, a member of the famous

Virginia dynasty of Taylors, was along the Kentucky. These surveyors were well out ahead of the rush which was to come. Daniel Boone and a band of neighbors attempted to plant a settlement in Kentucky in 1773, but the Cherokees bluffed them away.

In late spring the edge of the great plateau sloping down to the Salt River valley was a beautiful land. There were thick woods with towering trees of monstrous girth. Patches of rich grass and trim cane elbowed their way into the forests. These fattened deer, elk, and buffalo. The McAfee brothers scored trees across the Bluegrass to assert prior claims to land. They wandered up the little Salt to block out more claims for the numerous McAfee clan. No doubt they dreamed of a day when the bottoms before them would grow corn and tobacco, and blossom in rich pastures. About them was an American Eden. These first-comers crossed the narrow ridge between the Kentucky and the Salt and no doubt went by the spring which became a focal center of later Harrodstown.

In June, 1774, James Harrod, a Pennsylvania trader of long and rugged frontier experience, came at the head of a surveying party of forty Virginians to lay out a western town. On their way they blazed a tree at Cedar Creek, striking the first lick in the founding of Cincinnati. Downriver they entered Kentucky by way of the Kentucky River and followed it up to the high palisades. They, too, went south overland toward the Salt. The woods and meadows were in full bloom. Atop the great rock wall thousands of fertile acres awaited the conquering march of backwoods trader and land hunter.

Harrod and his men had come to establish permanent claims. They began to clear away the woods, to build log cabins, and to establish permanent land surveys. Spring days passed on into early summer without incident. Men came and went in the woods without interference; then Daniel Boone and Michael Holsteiner came on their explorations to warn Bullitt's men of the outbreak of Dunmore's War. This was a warning; the Indians struck. After all the Kentucky Eden had its serpent.

At Harrod's camp Daniel Boone saw his dream of being the first settler of Kentucky fading. If, however, he could not lead the first band of settlers to the land, he would join forces with Harrod. In partnership with Evan Hinton he lingered long enough to build a log cabin before going back to Virginia.

On a quiet July morning there were shots from behind a tree. One settler lay dead where he had been drying his land papers after a rain. War against Harrodstown had begun, and the settlers withdrew to join the frontier army pushing up from the Watauga settlements in eastern Tennessee to strike the Indians on the Ohio. Back along the Salt, they had made a shaky beginning of settlement. They had cut a tiny hole in the vast wilderness, and scored trees to memorialize land claims.

The friction between white man and Indian which caused Dunmore's War took place far away from Harrod's cabins in the wilderness where the Shawnee tribe struck in an effort to check settler pressure against their hunting grounds in what is present-day West Virginia. By August, 1774, militiamen from Virginia closed in against the Indians at Fort Pitt and along the Kanawha. The war was of short duration, but it was serious enough to halt activities at Harrodstown.

For Harrod and his partners it was useless to return to their half-built cabins to shiver out a cold winter. Spring was time enough, and in May, 1775, the settlers were back to stay. Quickly they helped open the land to a flood of settlers who came by river and trail to gobble up the vast reservoir of cheap land.

If the war had not accomplished the subjection of the Indians, it did stir up the frontiersmen. Stories told by Daniel Boone, Simon Kenton, the McAfee brothers, Thomas Bullitt, and Harrod's men traveled far. One of the scouts accompanying Lord Dunmore was a redheaded lad from Albemarle County, Virginia, who listened attentively to the yarns of his fellow scouts. Already George Rogers Clark had an insatiable land hunger, and in the spring of 1775 he popped out of the woods at Harrodstown. He startled young James Ray, a sixteen-year-old lad who had just roasted a duck and was ready to enjoy it. The stranger accepted the duck from the boy and stripped the bones clean.

Little did either youth realize what the future held for them. Clark was a natural leader of men. Quickly he was made commander of frontier militiamen. But his business was land hunting. He scouted the nearby countryside and left his marks on desirable tracts, intending no doubt to become in time a highly domesticated settler, which he was never to be.

While Harrod and Clark and others busied themselves at Harrodstown, Daniel Boone and Richard Henderson were building Boonesboro and so beginning a private empire in the West. In March, 1775, Henderson, in the Treaty of Sycamore Shoals, traded the Cherokees out of all the land below the Kentucky River, including the site of Harrodstown. While sweaty woodsmen raised log cabins on the south bank of the Kentucky, Henderson began the organization of a new colony.

In the meantime the trail up from Cumberland Gap disgorged new settlers to begin other settlements in Kentucky. Three families traveling with Daniel Boone and his womenfolk turned off at the Hazlepatch and made their way to Harrodstown. These men, their wives and children, brought the first touch of domesticity to the settlement. Among them was the most irascible of all Kentuckians, Hugh McGary, whose life in Kentucky was to be marked by one hot-tempered outburst after another.

The coming of women and children to Harrodstown created new anxieties. Men could run and hide or stand and fight it out when a sneaking Indian crept up to snatch a scalp. Women and children needed more protection than even cabins afforded. Every month there were increasing signs of Indian troubles. Already the Revolutionary War had begun, and the British in Detroit were spurring their Indian allies on to new attacks against the Kentucky settlers.

Wyandottes, Delawares, Shawnees, and Cherokees knew the "Big Knives" had been pushing west for more than a century. Wherever they came, they stayed. The braves readily accepted the war belt in 1776, and raided the new settlements at will. For the Kentuckians the time had come to build fortresses and to condition themselves for long sieges. Resolution, however, was weak among the settlers. When no raids occurred, they wishfully concluded the troubles had ended. Their hearts were in the land, and they wanted to get on with opening farms.

George Rogers Clark was more comprehending than his fellows at Harrod. The first problem to be settled was that of Henderson and his colony. This activity threatened Virginia's authority, and it could invalidate all the land claims granted by that state. In June, 1776, an assembly of settlers at Harrodstown elected John Gabriel Jones and George Rogers Clark to present the western problems to the general assembly sitting in Richmond. These delegates were successful in their mission, and on December 7, 1776, Kentucky County was created, with Harrodstown as its county seat. This was the first time the name Kentucky was used officially. In Harrodstown a court was created, and there were seated the sheriff, court clerks, county lieutenant, and court of magistrates.

Establishment of Virginia officially beyond the Appalachians solved a major political problem, but in no way lessened the British-Indian menace. Clark and Jones were given a meager amount of gunpowder, to be delivered to them at Fort Pitt, for the protection of the western settlements. This precious ammunition was drifted down the Ohio aboard a canoe and, after an Indian raid which resulted in Jones' death, was delivered to Harrodstown.

Clark understood clearly the nature of growing Indian pressures. The raids were becoming more than hit-and-run scalping affairs. Beyond the Ohio, the British were encouraging the Indians to carry out their raids at Detroit, Vincennes, and Kaskaskia, mainsprings of British influence. For the settlers the Indian territory beyond the Ohio was one of dark mystery. Indians drifted across the river into Kentucky as quietly as the spreading fog of night, then fired on settlers and ran. No one had any dependable information as to what was happening about the British posts. Rumor and gossip pictured them as being infernal places of plots and schemes. Clark sat in his corner blockhouse at Harrod's Fort and planned a campaign. He summoned three trusted woodsmen to meet with him, Simon Kenton, William Linn, and Samuel Moore, from whom he would choose two to spy on the British posts. By drawing the long straws Moore and Linn were chosen, and during the next two months they visited the old French strongholds of Vincennes and Kaskaskia where they gathered information. These places were unfortified, and Lieutenant Governor of Detroit Henry Hamilton planned to send troops armed with a cannon against the Kentucky settlements. This information confirmed Clark in his determination to lead a secret campaign into the Northwest.

Before Clark set out for Virginia in the early fall, Harrodstown settlers had their first full-scale frolic. William Linn, the returned spy, took a bride and this called for a rollicking celebration. Settlers danced puncheon floors slick, and ate themselves into a stupor. Clark could not wait to sleep off the fatigue of the party. Bright and early on October 1, 1777, he headed for Virginia to persuade Governor Patrick Henry and the Assembly to support his proposed Northwest campaign.

The Kentuckian could describe to the Virginians the horrors of an Indian attack, because settlers had been fired on. One, William Ray, had been killed. All that summer Indians had besieged Harrod's Fort. They had driven off the cows and horses. Only one nag was saved, and this one was used on hunting expeditions to secure meat for the settlers. Shawnees were everywhere. On one occasion James Harrod was treed by them, and only by the ruse of shaking his hat on the end of a ramrod was he able to draw the Indians' fire and kill two of them.

Clark never returned to Harrodstown after he left for Virginia. His influence, however, was to linger on. While he was away in the Northwest the settlers were further harassed by Indian raids. For seven years they lived under this pressure and men from Harrodstown were constantly called upon to aid neighboring settlements. John Bowman, Kentucky's first county lieutenant, early in the summer of 1779 led a secret war party against the Piqua towns of the Shawnees above the Ohio. Will Harrod was in command of the wild Mononghahelans as the Pennsylvanians were called. Before the expedition started up the Ohio, the frontiersmen had agreed to divide the rich loot they would take. An Indian hunter discovered the whites before the Piqua towns and the raid never took place. Bowman was charged with failure. Harrodstown was even more disturbed by the fear of surprise attack and possible annihilation.

The presence of women and children in the fort gave Harrodstown an atmosphere of permanency. Mrs. William Coomes began a school in which she corralled the children and taught them the elementary three R's. A head count in late 1777 revealed a population of 198 people, among whom were 85 men, 24 women, 22 children under sixteen years of age, and 19 slaves. This number increased despite the fear of the raids.

During the gloomy months of bloody 1777 most of the population of Harrod's settlement was huddled together in the small fortress compound. Tiny one-room cabins along the main walls, and large blockhouse corners offered safety. A spring in the corner of the enclosure supplied water. Something of the character of the people huddled in this stifling island of safety can be gathered from the description of the pioneers of nearby Boonesboro by that crotchety British observer J. F. D. Smythe. In 1780 he wandered far afield to the Kentucky. There he said, "Although the inhabitants are in reality a rude, barbarous and unsophisticated set of men, yet you will frequently find pleasure in their conversation; their ideas are bold and spirited, but their sentiments are not liberal. However, they are certainly a sensible, enterprising, hardy unspoiled race, yet open, free and hospitable."

Life in the Harrodstown compound never could have been pleasant. People and their animals were crowded together. Quarrelsome inhabitants could always find something to ruffle their feelings. Colonel William Fleming, a Virginia land-office official, gave a graphic description of conditions in the chilling winter of 1780. "The spring at this place," he wrote, "is below the Fort and fed by ponds above the Fort so that the whole dirt and filth of the Fort, putrefied flesh, dead dogs, horse, cow, hog excrements and human odour [ordure] all wash into the spring which with the ashes and sweepings of filthy cabins, the dirtiness of the people, steeping skins to dress and washing every sort of dirty rags and clothes in the spring perfectly poisons the water and makes most filthy nauseous potation of the water imaginable and will certainly contribute to render the inhabitants of this place sickly."

Equally as interesting as Colonel Fleming's raw description of conditions inside Harrod's fort was his notation that the land commissioners finished their work in February and that the court had granted certificates for 1,096,650 acres of land. This was certification for perhaps three times the amount of land lying within a radius of one hundred and fifty miles about the town.

The puncheon wall fort was never intended to be a place of permanent residence. Just as soon as the Indians were driven back families rushed out to the open country. Almost on the heels of the retreating warriors men again slashed at the woods in their clearings, and women were ordering crude cabins for family living. Like a summer-spent hornet's nest, the tenants had fled, and the old compound at Harrod's lay barren and trampled, and in the first stages of decay. Because it was the first settlement planted in the Kentucky littoral, it was a place of beginnings, a fact its inhabitants would ever value as a central part of the glory of their community.

*On sun-dappled lawns, these Harrodsburg ladies only three generations away from log cabins assumed a graciously Victorian pose near their spacious homes.*

Harrodstown ended its pioneer days quietly. It became Harrodsburg, the seat of Mercer County, in 1785. Its population grew and the fertile soil about it offered economic security. Among the new settlers who came to the place were the Robards of Virginia, who accumulated large holdings of land and built themselves a fine stone house. One son, Lewis, an active land speculator, married Rachel Donelson, the buxom daughter of another land hunter, John Donelson of the Cumberland valley. She was an attractive lass of medium height, with beautifully molded form, full red lips, a glowing olive-shaded face which rippled with smiles and laughter. A plucky girl, she had made the harrowing journey down the Tennessee and up the Ohio and Cumberland aboard the flatboat *Adventure* with the Watauga settlers on their way to settle Nashville.

Rachel became the belle of the lower Cumberland and could have taken her choice of suitors. Instead she married Captain Robards of Harrodsburg, a sensitive, jealous man —too jealous to be married to a beautifully molded form with full red lips. He took his bride home to the big stone house and his mother. Rachel flirted with Mother Robards' visitors and on one occasion was caught by Lewis having a cheek-by-cheek tete-à-tete with Peyton Short, a lively young trader. Robards' outburst against Rachel and Short made public the secretly whispered gossip that he was unhappy in his marriage.

Robards, after the Short incident, ordered his wife home to Nashville and out of his sight forever. He requested the Donelsons to send for her, and Samuel Donelson accompanied his sister home through the two hundred miles of Kentucky and Tennessee wilderness. Rachel had hardly reached Nashville before her mother accepted as a boarder the young frontier lawyer and federal district attorney, Andrew Jackson, fresh from North Carolina. Attorney Jackson was attracted at once to the pretty Mrs. Robards of Harrodsburg. In a short time John Overton appeared in Nashville to practice law, and one of his first commissions was to seek Rachel's forgiveness of her impetuous husband. Lewis Robards did crave again the sight of his Rachel, and he came to Nashville and began improving his land claim. Again he became jealous, this time of Andrew Jackson. The Donelson household was upset, but Rachel foolishly returned to Harrodsburg with Lewis only to experience another emotional upheaval. This time Andrew Jackson came to take her home.

In Kentucky, Jackson threatened to cut off Robards' ears if he associated the lawyer's name with Rachel's. This led to a comic arraignment of Jackson before a magistrate to be placed under a peace bond. It is said the Tennessean borrowed a knife from the magistrate and looked Robards straight in the eye while he ran his thumb over the blade. The captain ran away, but Magistrate Robert Weakley upheld the dignity of his court by issuing the bond. Jackson took Rachel home to Nashville. In the meantime he had

Jack Jouett, of Revolutionary War fame, seek a divorce in the Virginia Legislature. In time Robards raised such a howl that he created one of the most virulent social scandals in early nineteenth-century American history. In future political campaigns enemies made charges of open adultery against Andrew and Rachel from the stump, in the columns of newspapers, and through the pamphlet press. Back in Harrodsburg the stormy Robards fed the gossip mills with his jealous charges, but he had lost his Rachel by his own misdeeds.

At the time when Rachel and Lewis Robards were growing apart, delegates were meeting in nearby Danville, preparing for the separation of Kentucky from Virginia. The struggle with political and constitutional issues was almost as rugged as were those with the Indians and elements. At the end of eight years and ten conventions, frontier statesmen affected a separation from the mother state, and Kentucky became an independent commonwealth in 1792. Harrodsburg became a county-seat town in a new state that created counties as fast as it had established frontier stations in earlier years.

The surrounding land set the pattern for life in Harrodsburg. When farmers prospered, the town boomed; when their crops failed, the pace of life was slowed. Horses, mules, cattle, sheep, hogs, tobacco, and hemp yielded rich returns. Where the McAfees, Harrods, McGarys, and Coomes planted piddling little patches of corn to validate land claims, there were, in 1810, ever-widening fields of corn, wheat, tobacco, and hemp. Across the rolling hills in harvest season, and on the Indians' old hunting grounds, tepees of hempen stalks and corn trailed across the horizon. Barns bulged with heavily sprung tier rails of curing tobacco, and orchards yielded bountiful harvest of fruits to be made into liquors.

Pastures were slashed out of cane and woodland. Descendants of those wild cows which had signaled the approach of Indians by scurrying home with bells clanging and tails curled high over their backs, now grazed calmly in rich meadows. Every county-court day brought more animals than people to town. Jockey row, hitching rack, and side lots became bawling, neighing, bleating bedlams. Thousands of complacent hogs were herded into town to be driven over the old pioneer trails back to the East. Droves of young mules were led away from their pastures to be sold south to turn the new cotton lands. Along with them went the surplus Kentucky slaves to be sold to cotton farmers in delta and black belt.

Harrodsburg was a county town, resembling those of Virginia, and in turn those of England. Many of its most prominent citizens were farmers who built mansions within the town limits or on nearby lands. Some of these, like the James Neal and Thompson homes, Diamond Point and Wildwood, Cherry Hill, the old MaGoffin place, the stately Harrodsburg Academy, and the elaborate Southern-type

*The stately resort of Graham Springs, standing close to the original stockade a scant forty years after the pioneers' ordeal, was an unsurpassed spa in the pre-war South.*

hotel at Graham's Springs all symbolized a rising agricultural wealth. The first houses reflected the influence of Virginia Georgian, but after 1830 and the introduction of the Greek-revival design, Harrodsburg was caught in a wave of neoclassicism. In cultural spirit Harrodsburg lived suspended between affluent Valley Virginia, and a throbbing, growing, raw Ohio valley. Outwardly it compounded the grace of the Virginia country town with the bubbling optimism of the New West, and the unpolished ruggedness of the backwoods. Mercer was a Bluegrass county which, with some frontier seasoning, duplicated west of the mountains, the social and economic patterns of Virginia. Some of the first settlers brought their slaves with them. When John Cowan prepared his census of Harrodstown in 1777 he listed nineteen slaves among the inhabitants. As the fertile lands were brought under cultivation the number of slaves was increased. For more than a half century they labored in hemp and tobacco fields. Some of them, sold South, were separated from their families in those deeply emotional dramas which so bitterly damned the system. Others lived happily on farm and plantation, or in town, as well adjusted to the land as were their masters.

An enduring symbol of Harrodsburg's social maturity was the relaxed atmosphere centered about the elaborate old Graham Springs Hotel. Shaded by a grove of massive virgin oak, ash, elm, and maple, the mineral springs bubbled only a short piece away from the one which had sustained the pioneers in the stinking fort during the hard years. Graham's had just enough of a mineral flavor to suggest a cure for social loneliness, to give a fillip to social climbing, to encourage unbridled flirtation, to foster a little philandering, and to stimulate endless discussions of crops, horses, slaves, and fox hounds.

Dr. Christopher Columbus Graham, man of many parts and talents, arrived in Harrodsburg with a fresh doctor-of-medicine degree and an insatiable ambition to get on in the world. He was self-proclaimed world's champion rifle-shot. His heroic record in the War of 1812 was never allowed to be forgotten, and quickly it was known that he had more on his mind than the woes of the lonely and the afflicted. He sought a likely Harrodsburg belle to make his wife and secure his social position. With more tangible promise of wealth, he wooed the mineral springs. He sought the patronage not only of bored Kentuckians but that of fever-ridden Lower Southerners.

To enhance the beauty of his rich natural setting and his great columned hotel, Dr. Graham hauled down by flat-boat from the high country about the head of the Kentucky River a variety of mountain trees and shrubs. He was one of the first Kentuckians to lay out a large formal garden, and to develop aesthetically the surrounding woodlands. About his springs he attempted to create a perfect setting for romance and love-making, and this he accomplished in masterly fashion.

One of the Rowan girls from Bardstown described joys of the springs to one of Judge Bibbs' daughters. She wrote: "I have just left the ballroom. If I could only describe to you this lovely place, the many comforts and luxuries we have, together with the interesting gentlemen. There are two gentlemen worth more than a million apiece." There was more to Dr. Graham's fairyland that appealed to young girls. Along with eligible rich men there was plenty to eat. "The table," wrote Miss Rowan, "is the best I ever sat down to at any place: *Ice* Cream in profusion, and cottages with large closets." This was all that a frolicking clientele could ask.

Visitors to the mineral springs of America in the first half of the nineteenth century were, on the surface, easily satisfied. They strolled through the groves, and sat on the porches for hours. They discussed politics incessantly, and damned or praised, as their moods dictated, the administrations in Frankfort and Washington. There was more to their visits, however. Harrodsburg, along with the other watering places, early gained a reputation for gambling. A newspaper reporter in 1905 said that when expert gamblers were needed at other places, proprietors of resort hotels requested Harrodsburg to supply them. If this was a fact, Dr. Graham was as careful as a Mississippi steamboat captain not to advertise it.

Graham's Springs relied on the traveling theatrical companies to provide entertainment. In time many famous actors touring the Western circuit appeared on the hotel's stage. Professor Koumar, a German violinist, enlivened the entertainment with his thick guttural renditions of the "Woodpecker Song" to his own accompaniment. If Professor Koumar stirred a humorous vein, the famous musical waiters of the hotel, Henry, Reuben, and George, wafted visitors into romantic moods with their harmonious plantation songs. In 1841, Dr. Graham sent this trio of slaves to Lexington to entertain President-elect William Henry Harrison. When they had sung Old Tippecanoe into mellow drowsiness, the waiters packed their fancy jackets and headed for Canada by way of Louisville and the steamer *Zebulon M. Pike.* Their master in hot pursuit almost lost his life at the hands of freedom-loving bystanders who tried to prevent him from recovering his property. He sued the owners of the steamboat, and the case reached the United States Supreme Court which awarded damages of $300.

Many a famous name of the early American stage appeared on the bill of the hotel's theater. Among these were the Drake family, James Douglas, Samuel, Martha, Julia, and Alexander; Harry Vaught, Noah M. Ludlow, Harry Forbes, Jenny Lind, and Sol Smith. N. Parker Willis, poet and traveler, stopped on his way to the tropics to take the waters at Harrodsburg and later wrote of his pleasant experiences.

Rolling through Dr. Graham's gateway, guarded by a pair of bronze lions, came the stylish carriages of cotton planters, wealthy businessmen, Kentucky farmers, and politicians. Henry Clay was there, as were his fellow Kentuckians John Rowan, Judge George Bibb, the roistering Cassius M. Clay (whose slave took his name, which was passed down directly to a prize fighter), "Swearing Bob"

Letcher, Governor John J. Crittenden, George D. Prentice, and William Preston. Glendy Burke, a flashy merchant prince of Cincinnati, followed in the wake of the Queen City beauty, Alice Carneal. Alice, however, had to share queenly honors with Louisville's buxom and oft-married widow, Sally Ward.

George D. Prentice was a visitor to Graham's Springs in August 1845. He wrote that, "a more lovely resort than the Harrodsburg [Graham's] Springs is not to be found in America. The lot, in which the mineral springs is situated, consists of at least 100 acres, all thickly covered with trees and shrubbery, the spontaneous growth of the soil, and the whole is interspersed in every direction with the most beautiful paths laid out with great taste and labor and at much expense, so that lovers or those who seek retirement may wander at will for hours, unseen but by the thousand birds that sing and flutter over their heads.

"The palace-like hotel is the admiration of all who see it. The hotel, the cottages, and the rich shrubbery of the yard constitute a scene of beauty that can hardly be surpassed. We sat for hours one evening gazing at the hundred lights that glowed from all directions through the thick foliage, and the whole scene appeared more fairy vision than real."

These were the years when part of Harrodsburg society lived up to the hilt in the moonlight and roses tradition of the ante-bellum South. More than 10,000 persons flocked to the springs. Fierce and romantic militia companies, with their flashy uniforms and comical goose steps, came from all over the Bluegrass to parade on the grounds, and to carry on flirtations in the shadows. But like the prophetic line in Stephen Foster's "My Old Kentucky Home," a shadow crept over the Springs and its ebullient master. By 1853 the belles went elsewhere to bestow their favors, and the militiamen temporarily stacked their arms, leaving a monumental hotel building in simulated Greek-revival tradition, and a lone grave beneath the oaks.

A plain little tombstone marks the grave of a mysterious maid who was said to have danced herself to death on the ballroom floor. The romantics have called the grave that of an "unknown belle." A fine web of legend has been spun over the years about this lass and her background. One account said she was Mollie Black of Tazewell, Tennessee, who had married the itinerant actor, Joe Sewell. She had run away from Joe, a bawling infant, and a nagging mother-in-law to take a fling at Graham's Springs. Whoever she was, she created for Harrodsburg an enduring and romantic mystery.

For most of the people of Harrodsburg, Dr. Graham's palatial resort lay beyond the pale of their everyday lives. They were too busy selling goods, running for office, visiting, gossiping, and going to church to envy the visitors to the hotel. Presbyterians, Methodists, Disciples of Christ, and Baptists herded flocks of members through their church doors. To a large extent individual social standing was gauged by membership in a local church. Presbyterians were first to arive at Harrodstown. The Harrods, McAfee brothers, Robards, and others sprang from stern Scotch Calvinist backgrounds. Father David Rice, pioneer missionary to the backwoods, preached a doctrine of economic thrift and spiritual fidelity.

The same voices which shouted angry defiance at Indian marauders invoked the blessings of God on the settlement. From the outset organized religion was a pronounced fact in the lives of the people. Denominations settled side by side, keeping an unspoken truce, but holding vigorous differences of views. Among the hardy old frontier campaigners who came to live in Harrodsburg was the Reverend Jesse Head. Brother Head, a circuit rider from nearby Washington County, had carved himself a modest niche in history by joining Nancy Hanks and Tom Lincoln in marriage. He was neither able nor satisfied to live by the simple role of mendicant circuit rider, and in the ferment of the early Jacksonian years took up the editorial pen in behalf of his hero. Jousting with his neighbors, especially George D. Prentice of the Louisville *Journal,* he often forgot the admonitions of the gentle John Wesley of Lincoln College, Oxford.

It mattered little whether one was Presbyterian or Disciple of Christ in general acceptance in the town. The bastion of orthodox form and churchly dignity was disturbed, however, by Mother Ann Lee's Shaker disciples at Pleasant Hill. There, overlooking the Kentucky River, this community of mystics entertained visitations in spirit of the Prophet Moses, General George Washington, Chief Cornstalk, and scores of others. These plain people of the jubilant faith often walked the streets of Harrodsburg selling their jellies, jams, garden seeds, and sturdy furniture. Sometimes they were there to defend themselves against the forays of tax collector and sheriff. It was not unusual for the shiftless of the town to profess Shaker conversion at the outset of biting cold winter in order to enjoy the warm comforts of a free bedroom and the joys of a well-stocked pantry. Perhaps others sought solace of a more personal nature. At least the colony's irate recorder at the outset of spring, on one occasion, flung after a departing "winter sister" the epithet, "Harlot of Harrodsburg."

The adventures of Harrodsburg natives extended far beyond the well-kept meadows of Shakertown and the Kentucky River. There was James Wiley MaGoffin, who helped to open the Santa Fe trade and to colonize Americans in the Mexican Southwest. A jovial Irishman, steeped in the intimate ways of frontier life, MaGoffin became the "Don Santiago" of the far-flung border.

Behind in Harrodsburg, Don Santiago's less venturesome brother cast his lot on the murky waters of local politics. Beriah MaGoffin, lawyer, officeholder, politician, and political kingmaker, was elected in 1859 to the governorship of Kentucky. Southerner at heart, he was faced with decisions which sometimes did not express his personal sentiments. Left to his own devices, he no doubt would have led Kentucky into the Confederacy, and deeper into the bloody chaos of Civil War. As it was, Harrodsburg was to see and hear enough of the war. Its sons rode away to fight on both sides. Raiders clattered back and forth through its streets, and in October, 1862, the roar of battle came near its borders when the armies of Don Carlos Buell and Braxton Bragg stumbled into conflict at Perryville.

Near Harrodsburg was Camp Nelson where the first Union forces in Kentucky were organized. Into this camp poured volunteers from Mercer County and Harrodsburg, and before the Civil War ended some of them had fought at Shiloh, Vicksburg, Chattanooga, and Atlanta. Harrodsburg boys rode with Morgan's cavalry and fought in Bragg's army at nearby Perryville. Brothers had gone into opposing armies, and Harrodsburg families found themselves emotionally divided during the war, hoping that sons would not, by the ill fortunes of war, confront each other in murderous combat on the battlefield.

At the end of the Civil War, men came back to Harrodsburg to pick up their lives and to mend their fortunes. Unlike most veterans of the Southern cause, they found their countryside intact and productive. The slaves were freed, but they were still there to work as laborers. The fields blossomed with promise of a fresh harvest, the courthouse square was astir with mules and traders. Crops and livestock still brought cash money to farmer and merchant. The old differences of the war were quickly forgotten, and Harrodsburg became a highly self-contained island of social intimacy. Families found within themselves resources to brighten their lives and, as in all Bluegrass Kentucky, social intercourse went at a lively clip. Dances, athletic contests, barbecues, house parties, and family gatherings sweetened the passing seasons.

Large numbers of Harrodsburg families lived graciously. While the parlors of the old mansions were scenes of gaiety, the dining rooms reflected even more a plenteous mode of living. A list of foods served at a family dinner represented a capital feast, indeed. Matrons of the town prided themselves on their mature art of cooking. From baking country ham to making frothy Christmas eggnog they used lavish hands. They never heard of *Cordon Bleu,* but they were trained strictly within the tastes and modes of a rich land.

Harrodsburg could not be of frontier origin and escape human tragedies. Murders, assaults, and fires discolored an otherwise pleasant local history. Soldiers home from the Civil War were restive and sometimes bored with the quiet ways of the community. They brought back with them stories of high adventure in the war. Some had ridden with

*A Bluegrass legend, Captain Phil B. Thompson, here an old man, had exercised frontier lawlessness, when as a lawyer and Congressman, he had shot and killed two foes.*

the impetuous John Hunt Morgan who had raided across Kentucky on several occasions. These veterans in return to civilian life became the colonels, majors, and captains of the titled aristocracy. Among these were Colonel Phil B. Thompson, Sr. and his son Captain Phil B. Thompson, Jr. They were lawyers and important local political figures.

In 1867 a chain of events was begun which resulted in a mass killing before the bar of the circuit court itself. Theodore Daviess, Sr., borrowed a large sum of money from a usurious moneylender for which he had to pay the interest at the outset. A year later he paid Colonel Thompson, his lawyer, the entire sum of the debt. Following this he was sued by the shylock for payment, and in the ensuing trial documents were produced to show that Thompson had collected the money and kept it. A gun fight broke out in the courtroom during which the Thompsons killed the elder Daviess and two of his sons. Captain Phil B. Thompson was accused of shooting Theodore Daviess in the back. A desultory hearing was held, but Captain Thompson was never even indicted or brought to trial. In the postwar years Kentuckians, of Bluegrass and mountain alike, carried pistols as casually as they did penknives, so on that dreary morning in Harrodsburg there was no expression of surprise that so many people carried pistols in the courtroom; rather the amazement was that no more people were killed.

In time "Little" Phil Thompson was elected to Congress, and as a member of that body he established a reputation for hard work and friendliness. These qualities won

him steadfast friends, one of whom was the eloquent Senator Daniel Voorhies of Indiana.

On his journeys to Washington, "Little" Phil Thompson traveled by way of the Southern Railway, stopping off in Cincinnati, and sometimes his wife accompanied him. Kentuckians, visiting Cincinnati, flocked to the Burnet House and Gibson Hotel to enjoy the parties and visiting. Unhappily for Phil Thompson his wife was an alcoholic, a fact which had necessitated placing his daughter in a convent school in Washington. In January, 1883, "Little" Phil left his wife in Cincinnati and went on to Washington to the reconvening of Congress. In the St. Clair Hotel, where she was staying with her friend, Jennie Buckner, she met Walter Davis of Harrodsburg, and Jennie Buckner reported to Congressman Thompson that Davis had debauched his drunken wife.

In April, Captain Thompson was back in Harrodsburg where gossip was on every tongue. On April 27 he started for Lexington aboard the shuttle train which connected Harrodsburg with the Southern Railway. Aboard the train were several Harrodsburg men, including Walter Davis. At the junction Davis had undertaken to shake hands with Thompson, but the captain refused his greeting, saying, "You damned son-of-a-bitch, do you dare speak to me after debauching my wife?" Davis rushed off the train, but Captain Thompson shot and killed him.

The shuttle train returned to Harrodsburg with both men aboard, Davis a corpse and Captain Thompson on his way to court to report his crime. In a highly unusual proceeding "Little" Phil strode into the circuit-court room, disrupted proceedings, and pleaded the "unwritten law." A skilled trial lawyer, he delivered an eloquent plea of extenuating circumstances.

A fortnight later the case Commonwealth *versus* Phil B. Thompson, Jr., was brought to trial. Present to participate was a battery of the ablest lawyers ever assembled in a single Kentucky circuit-court room. The Commonwealth was represented by counsel that had on numerous occasions brought jurors to tears and favorable decisions. The defense was led by United States Senators Daniel Voorhies and J. C. S. Blackburn. Both were spread-eagle orators, who could wring the last emotional quiver out of manly honor, home, mother, family, and fireside. The secondary defense was hardly less capable. Benches were filled with lawyers from all over Kentucky, come to hear the arguments. A jury of Mercer County farmers was sworn to assess the evidence and to render a decision.

For eight days the legal tug of war went on with clever maneuvers and grilling of witnesses. A succession of individuals had their moment in the box. Every sordid detail of what happened in Cincinnati was reviewed. Jennie Buckner was questioned long and savagely because only recently she herself had caused a scandal in Louisville. The defense attempted both to invalidate her testimony and to besmirch her character. At a tense moment in the trial

Mrs. Walter Davis, draped in heavy mourning, came into the courtroom and sat with bowed head. Rumor went about that the prosecution would also have Mrs. Thompson come to the bar and fling herself down before the judge and make a public confession.

When the last witness had recited his sorry tale, the case was turned over to the orators. Each side had eight hours in which to present arguments. Lieutenant Governor J. C. Cantrill, Judge Jere Morton, and Colonel George Denny pleaded for conviction. The great Voorhies rattled the windows of the room with his booming defense of "Little" Phil. Neither jury nor audience was fully rational in his presence. They sat on the edges of the benches with mouths agape, and were incapable of weighing objectively the facts of the case.

Voorhies was a warm-up lawyer. The most eloquent plea was made by the long-winded Blackburn from nearby Versailles. He knew the turn of mind of jury and audience. He also knew that no Kentuckian would vote to convict another for defending his home and good name. Mother and wife were sacred words which he uttered in tremulo voice. His unctuous references to the idols of Kentucky erased the last vestige of reason on the part of the jury. Beyond the courtroom twenty thousand southern Kentuckians about the border town of Guthrie wired that Little Phil had acted honorably, and they were ready to give him their support.

*Forming a tradition, farmers with increased leisure took sulkies and riding horses out for sport in the late 1800's. Riding remains a popular local activity.*

*For a holiday outing, young people in the 1910's drove in their elaborate automobiles to a new Graham Springs, which lasted briefly with less grandeur than the original.*

At last the fate of Captain Thompson was in the hand of the farmer-jurors. They were convinced before they left their box that "Little" Phil had properly invoked the unwritten law, as every man should in defense of his home, and soon let this decision be known.

The audience which listened to the heavy legal cannonading was near physical exhaustion. The town itself was burned out. In fact an incendiary had set fire to a lumberyard and Harrodsburg had all but burned to the ground just before the jury began deliberations. An alarm eventually brought out the volunteer fire company, but not until its members had dressed themselves in fancy uniforms and put on a parade. Critics said their old engine was out of repair and useless. There were heroes, however, among the unorganized volunteers, among them Captain Thompson, who on the morrow would await the decision of a jury as to his fate.

Harrodsburg in time recovered from both the oratory of the Thompson trial and the devastating fire, which had no connection except that the two moments of great excitement occurred simultaneously. Main Street again was lined with stores, and tobacco and livestock markets produced a rich annual income which helped to erase the tragedy of the fire. For the next fifty years the population of the town grew at an almost imperceptible rate. Its people settled down to the quiet, undisturbed routine of small-town life without being further troubled by either scandal or disaster.

The twentieth century, however, was to involve the sons of the town in wars, as had the Revolution, the War of 1812, and the Mexican and Civil wars. Harrodsburg boys went away to fight in France in the First World War, but it was the Second which dealt the town a staggering blow. Sixty-six local boys were members of the 38th Tank Company of the Kentucky State Guard. In December, 1940, they were called up to participate in armored maneuvers in Louisiana. At Fort Knox they were organized into Company D of the 192nd Battalion. General George C. Marshall personally selected the 192nd to be sent to the Philippines to guard Clark Field against a surprise airborne attack. On December 7 a Japanese bombing raid devastated Clark Field and led to the chain of events which included the horrible death march on Bataan in April, 1942, and the surrender of Corregidor. For three months the Americans had held the Japanese at bay, but, for the survivors, the surrender began a long and beastly story of sadistic bayonetings, beatings, shootings, and starvation in prisons in Japan and Manchuria. Out of the original sixty-six Harrodsburg boys who went from the Louisiana maneuvers to the Philippines, twenty-nine had died. The thirty-seven who came home had all suffered monstrously in prison and work camps. The stories they told of Japanese brutality and inhumanity taxed human comprehension. Few or no other American towns suffered so hard a blow as did Harrodsburg. Not until the war ended were the people certain that any one of the sixty-six boys would ever return.

Today many of the veterans of Bataan and Corregidor live in and around Harrodsburg. They came home and fitted themselves into the normal course of life about them. A tank bearing a list of their names stands in a small veterans' park, and nearby is the elegant granite national memorial to Clark's Northwest Expedition. Few American towns can claim so full a history of civilian soldiers fighting so gallantly. Men have been going away from Harrodsburg to fight for their homes ever since James Harrod first led his tiny party up the Ohio to participate in Dunmore's War.

At this point in the twentieth century Harrodsburg with a population of 6,061 people in 1960 has been caught up in the general swirl of American industrial expansion. Rings of new ranch-style and split-level houses spiral out in the surrounding meadows about their town. Glass and textile factories supplement the local service industries in shaping a new economy. Publications of the Chamber of Commerce reveal with great intimacy the statistical ribs of the town and its trading community. Income is now a big factor in this historic town's approach to the future.

Nevertheless, Harrodsburg teeters between reverence for the past and anticipation of the future. In early 1963 the town's civic leaders hoped they could make the past serve the future by staging an outdoor drama, *Home is the Hunter,* and reap a harvest of tourist dollars. In a somewhat more direct manner the Chamber of Commerce says, "Despite its daily association with, and pride in, the romantic, by-gone doings of Harrod, Clark, and Boone, the Harrodsburg of today is looking ahead, not back. It has become a city in which the past and the present, the old and the new, blend in harmony. Now, with its citizens actively seeking industry, the city may well be standing on the threshold of a great future."

Frankly, many people of the town would rather have the transient tourist than industrial settlers. There would be no permanent responsibility for the former. There are people in Harrodsburg who are most reluctant to view their future through industrial eyes. Their town has had its own special values which long ago were formulated in a pattern of unhurried life. These values people are most hesitant to surrender in exchange for a set of statistical tables which reflect wealth and economic promise. Fervently many Harrodsburg people hope history will become sufficiently salable so that their traditional mode of life will not be disrupted.

*An artful ease, cultivated in the 1850's, survived the Civil War, poverty, and a plague to inspire this scene on a lakeside porch in 1897.*

# A Proud Struggle for Grace

—

## *Holly Springs, Mississippi*

—

### BY HODDING CARTER

If you should chance by and be made welcome in this suspended place, there are certain things which you would be shown—old homes, small new industrial plants, a brooding cemetery, an unbelievable art museum, a courthouse square whereon time stopped, family scrapbooks, two Negro institutions of higher learning, and the ruins or reminders of earlier centers of learning from a day in which almost no slave could find a tutor. You will also witness the difference between properly and improperly used farmlands.

And you will come to know, however slightly, the welcoming people here. Good people into whom and from whom flows a distillate of the best of a past that is persistent. The name of this town on a once remote Mississippi ridge is Holly Springs.

The forebears were also good people who came in the 1830's to the land of the Chickasaw Cession, a verdant and virginal region of fertile tablelands and creek and river bottoms. What was to be the vital center of the Cession lay less than thirty miles from where northwest Mississippi joined the Tennessee line, with lusty Memphis, roaring down from its bluffs at the Mississippi River, only forty miles away.

The white men had no need to kill here, only to deprive. The conquering rifle was not heard nor did the arrow or the tomahawk or the knife strive to make unequal answer. This too left a mark. If these settlers were too often indifferent to the rights of the copper-tinted people of the forest, they were not unique in this. And while some came only to trade or hunt or speculate in the holdings of the despoiled Chickasaws, many more journeyed by trail and river from the homeplaces of the Atlantic seaboard and Kentucky and Tennessee with their families and chattels and slaves and not a few with books and musical instruments. Others, less fortunate, came only with ax and plow and rifle and perhaps a few cows and mules and horses, together with hoe and spade and garden seed. Some of the descendants of these latter folk, not rising above their indifferent starts, would be called rednecks. But here in the Chickasaw country they have earned a better label, for by and large the shiftless moved on. The rest clung aid more often than not added acreage to the small farms that outnumbered the great cotton estates.

Together the educated and well-to-do and the poorer whites would build on the forested Pontotoc Ridge a settlement which would first be named Clarendon, then Paris, and at the early last Holly Springs, from the Chickasaw designation. Here, in a dell on this ridge, higher by an invigorating 700 feet than the bordering expanse to the west and south, there flowed in a holly grove a large spring that measured 30 feet wide and 10 feet deep, so high was the water table. Since time immemorial the spring had been a camp site for the tribal hunters of the Chickasaw Nation on their way to and from the hunting grounds in the flat country and swamps that lay between the Yazoo and Mississippi rivers. Beside the bubbling water of this spring, within easy reach of the Chickasaw tribal seat at Pontotoc, the itinerant white traders also camped and bartered.

It was a lovely land of rolling hills and sweet rivers and intermittent open prairie. Seemingly the forest extended unendingly, the magnolia and pine, the hickory and oak, enmeshed by the scuppernong and muscadine and carpeted with all manner of wild flowers, so lushly that an early spellbound horseman would set down with poetic simplicity: "The daisies rose up to my stirrups."

This was not ordinary forest land. To make the prey of the hunter more vulnerable, or to improve the grazing, or both, the Chickasaws kept much of the forest cleared of underbrush and rank growth so that the expanses were more like the wooded parks of the old world than the wilderness of the new. But because the white men came to grow cotton, great areas of the forest were soon cleared away and homes were built of the felled timber and of the brick that was created from the red clay.

De Soto may have passed this way, and it is certain that white hunters saw the land before the first white settler built a two-room cabin in 1830. He was Robert Burrell Alexander, a Virginian, who bought his land from the Indians and cleared it. He also built, about five years later, a two-room log tavern that looked down upon the spring. It was the first building on the site upon which William S. Randolph of the notable Virginia family would determine to lay out a town.

Two years after the arrival of Alexander, the agents of the Great White Father persuaded the Indians to open their lands to the white man. By 1834 the area was well enough known for Alexander C. McEwen, pioneer planter and co-founder of Holly Springs, to have supplies needed in building his home consigned to "the Holly Springs." By 1836, Chickasaw Cession territory had been divided into counties, the largest of which was Marshall, into which the land hungry poured by the hundreds. The eyes of some of them shone with the frenzy of speculation, none the less compelling because it was dirt, not gold, they sought. That same year Holly Springs itself was established as the Marshall County seat, with a town square designated and Spring Street, the first to be laid off, a reality alternatively of dust and mud. It was only fitting that the first brick building was the land office.

To the land office flocked the newcomers, some of them grasping or litigious or troubled because the land changed hands faster than the records the surveyors tried to keep. In 1838, there were 1200 cases on the docket of the March term of Circuit Court, mostly having to do with land claims. So began the bonanza times for the lawyers who in 1840 numbered forty, one for each ten white men of the population. In the end Holly Springs would be fortunate because of her lawyers, for they were men of education and breeding, with a will and the power to command. Greatly because of them, it would not know the roistering, brawling days that marked so much of the Southern frontier.

Three years after the founding of the town, President Thomas Johnson of the new Female Institute was able to write:

"Holly Springs, four years ago, was a cotton plantation; now we number a population of 2,500 . . . Our population consists not of adventurers who came to the South for the purpose of regaining a lost fortune, but of substantial men who brought their fortunes, and better still, their intelligence, with them, and who believed they could enjoy in a substantial degree the advantages of cultivating the great staple commodity of the South and at the same time breathe the pure, healthy, invigorating atmosphere, and they were not mistaken. . ."

Typifying the substance of so many of these early comers was William Lumpkin who in 1837 wrote back from Athens, Georgia, to his sons with whom he had earlier

*The rural atmosphere of the prewar years lingered in a town that kept its cultural aspirations. Here, in 1900, sheep were driven behind the Opera House (center).*

traveled to purchase and clear land in the new Marshall County:

"I have turned almost all my notes into money at a moderate discount and have sold our furniture and other property I could not remove as well as could be expected. . . . .we shall have upwards of 60 negroes, 32 horses and mules, about 50 head of cattle besides the white family, consisting of your mother and myself, 4 daughters, 4 grandchildren, Mr. Mayer [his son-in-law] and I, and perhaps 2 young white men. I have a coach and 4 white horses, two large waggons 5 mules in each, and a 2 horse waggon and a Dearborn waggon, and my Sulkey. Mr. Mayer has 2 large waggons, a coachee, and cart and 14 head of horses and mules. So you see we shall have a very large cavalcade, and a very expensive one—Through Divine Mercy and goodness we are generally in good health thanks be God. . . .We shall need considerable house room for the negroes. Also the large field opened and fodder and corn secured so we may turn whatever cattle, and mules in. . . ."

Such men as these and their heirs would, like the lawyers, give a special identity to the little community. The homes the prospering settlers of town and countryside began building in the late 30's were sometimes modest and sometimes pretentious; but most of them were alike in the good taste in architecture and furnishings that the settlers brought with them or sent for afterward. Even casual visitors were impressed with the refinement of the town.

And a town and a county began to grow. Not only planters and yeoman farmers came to the ridgelands. Civilization needed editors and merchants, doctors and preachers, blacksmiths, craftsmen of every kind, teachers. These came too, and for the most part they were several cuts above most of those who were peopling the wilderness Deep South and Southwest.

One proof of this was the institution-mindedness of these people, which will be more closely noted. Even before the town's incorporation, they voted in a town meeting to establish the Holly Springs Female Institute and before it was built they had erected a home for the Literary Institute for boys.

Nor did they neglect religion. The Presbyterians were first to organize, followed closely by the Methodists, the Baptists, and the Episcopalians.

Holly Springs' Bank of McEwen, King and Company was the first in northern Mississippi and there were others. They failed with temporary dire results in the wake of the national panic of 1837. Wrote the Holly Springs *Gazette* a few years later: "The two real estate banks exploded . . . and with them stopped the improvement of our town. The reaction was severe and fell heavily on many of our best citizens. Some were forced to flee to Texas [to escape their creditors]. Some retired to the country. And those who remained were generally of the most solvent class."

Holly Springs survived the economic disaster and the Northern Bank of Mississippi, incorporated in 1837 with a quarter of a million dollars in capital, was to last until the next great national catastrophe, the War Between the States.

Despite panic and failures and intricacies of doing business with the local currencies issued by various banks and businesses, the Holly Springs boom was not halted for long, for its impetus came from cotton and cotton was king. In 1838, the west side of the square counted no fewer than eight brick buildings and the south side, a new barroom. Six brick stores were nearing completion on the south and spacious wooden business and office buildings stood between the brick edifices. In the center of the square rose the columned court house with a cupola surmounting its two stories. Communication with the outside world was assured by the formation of the Holly Springs and Mississippi River Turnpike Company to provide improved access to the Mississippi River, the life line of the mid-continent.

In the transforming wilderness, Holly Springs' commanding position seemed assured. And so it would be until the time of war and of later pestilence.

The signs of civilization were everywhere apparent.

The *Southern Banner* in 1839 reported that the stock of whiskey "is fair and the demand good at 50¢ to 60¢ a gallon," which, with cotton selling at 13¢ to 16¢ a pound seemed amazingly cheap. The citizens were enjoying the races at the Holly Springs race course. Three years after the town's founding, a drama group was formed which called itself the Thespians and entranced its audiences with such fare as "John Bull or the Englishman's Fireside" and "Fortune's Frolic, or the Mistakes of a Knife" and "The Fall of the Alamo or The Death of Davy Crockett." The players even essayed a presentation of "She Stoops to Conquer." And supplementing the home-town actors were traveling troupes with such thrillers as "Husband at Sight," and "Bath Reed or Married Yesterday," and "Loan of a Lover." Itinerant artists and bootmakers stopped at the Union House or the Marshall Inn to cajole customers, and a local artist, George P. Young, proved that the arts were at home in Holly Springs; his opus, "The Destruc-

tion of Jerusalem by Titus," a 9-by-15-foot canvas, was considered by some critics to bear the mark of genius.

Politics came in for close attention, too. The political atmosphere of Holly Springs, unlike that of some of its neighboring communities, was conservative, with the Whigs generally in the saddle throughout Marshall County. The politicians reveled in the dinners which were held in honor of any and every visiting notable with much toasting in strong drink, long speeches, and too much to eat. At one such dinner thirteen toasts were drunk to:

The heroes of the Revolution
The Southern states of the Confederacy [the national compact was even then looked upon in the South as a confederacy rather than a union]
Thomas Jefferson
Our guest, Judge E. C. Wilkinson
The memory of General George Washington
The Governor of Maine
James Madison
The 26 stars in our political galaxy
Our national honor
The Navy
The memory of Lafayette and DeKalb
The State of Mississippi
And the Ladies, "in prosperity our purest source of pleasure, in adversity our best and truest friends."

HOLLY SPRINGS GARDEN CLUB

*Medicine shows featuring a minstrel still packed the square during the early 1900's in front of the remodeled court house, gutted by the war. The medicine was for the blood and liver.*

The churchgoers had their choice of eight sermons every Sunday. And for those to whom cleanliness was next to godliness, the public bathhouse of Aaron Woodruff, the gunsmith, was open regularly and advertised as having Fridays reserved for the ladies. There was little to grumble about other than the mudholes and dead dogs in the streets, no great irritants in a community which now had nine drygoods stores, five grocery stores, a jeweler, three hotels, six doctors' offices, fourteen law offices. With most land acquisitions completed the number of lawyers had decreased.

So much for the community life in a new Mississippi town, its fortune resting mainly on cotton and its prosperity a compound of trade, professional services, and income from land. By 1840, with a little more than twenty years of happy times to be enjoyed before the war, the population of Marshall County, exclusive of the remaining Chickasaws was 17,536—in an area where only one white man had been living less than ten years earlier. Of these 9,268 were whites, 8 were free Negroes, and the rest slaves—an unusually high ratio of whites to Negroes in the cotton kingdom, which indicates that the number of small landholders was unusually high. And Holly Springs itself could count 1,117 citizens, a little more than half of whom were men.

There was from its inception an Athenian quality to the little town, with its emphasis on education. The boys' Literary Institute, a two-story brick building, would soon bear the august title of The University of Holly Springs, the first such in Mississippi. When the university died in 1843, a New Yorker, Dr. Francis Lister Hawks, one of the most prominent Episcopalian ministers in the United States, then serving as rector of Christ Church, Holly Springs, became president of a new boys' academy, St. Thomas Hall. After his departure to become president of what would become Tulane University in New Orleans, the school was again reorganized, this time as a military academy. Through its brick portals would march many a future officer of the Confederacy. The university's original brick building was occupied from 1850 to 1879 by a new school, Chalmers Institute. Most of the boys at the western end of town attended Chalmers Institute, while those in the eastern and northern part went to St. Thomas Hall.

In the 1840's, the Female Institute, by now called the Holly Springs Collegiate Institute, moved into a two-story building with a 64-foot front whose cornerstone was laid with Masonic rites. Here it awarded the degree of Mistress of Polite Literature. By 1850 the Franklin Female College was in competition with it and Marshall County was spending more on higher education than the rest of the state put together, excluding the budget for the University of Mississippi. That university had been established at Oxford, twenty-eight miles to the south, with the intellectual and financial assistance of many leading Holly Springs citizens.

Additionally, in these prewar years, there were at least eight other shorter-lived academies and institutes; thirteen rudimentary public schools with thirteen teachers; and a

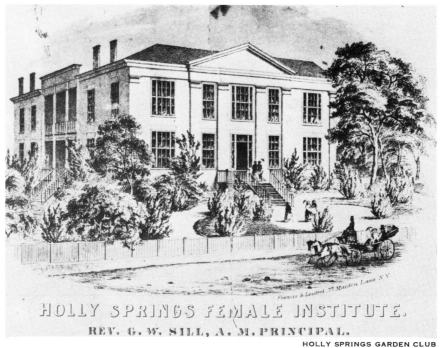

HOLLY SPRINGS FEMALE INSTITUTE.
REV. G. W. SILL, A. M. PRINCIPAL.

HOLLY SPRINGS GARDEN CLUB

*The Female Institute in 1870 carried on the town's traditional commitment to education. Started by the first settlers, it had been one of eleven academies during the prosperous 1850's.*

varying number of professors of music, mathematics, art, languages, and rhetoric who taught privately. And on the plantations the families employed tutors for their children who could not get in to town to school.

In 1843, Thomas Falconer's Holly Springs *Gazette* advertised the Female Institute's educational offerings, together with announcements of new barristers, a dentist, and a doctor. Six years later the *Gazette's* advertising columns bore witness to the diversity of the mercantile and professional activities of the thriving trading center. It contained notices of candidacies for judge, district attorney, vice chancery clerk, sheriff, probate judge, and assessor. A dentist advertised: "Nothing but the best of teeth will be used . . . and the finest gold to set the teeth in." Six lawyers published card advertisements while a life-insurance company, a barber and hairdresser, a drugstore, a hatter, a grocery, a saddlery selling Spanish and Comanche saddles, a carriage maker and a Memphis bookseller made known their wares. Those who needed such reminders were advised to buy Jew David's Hebrew Plaster for almost any ill or Wistar's Balsam for lung complaints, liver affections, and pains of the back or side.

By now the town had a certain martial air and many of its younger men could talk with relish and personal knowledge of such faraway places as Monterrey and Buena Vista in Mexico, for in concert with many another Mississippi war hawk, the Marshall Guards had, as volunteers, marched away to fight against Mexico and for Texas and manifest destiny. The brave farewells had been said on the planked streets surrounding the courthouse. The Guards then departed for Vicksburg under their elected captain, the veteran Alexander B. Bradford, whom they called general out of respect for his services in the War of 1812 and Andy Jackson's Seminole War. At Vicksburg the Guards joined other state units to become the famous First Mississippi. Holly Springs' General Bradford received there 350 votes for the colonelcy of the regiment to Jeff Davis' 300, but because that vote represented only a plurality of those cast for several candidates Bradford declined in Davis' favor. At Buena Vista, desperately wanting to be wounded "for political reasons," the fiery old soldier deliberately and repeatedly exposed himself to enemy fire, muttering "My God! Can't one bullet hit me?"

The losses of the Marshall Guards and the Marshall Relief Guards who followed them were severe. From those who returned would come much of the county's officer personnel of a bloodier ordeal.

The Mexicans, however, had been no new enemies to some of the men of Marshall County. Four years before Zachary Taylor crossed the Rio Grande, forty of the county's hot bloods, ostentatiously calling themselves Wolf Hunters, to circumvent America's neutrality law, had sailed from New Orleans to Galveston to offer themselves for the defense of the still threatened young Republic of Texas.

In the waning 40's dawned the halcyon days. The fruitful farms of Marshall County not only produced more cotton than any like number of acres anywhere in the world but also practiced a diversification that would not be noted less than a half century later. The crops included vegetables for the laden tables at home and for the market place; raspberries, strawberries, cherries, figs and other fruit in abundance; beef and pork and poultry; lambs for wool and for consumption; wheat for bread, and corn for man and beast. There was no reason for master or slave or yeoman farmer to go hungry. Taxes were almost nonexistent. Good land could be had for from $10 to $15 an acre but a prime slave cost a minimum of $700.

Townsmen and countrymen alike were more at home in the saddle and the chase than in the drawing room and high among their recreational pursuits was a modified version of knightly tilting. The men liked cockfighting and card playing, either at home or in the public gambling places. The saloons did a thriving business. Sometimes the more rambunctious blades, in or out of their cups, settled their differences with firearms. Fishing occupied both sexes for an extraordinary number of hours a week.

In addition to these frontier diversions, young and old delighted in spelling bees, all-day visiting and home musicals—pianos having been brought in by oxcart after their arrival by river at Memphis. Despite the admonitions of their clergymen, many members of the gentry enjoyed cotillions. At a later date one of the socially impeccable elders demanded that the Presbyterian session excommunicate him from all privileges of the church because he had "done one thing censurable by the church which is a sufficient cause for expulsion, *viz.* dancing at a private party of ladies and gentlemen and declaring the act censurable neither by religion nor sound morals." Regretfully the session held to its policy and expelled him.

For the white folks of Holly Springs and Marshall County, life as a whole was delightfully bucolic, nor would that atmosphere have greatly changed a hundred years later.

The late 1850's marked the peak of the region's prosperity and a tremendous burst in building. The Episcopalians erected their present Christ Church, an exquisite Gothic chapel with eight stained-glass windows on either side and a spire surmounted by a ball and cross. Here ministered the Reverend Joseph Holt Ingraham of Maine who had previously written, among many novels, *The Prince of the House of David*, reputedly the first fictional use of Biblical material. The earlier church was purchased by the recently organized Roman Catholic parish. The Presbyterians started their fourth sanctuary, which by the outbreak of the war had been finished. In their third church where the famous evangelist, the Reverend Dan Baker, favorite preacher of John Quincy Adams and Andrew Jackson, had served. The Methodists made improvements to their edifice completed in 1849.

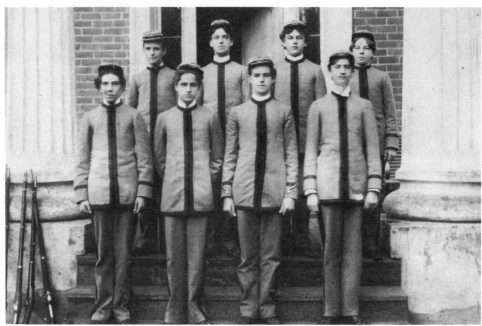

*Cadets of the surviving boy's school, St. Thomas' Hall, studied in the 1890's in the spirit of the prewar culture. The school had trained many Confederate officers.*

The years from 1855 to the beginning of the war were those during which many of the museum-piece homes of Holly Springs were built. White-columned Georgian, or iron-laced and Gothic, in respectful admiration of Sir Walter Scott, they added a magnificent supplement to the simple architectural beauty of English basement-type cottages and large clapboard-covered log houses of ten and twenty years earlier.

Brick predominated because of the fortuitous way in which native clay was employed for building. The red earth of the Pontotoc Ridge remains today possibly the best brick-making soil in America. The housebuilders simply excavated the cellar areas of their homes-to-be and with portable equipment and the labor of artisan slaves they made their bricks on the spot. The houses literally were born from the land on which they rose. The result was not only handsomer and more durable buildings, but the expense was far less than had trees been felled in the forests, transported, and sawed into boards.

And, by and large, to the extent of their means, the builders furnished them with a combination of family heirlooms, china and silver, selected pieces and bric-a-brac from as far away as Europe, and not inconsequential articles fashioned by white and Negro craftsmen in Memphis and even in Holly Springs itself. The graciousness which was created is today the rare hallmark of the homes of Holly Springs.

The business and professional men and farmers happily offered up a goodly part of the money they were making— and some were accumulating small fortunes—as tribute to the idols of the hearth.

Many of the homes that rose then and earlier no longer stand. Fire, abandonment within a quarter of a century after yellow fever struck, razing in the name of progress, all took their toll. But in 1861 Holly Springs was a small architectural paradise.

And there existed other dreams, the grandest of which had to do with the building of a railroad. Throughout America, railroad fever possessed its leaders. A young Illinois politician, Abraham Lincoln, entering the House of Representatives in 1847 made his second address before that body a plea for land-grant aid for a proposed Central Railroad "connecting the Upper and Lower Mississippi Rivers with a chain of lakes at Chicago." As early as 1841 Marshall countians sought to incorporate a railroad. They were dissatisfied with the twelve hours it took the four-horse post coach to go from the Marshall Inn on the square to the Memphis bluffs, and with the oxcart transportation of cotton to the Tallahatchie River twenty miles from Holly Springs.

After two abortive efforts, the Mississippi Central Railroad received a charter from the Mississippi legislature and opened its headquarters in Holly Springs in 1852. The purpose of its founders—such men as Walter Goodman, who was known as the father of the line, Harvey Washington Walter, a distinguished lawyer who would rise to a colonelcy in the Civil War, J. W. Clapp, A. M. Clayton and other citizens—was that their cotton should move by rail and the rich farming land be connected with the rest of the nation. Soon they were driven by the heady vision of a line which would split the wilderness of mid-America from

Illinois to New Orleans. Through their efforts the last gap in this line was closed in 1860. And in subsequent years, by merger of other short lines, the Illinois Central Railroad came into being.

But in the 1850's, with only such financing as the prosperous area could itself produce, the directors undertook the task of laying two hundred miles of railroad in central Mississippi. When the initial ground-breaking ceremony took place in Holly Springs on November 16, 1853, more than 6,000 persons, including the Masons, the Odd Fellows, St. Thomas Hall cadets, dignitaries from throughout the state, ladies and gentlemen, old and young, attended the barbecue. H. W. Walter turned the first shovel of dirt. After appropriate state legislation, landowners along the proposed right of way were taxed 5 per cent on the value of their land and were given a corresponding amount of stock in the company. Black laborers well dosed with precautionary quinine and fed a heavy basic diet of cornmeal, pork, and molasses built the bed with pick and shovel, wheelbarrow and wagon, while Mr. Goodman and the other directors rode up and down the future line exhorting and cajoling the landowners to provide crosstie timber, the use of mule teams and ox teams for carting materials and supplies and the labor of their slaves in exchange for stock.

In May, 1855, two beautiful and highly polished locomotives, ornamented with brass and gold leaf, arrived in Memphis. Three years later the line was operating northward from Water Valley, Mississippi, through Holly Springs to Grand Junction in Tennessee, where the east-west Memphis and Charleston line, today's Southern Railroad, crossed, and southward twenty-eight miles from the designated town of Goodman to Canton, Mississippi. But between was an eighty-six-mile gap traversed by stagecoach and known as the "Big Gap."

To fill this, Goodman had to go to London to get financing through George Peabody, a partner of J. P. Morgan's father. Finally, on January 31, 1860, Walter, who had turned the first shovel of dirt, drove the last spike of the Mississippi Central Railroad, south of Winona, and the people of Holly Springs could travel by railroad as far as Bangor, Maine, Chicago and New Orleans, save for an eighteen-mile steamboat-ferry passage from Columbus, Kentucky, to Cairo, Illinois. The determination of Holly Springs helped make the great dream come true.

The Mississippi Central's main offices and its shops were in Holly Springs. The telegraph wires along the right of way, vital to operation of the railroad, provided swift communication with the rest of the nation. The world might well pivot on the town, or so it seemed, so exhilarating was the achievement.

As a first fruit of the Mississippi Central, there was established in 1859 Marshall County's only truly industrial plant, the Jones, McElwain and Co.'s iron foundry, an enterprise which, together with the railroad, would make Holly Springs a minor military target in a war for which

the more hotheaded had long been clamoring. Situated a mile and a half north of town, its 300-foot, two-story main building with two 150-foot wings would be dominated by two tall stacks. Nearby would be the 170-foot-long blacksmith and barrel mill with a 132-foot wing. Even before war orders skyrocketed its production, two hundred workers were employed. Within two years the foundry's production of ornamental iron grillwork and railings would be halted and the foundry become an armory, the first to manufacture small arms for the Confederacy under contract.

Over farms and homes and town square and railroad yard the clouds of impending conflict hung menacingly low. The more conservative leadership of the old Whigs had been supplanted for a decade before the outbreak of war by that of the no-compromise Democrats. In 1851, when the Congressional compromises and the question of secession or union were paramount in Mississippi, Marshall County's Whigs were barely returned to the legislature. Soon thereafter the Whig party was dead and not only in Mississippi. The sole question in the minds of the rampaging secessionists was whether a man should agree with Jefferson on the right of secession or with Madison on the right of revolution, or with both. Neither in Holly Springs nor anywhere else in the South would prevail the persevering, surprisingly strong minority of Southerners who believed in the preservation of the Union. In 1861, just before the bombardment of Fort Sumter, Alexander M. Clayton of Holly Springs and L. Q. C. Lamar, Mississippi's noblest statesman, who later practiced law in Holly Springs, were to write the state's Ordinance of Secession. As Clayton was to comment: "All the members [who voted for it] were for it with a deep conviction of the vast responsibility it involved, but a still deeper conviction of its necessity, if the doctrine of states rights was not to be abandoned; and the immense value of slave property was not to be given up."

So approached the nation's supreme tragedy, its character as Grecian as the columns of the soon-to-be-humbled mansions of Holly Springs.

To tell of a war in terms of a single town or county means the elimination of grand strategy and the over-all desolation of defeat. For Holly Springs it can be told with the death of a young man who was only one of the more than 300,000 who fell in the South's behalf, with the tale of a daring Confederate raid, the letter of a high-spirited pretty girl who fought the Yankees to a standstill with her tongue, and the destruction of a home.

The men and boys of Holly Springs and Marshall County were as ready to fight as any in the South and as confident that since one Southerner could whip 20 Yankees, the war would be a lark that might even end before they could enjoy it. Among these confident young men—

who were better fighters than they were disciplined soldiers —were the Confederate Guards whose captain became General Winfield Scott Featherston. From beginning to end, 150 joined the Confederate Guards to teach the Abolitionists a lesson. Most were farmers, but the roster also included students, railroaders, clerks, carpenters, schoolteachers, merchants, doctors, mechanics, harness makers, a gin maker, a military instructor, a painter, a printer, a lawyer. Forty-eight did not return. Of these, 30 were killed in battle or died of their wounds and 18 succumbed to disease. More than half of those on the roster were wounded. Casualties were as high in other units that Marshall County boys joined.

Robert Moore was among those who fell. The seventh of ten children, he was a member of a farming family which, while not wealthy, was more than passably well off. The Moores, owners of a few slaves, lived eight miles north of town in a two-story frame house with enormous chimneys at either end and a columned front porch surmounted by a second-floor balcony. Robert, like his brothers, was sent to St. Thomas Hall to school and, at twenty-three, was farming with his father when he enlisted as a private in the Confederate Guards. He was only two years older and a lieutenant when he died.

Robert Moore kept a diary revealing an exuberant young man who did not take overly well to discipline and liked a pretty face but, perhaps with a premonition of death, turned to religion before a musket ball cut him down in Virginia.

He wrote rarely of his personal combat experiences. He narrated that "I was in among the canonballs at Mitchell's ford" and dismissed Gettysburg briefly: ". . . we had a desperate encounter with the enemy this evening for two hours, drove them before us for one and ¼ miles. We were forced to fall back for lack of support. Captured several batteries and stand of colors. Our loss was heavy in the regt. 223 killed and wounded, in our co. 29. Several of them were my dear friends. Every man acted the hero. Miss. has lost many of her best and bravest sons. How thankful we should all be to God who have escaped. Oh! the horrors of war."

There were lighter entries. He "fell in love with a young lady with a yellow dress on" and "had an eggnog tonight but did not enjoy it much as we had no ladies to share it with us." Once he "came near shooting a loose horse tonight because he would not halt and give the counter sign." After the wind blew down the regiment's tents he reported "the col. is sitting on the floor of his tent looking like an old dove whose nest has been robbed." With inclement weather he found "the drams are a little too small for the weather."

Once, when forbidden to leave camp, "I passed the line with a wagon going in for straw and went into town." And another time "we stayed in camp without leave and . . . must go on police in a few days."

But he records that when the soldiers discuss the war "we always close by coming to the conclusion that we will after much hard fighting succeed in establishing our independence."

In the year of his death he became devoutly religious. "Have been seeking salvation of my soul for several days past. Oh what trials does the devil throw in the way of one."

The Confederate Guards fought across Tennessee and Virginia for two more years after Robert Moore was slain, many of them barefoot, all of them hungry. But their spirits remained incredibly high. At New Market they re-enlisted for four years or the duration of the war. The conflict was not to last that long. The Guards stacked their arms at Appomatox and turned homeward. They had done well. Their foes had done no better, but there were more of them and if they had not had more to fight for, assuredly they had more to fight with. This the men of Marshall County had not foreseen.

Though Holly Springs changed hands at least 59 times during the war and was used throughout most of it as a hospital center for Confederate or Union soldiers, no pitched battles were fought in or near the town. But it was the scene of an amazing Confederate raid under General Earl Van Dorn on December 20, 1862, in which more than $6,000,000 of Federal supplies intended for use in the forthcoming Vicksburg campaign were destroyed.

Earlier in the fall, General U. S. Grant had begun putting into effect his plan to take Vicksburg by a combined land and river operation. One Federal force was to be moved by transports down the Mississippi from Memphis. Grant ordered the major part of his army down the Mississippi Central while the Confederates who had maintained a considerable number of troops in and near Holly Springs retired to a more defensible position on the Yalobusha River. Before Grant's army reached Holly Springs, the Confederate Government had removed all possible equipment from the converted McElwain and Jones foundry and partly destroyed the armory itself.

At Holly Springs, Grant assembled huge stores of weapons, ammunition, food stuff, and much else, and for a while maintained headquarters in the town. After his men moved southward, late in the fall, he left a small body of troops to guard the material which filled every public building, the Masonic Temple, churches, stores, and even private homes. The Federal command did not dream that any sizable number of Confederates would venture so far behind the main body of Union forces.

And then, soon after daybreak on the cold December morning, Van Dorn and 2,500 cavalrymen rode into the town, meeting with almost no resistance from the outnumbered and surprised Northerners, who quickly surrendered and were paroled. The work of destruction continued until four in the afternoon when the Confederate cavalrymen galloped triumphantly away, leaving many of the buildings in the business section destroyed or badly damaged, and the abandoned armory, which the Union had planned to convert into a 2,000-bed hospital, burned to the ground.

With his supplies all but wiped out, Grant fell back on Holly Springs and from there retired to Memphis from where he would go downriver for his third and final descent upon Vicksburg. The coup delayed the fall of Vicksburg for months.

J. G. Deupree, trooper of the 1st Mississippi Cavalry, and a participant in the raid, wrote, after the war, the best story of the raid. He said in part:

> The women of Holly Springs, many of them still in their nightclothes, and with their dishevelled hair floating in the winter wind, clapped their hands with joy and shouted encouragement to the raiders. The scene was indescribable, with Federals running, Confederates yelling, tents and buildings burning, torches flaming, guns popping, sabres clanking, negroes and abolitionists begging for mercy. . . . By a little after 4 P.M. all Federal property, save what could be appropriated, had been destroyed, the prisoners had been paroled and Van Dorn resumed his march Northward.

Sure of eventual victory, townsmen and cavalrymen were alike contemptuous of the enemy treasure, the quartermaster's payroll money stored in sheets of uncut currency. That is, with one recorded exception. He was an English blacksmith who made a saddle blanket for his mule out of a stack of Yankee paper money and rode off on it. It became the foundation of a not inconsiderable Mississippi family fortune after the war.

It may have been that some Northern officers playfully teased or flirted with Cordelia Scales, a pretty and saucy young lady, who fought for the South with her tongue.

The Scales lived out the war at their homeplace, Oakland, near the town and in Holly Springs. Whether at the plantation or in town, Cordelia took on any Yankees who crossed her path; and more often than not they must have delighted in the eighteen-year-old Secesh belle. Intermittently she wrote to her dearest friend, Lou. It is a pity that all of her letters, now in a thesis by William Baskerville Hamilton, can't be used. One must suffice. It was written when town and county were temporarily in Confederate hands, October 29, 1862.

> . . . I wish you could see me now with my hair parted on the side and with my black velvet Zouave on and pistol by my side and riding my fine colt, Beula. I know you would take me for a Guerrilla. I never ride now or walk without my pistol. Quite warlike, you see. . . .
> . . . I must tell you about the Yankees as you are so anxious to know how they behaved. . . . They came and stayed in our yard all the time. Their camp was where our soldiers are now. And they used to order the milk to be churned and they took cornfodder, ruined the garden and took everything in the poultry line. Hulberts division the very worse stayed here with us

*With occupying Union officers on the square, Holly Springs in this 1862 sketch was outwardly placid. Its citizens were staunch Confederates. It was daringly raided and changed hands often.*

Railroad Depot.

*The railroad that linked the town to the nation in 1860 represented the effort and aspiration of local leaders. A Union target, the road was wrecked in the war.*

Rebel Armory.

*This local foundry, which made fancy iron work during the 1850's, became the first small-arms factory for the Confederacy. Captured by the Union, it was burned down by Southern raiders.*

nearly all the time. I never heard such profanity in all my life and so impudent they would walk around the house and look up at the windows and say 'wonder how many dam Secess gals they got up there. I did not have my pistol and Ma would not let me go where they were but one evening she was so worn out she sent me down to attend to the skimming of some wine and other household matters when she thought they had all left. Just as I got out in the yard two cavalry men and six infantry came up and surrounded me. Ma and Sis Lucy were looking on and were frightened very much for they knew I would speak my mind to them if they provoked me. The first Lieut. asked me if we had any chickens. I told him no any milk I said no that some of his tribe had been there that morning and got everything in that line. He smiled and said 'they did not pay you for them, did they?' I told him a few pretended to pay by giving us Federal money, but that I preferred leaves to that, he said 'why, Federal money don't seem to be in demand! I said not down this way sure. The second Lieut. a redheaded ugly pert thing commenced to laugh about our men running from Holly Springs and said 'our men never run, Miss' I told him no we all know what a orderly retreat they made from Bull Run, Mannassas, and Leighburg, that it did their army a great deal of credit and I hope they felt proud of it. One of the pickets then remarked 'Oh! Hush Tom, you don't know how to talk to secess gals' I turned to him and thanked him that we were all ladies in the South. The 2nd Lt. got very mad at what I said about their men running said I can inform you Miss that I was in the battle of Leighsburg and our men did not run far. I told him I knew they did not they ran as far as they could and then jumped in the river. The first Lt. broke out in a laugh and said 'Ah! Tom, shes got you now' and turned to me and said 'I admire your candor very much. I had much rather see you so brave than for you to pretend to entertain Union Sentiments! I told him there wasn't a Union man, woman or child in the State of Mississippi and the first man that said he was to shoot him, right there for he did it only to protect his property. He said he would and wanted to know if all the ladies were that brave, and I informed him they were and if they whipped this part of our army that we had boys and girls enough to whip them. One of the soldiers said 'I think you had better inspire some of your men with your bravery' I told him that our men need no inspiration whatever. The Lt. then said to me 'Now Miss you Southern ladies would not fight You are too good natured. I said we were very good natured but when our soil was invaded and by such creatures as they were it was enough to arouse anyone—he wanted to know what I stilled them. I told him Yankees or negro thieves this made them very mad and they told me they were Western men. I told him that I judged people by the company they kept and that they fought with them and staid with them that 'birds of a feather would flock together' he remembered & turned & left them then. I wish you could have seen me I walked away just like the very ground was polluted by them, the first Lt. asked me for some water when he saw I was going I told him there was a spring on the place if he wanted any he then told me such bravery would be rewarded that nothing on the place should be touched he made all the men march before him and did not let them trouble anything. Just as I was walking away and congratulating myself that they had not cursed me, one of them said 'She is the damdest little secess I ever saw' and another 'she is a dam

pretty gal, I be-dog if she aint! I could write you a newspaper about them but I reckon you are tired now and it makes me so mad to think about them . . .

The letters of Cordelia Scales show that, despite her protestations of distaste, she found some Yankee officers tolerable. So did others who lived in Holly Springs itself, for they suffered little from Grant's occupying troops. But not so with the owners of many a county plantation or farmhouse across the South, for these and the produce and livestock of their acres were the principal and often wanton targets of the invader.

One such was Strawberry Plains, the finest plantation home in Marshall County, which Ebenezer Nelms Davis and his wife had built ten years before the war. What is told briefly here has been lovingly narrated by Hubert McAlexander, Jr., of Holly Springs, a member of the University of Mississippi English faculty whose love of the county's past is equaled only by his knowledge of it.

Ebenezer Davis came to Marshall County from North Carolina in the late 1830's with his parents. The place he bought a few miles out of Holly Springs, on Coldwater Creek, he named Strawberry Plains because of the wild strawberries which grew in profusion on the hundred-acre plateau behind the house. His first home on the place was a comfortable log house, which his slaves constructed shortly after the land was cleared. To this he brought his bride, Martha Trimble Greenlee of Clover Hills, Greenlee Ferry, Virginia.

Davis was a progressive and good man who established a school for the neighborhood overseers' children. He also built the only white church in the neighborhood and one for his slaves which, as Strawberry Church, lives on.

By 1860, Davis owned 113 slaves and land totaling 40,000 acres in Marshall County, the Yazoo-Mississippi Delta, Alabama, and Arkansas. In 1851, he had built the majestic two-and-a-half-story brick house with a columned portico and its many outbuildings. Not much but the bricks would be left less than fifteen years later, and they would be cracked and blackened. Downstairs were double parlors, a dining room, and a bedroom. Four bedrooms graced the second floor, and the third floor served as nursery. A covered walk connected kitchen to dining room.

The plantation buildings also included an icehouse, flour mill, blacksmith shop, carriage house, smokehouse, cotton gin and stables, slave quarters and a one-room schoolhouse for the Davis children.

Among the servants were a head nurse, a nurse for each child, maids, a butler, and three cooks, one for each meal. All were slaves as was the plantation overseer. The household servants were taught to read and write. For the many dances and parties at the house the plantation had its own Negro musicians.

Mrs. Davis had proposed selling their slaves before the Civil War. Even Davis opposed secession; but when war came they cast their lot with Mississippi and the Confederacy.

Too old to go to war, the planter moved to his Alabama lands to farm them, at the request of his wife, until the war's end. Mrs. Davis and the children remained behind. After Shiloh the family schoolhouse was used as a hospital.

With her husband's departure, Martha Greenlee Davis took over the responsibilities of head of the family in Marshall County. After a succession of raiders had taken all her livestock, she borrowed horses and with her oldest son rode off to LaGrange, Tennessee, to demand that the Yankees return her at least one horse. When all her baled cotton was burned, she and a nearby friend, Eliza Stephenson, fingered through the charred remnants and put together enough for two bales. Once, when one of a party of 18 soldiers made an obscene remark, Mrs. Davis shot him dead with her pistol and held the others at bay until the arrival of an officer who exonerated her and ordered the men off the place.

But there came the day when the officer in charge of another raiding party would not be as generous. Inside were her sick children. Outside were the Union soldiers, ready to set the house afire. She begged for a few days. Instead they gave her fifteen minutes to remove the children and any personal belongings she could. Some kinder Yankees carried out a few pieces of parlor furniture for her. She herself led the children from their doomed home while soldiers chopped her rosewood piano to bits to make kindling for the fire. As the flames consumed the draperies and began curling up the circular stair, one of the children remembered a jewelry box hidden in a column of the front portico. Seconds before the fire attacked the pillar, the boy removed a concealing wedge, reached inside, and took out the box. But a soldier who had seen him grabbed the small chest from his hands. Taking the jewelry with them, the raiders rode away, while the flames they had lit gutted the interior.

But Mrs. Davis did not desert Strawberry Plains. She sent the younger children to stay with relatives, and she and her oldest son moved into a log cabin. Later, when her family's home, Clover Hill in Virginia, was sold, she took her share of the proceeds and made Strawberry Plains habitable again. But barely so.

Only an elderly, unmarried granddaughter of Ebenezer and Martha Greenlee Davis lives today in the proud, sad, and haunting shell of the house which Yankee raiders left.

When the men of Marshall County who survived the war returned, they found most of the homes in Holly Springs had been more fortunate than the mansion of Strawberry Plains. But in the county, and even in the town, bushwhackers, deserters, or Union soldiers had taken their toll. Few public buildings, places of business, or even churches had come through unscathed. The courthouse was gutted beyond usefulness, not out of malice but because of a fire set in one of the rooms by some Yankee soldiers who were being held for military misconduct. The Mississippi Central Railroad was a nightmare of twisted steel rail, burned-out bridges and rolling stock. After the manner of Sherman's bummers, the troops heated the loosened rails above the crossties, which they set afire, and wrapped the pliable steel around tree trunks. The banks were closed. The currency of the Confederacy was without value. The slaves who represented from $7,000,000 to $10,000,000 of the former wealth of the planters, farmers, and townsmen were free, without the recompense to the owners which Abraham Lincoln had urged.

The land remained, which was just about all that had been here thirty years before. But the war had not spared even the rich earth. The erosion which had started because of inability to maintain proper drainage ditches would continue over large areas of Marshall County land for nearly three-fourths of a century. Few among the people did not mourn a kinsman and at the beginning of the peace, with Lincoln dead, little hope was held that the victors would be compassionate. The courthouse, the very symbol of law and order, had to be rebuilt out of funds scraped together by the citizens of the county, for the federal government refused to pay the $25,000 requested to replace the graceful structure. The new courthouse, greatly resembling the old, would remind a defeated people of the days of wealth and pride and dreaming.

In most of the South, Reconstruction brought the taste of gall and the memory still angers, though the period ended nearly ninety years ago. But apparently in Holly Springs most of the Republican overlords, both white and black, were not as avaricious or corrupt as their counterparts elsewhere, nor was the outrage of the white citizenry as violently or as implacably expressed, though this is not to say that they either liked the new order or intended for it to continue. Some of the best people of Holly Springs turned Republican themselves and participated in the Reconstruction government and not a few homes were opened to friendly carpetbaggers and Union officers whose social backgrounds were more acceptable than their politics. The community was even fortunate in its occupation garrison, for its commander, Major John Power, was universally liked.

Marshall County had counted many a Whig among its prewar leaders, and of these some turned after the war to the Republican party out of principle. Others, of course, wanted the offices that the Republicans could give.

There were some interesting cases. Take Dr. W. M. Compton, for example, who was editor of a Democratic paper in Holly Springs and one of the organizers of the local Ku Klux Klan in which he held the office of Grand Giant. Later in the Reconstruction era, he turned Republican and left the county to become superintendent of the insane asylum in Jackson. In time he returned to find welcoming hands and aid in his efforts to found a hospital.

Another who abandoned the Democrats was B. D. Nabors, a native Mississippian who as a Republican served as county clerk and county attorney without forfeiting his status. J. L. Burton, member of a wealthy Marshall County family, a Democrat before the war and a Confederate veteran, became the Republican treasurer of the county and made a large amount of money buying school warrants at a discount and selling them later at par. He became a United States marshal.

Among the outsiders who won social acceptance was C. Wiley Wells of New York who came to Marshall County after the war as a United States attorney for the northern district of Mississippi and proved himself a fair and liberal Republican.

A few gained more than just admission to the social life. Consider George M. Buchanan, a Kentuckian who had emigrated to Missouri and had joined the Confederate Second Missouri Regiment. It was not politics which drew him to Holly Springs after the war, where, as a Republican, he was elected sheriff. Cupid was his magnet. He had been wounded during the war and as a convalescent had met in Holly Springs the daughter of a prominent family. When he rejoined his regiment he proposed marriage by letter and was accepted. Though he never renounced his Republicanism, he ended up as a leading citizen.

But the principal carpetbagger, Nelson G. Gill of Illinois, was never welcomed. A masterly speaker and undisputed voice of the Republicans, he was cordially hated by the whites because he accepted the Negroes on terms of social equality. He later moved to Holmes County, Mississippi, and became a Democrat; then again to Los Angeles where, as a Republican, he won a term as sheriff. For a while he was in charge of the suspect Freedmen's Bureau in Holly Springs. So objectionable was his behaviour, especially in his conduct of Bureau court cases arising from complaints of Negroes against whites, that an angry delegation of Klansmen called upon him to give vigorous personal warning to mend his ways. With his wife he operated a Negro school which was first private and later public. Legend has it that she once had a considerable number of pictures of herself made and forced each of her pupils to buy one for two bits.

If the region was comparatively fortunate in the generally decent relationships between white Republican and white Democrat, the good behavior of a majority of the Negro politicians and rank and file made it even more so.

A minority even adhered to the Democratic party, among them Henry House, a former slave who had been taught to read and write by his owner's wife. House organized a Negro Democratic club and garnered many a Negro voter. During one of the later Reconstruction campaigns, the Democrats took up a collection after a torchlight parade to buy him a sound little house about a mile and half out of town.

Respected, too, by white political opponents was another former slave, James Hill, a Republican leader who became Mississippi's Secretary of State in 1874 and continued in office for three years after the Democrats regained control of the state in 1875. The Holly Springs folk never forgot that when his former master's family fell ill after the war James Hill helped nurse them and is said to have even given them financial assistance.

But the Negro who is remembered with most admiration in Holly Springs was not a native; he came to town after Reconstruction. His name was Hiram Rhodes Revels, a North Carolina-born slave who was educated in the Midwest and ordained a minister of the African Methodist Church in 1845. The organizer of two Negro regiments in Maryland, he served as an army chaplain and having come to know Mississippi during the war settled in Natchez soon thereafter.

His political ascendance was meteoric. Elected alderman in 1868, he went to the state senate in 1870 and then, in the same year, to the Senate of the United States where he occupied the seat left vacant by Jefferson Davis, thereby becoming the first of two Negroes to serve as United States Senator. The other, B. K. Bruce, also represented Mississippi during Reconstruction. Returning near Reconstruction's end, Revels became Secretary of State in Mississippi in 1873 and assumed the presidency of Alcorn, a new Negro college. In 1875, he moved to Holly Springs where he acted as district superintendent of the Methodist Episcopal Church. It was from here that he wrote his famous letter to President U. S. Grant, explaining his desertion of the Republicans in the election which threw out the Carpetbag government. It said in part:

"Since Reconstruction, the masses of my people have been as it were enslaved in mind by unprincipled adventurers, who, caring nothing for the country, were willing to stoop to anything, however infamous, to secure power to themselves and perpetuate it. My people are naturally Republicans, but as they grow older in freedom, so do they in wisdom. A great portion of them have learned that they were being used as mere tools; and as in the last election, not being able to correct the existing evil among themselves, they determined, by casting their ballots against these unprincipled adventurers, to overthrow them."

Though the Reconstruction period was relatively calm in Holly Springs, all was not harmonious. The Loyal League, a southwide Negro political organization given to incendiary leadership and fiery rituals and meetings, was troublesome. So, too, in a different way, was the Ku Klux Klan which, in Marshall County as elsewhere in Mississippi, wore red and black uniforms. There is no record of the Klan having killed Negroes in the county, but some were intimidated and whipped and relieved of their weapons through Klan raids. And in the end the whites of county and community resorted, as did their fellow white Democrats throughout most of the South, to vote-stealing and other chicanery in the elections through which the whites finally regained political control. It is noteworthy that there is no evidence of flagrant or massive fraud on the part of town or county carpetbagger, scalawag or Negro office holder. They were charged mainly with extravagance and perhaps part of the accusation came from the fact that they instituted the first universal public-school system the region had known.

What did the most lasting damage here as throughout the South was not politics but the nature of the inevitable new labor relationship between the former white master and his emancipated slaves. Master and slave became landowner and tenant. Those tenants who furnished everything except the land and improvements gave the owner one-fourth of the cotton and one-third of the corn they produced; when the landlord furnished land, seed, feed, implements and stock, the crop was divided equally. The system was almost never profitable for the Negro. And the landowner, burdened with the necessity of providing subsistence for the tenants, generally unable financially to follow good farm practices, and handicapped by the wartime depletion of his livestock and the erosion of his soil, was unable for seventy-five years and more to even approach the prosperity of his forebears. The value of farm products in the county fell from over a million dollars just before the war to only $225,568 in 1870.

Political Reconstruction and agricultural adjustment were not the only problems facing the Confederate veterans of Marshall County in those postwar years. Though most of them were far poorer than their fathers had been when they came to the area, they were nonetheless resolved to build their world anew.

Among the unaccustomed enterprises with which Holly Springs attempted to recoup its fortunes were a marble works, a pottery, a wagon and buggy factory which by 1877 was turning out a thousand vehicles a year, and a three-story whiskey distillery in the hollow near the old spring.

At the war's end the bonds of the Mississippi Central Railroad were worth ten cents on the dollar. From Oxford to Grand Junction its lines were a shambles. In desperation, the company leased them to the Southern Railway Association for sixteen years. But before the end of the lease, the Illinois Central absorbed the struggling company. In December, 1873, the first train from New Orleans chugged into Holly Springs on its way to Fillmore, Kentucky, where a ferry transported the cars to the Illinois side for the run to Chicago.

Nor was Holly Springs content only with a north-south railroad. No sooner was the war over than some local promoters began advocating possible east-west lines. This did not materialize until the 1880's.

The community's interest in higher education was also renewed. In 1867, the board of trustees of the Holly Springs Female Institute wrote the board of the Peabody Fund, beseeching money to rebuild the school which had been burned out during the war. Only the three-acre cam-

HOLLY SPRINGS GARDEN CLUB

*Local doctors like this survivor worked in vain against the yellow-fever toll in 1878*
*when the Samaritan town opened its doors to refugees from stricken areas.*

pus near the center of town remained. President J. B. Fant told the Peabody Fund directors that every public building in the town had either been greatly damaged or destroyed during the war and that the citizens were so impoverished that they would be unable to replace the structures for many a year. The trustees emphasized the "unequalled salubrity" of Holly Springs and the beauty of the town and requested $20,000 from the fund, the rest to be raised locally. The plea was not heeded. On faith, by August 10, 1878, the board had made a contract with the architects. A month later the yellow fever struck. The three principal members of the board died and with them the hope for restoring the institute. In the end, the land was sold for a public school.

One school whose influence would reach far into Mississippi and the Deep South for more than half a century had its roots in the postwar years in a Holly Springs back parlor. Mrs. Lizzie Watson, whose Confederate sweetheart died in battle, continued classes she had begun during the war out of concern for the education of young women. First known as Fenelon Hall and then as Maury Institute, her school aspired to be the Vassar of the South. When deafness forced her to retire in 1891 the Presbyterians took over her school and in 1902 the state's Presbyterian Synod reorganized it as the Mississippi Synodical College. The college sponsored such cultural events as performances of the Chicago Symphony and caused H. L. Mencken to call Holly Springs "an oasis in the Sahara of the beaux arts." Mississippi Synodical's buildings were razed in the depression of the 1930's and made room for a hospital.

The establishment of two other institutions, though well regarded today, was not the doing of the native whites. Both were for Negro students—and still are.

The first, known originally as Shaw University, was established in 1866 by A. C. McDonald, a northern Methodist minister who was a missionary for the Freedmen's Aid Society. It was taken over in 1870 by the northern dominated Mississippi Conference of the Methodist Church and survives today as Rust College, a four-year college on a pleasant 113-acre campus near the heart of town, with a teaching staff of 37, and an enrollment of 550. Its support comes today from the Methodist Church.

The second, founded in 1870, was the Mississippi Normal School, now Mississippi Industrial College. It was the creation of a remarkable Negro, Bishop Elias Cottrell. He had been befriended by his former master who gave him a house. As an adult in the first postwar years, he learned to read by the light of a pine-knot fire, and even became proficient in Hebrew, which a kindly Nashville rabbi taught him. Mississippi Industrial College today gives principally vocational training to its students.

In those postwar years, the Holly Springs people learned to enjoy themselves again. When the Holly Springs Dramatic Association was organized in the early 70's, the most proper women could take part in the presentations. The three-story Masonic building, which would burn in 1951, had just been completed on the site of the old one, destroyed during Van Dorn's raid and, as before, the second floor was a theater so that the edifice was properly known as the Opera House. The dramatic association leased it and spent the munificent sum of $2,500 on a curtain and thirteen sets of scenery. The production of "Everybody's Friend," the opening play, was the most notable social event since the war. Thereafter until the yellow fever epidemic of 1878 plays were presented every month.

But Holly Springs' most talked of and admired daughter was not one of the pretty amateurs who adorned the Masonic Temple's stage. She was Katherine Sherwood Bonner, as lovely as any belle of Holly Springs, but more importantly the best woman writer that the nineteenth-century South produced. Hers was a short and frequently unhappy life.

Born in 1849, she was the daughter of Dr. Charles Bonner, an educated Irishman who emigrated to Pennsylvania and then to Holly Springs where he married Mary Wilson. Sherwood Bonner's first published story appeared in the *Boston Ploughman* while she was still in her teens. She was paid a commendable $20 for it. She wrote one story for *Frank Leslie's Journal* and thereafter contributed frequently to *Harper's Magazine, The Youth's Companion* and other publications. Her marriage at twenty-one to Edward McDowell, to whom she bore a daughter, was not successful and after he failed in a Texas business venture, she went, in 1873, to Boston where she became secretary and friend of Henry Wadsworth Longfellow. At his suggestion she wrote the Southern tales for which she is best known. The New England poet dedicated one of his poems to the Mississippi girl and she in turn dedicated her only full length novel, *Like Unto Like,* to the Northern bard. Sherwood Bonner also came to know Ralph Waldo Emerson and her description of him is one of the best ever written.

It was Sherwood Bonner who so lovingly described the trait which as much as anything else enabled her kind to stand up to defeat and adversity. That characteristic was an uncommon pride in their Southernness. Wrote Sherwood of her Holly Springs compatriots:

They had the immense dignity of those who live in inherited homes, with the simplicity of manner that comes of an assured social position. They were handsome, healthy, full of physical force, as all people must be who ride horseback . . . and do not lie awake at night to wonder why they were born. That they were Southerners, was, of course, their first cause of congratulation. After a Northern trip, they were glad to be home and tell how they were recognized as Southerners everywhere—in the cars, and ships, and theaters. They felt their Southern accent a grace and a distinction, separating them from a people who walked fast, talked through their noses, and built railroads.

*In a rebirth of progress, the railroad that had been ruined during the war gained
a new station-hotel in the 1870's when the Illinois Central restored the line.*

In her forgetting, in the years of the South's trial, that her people had also built railroads, she was demonstrating her own Southernness.

Nothing—neither war nor Reconstruction nor crop failures nor economic disaster of any sort—ever struck Holly Springs as did yellow fever in the terrible epidemic of 1878.

Men could understand the how and the why of death in battle and political retaliation. But yellow jack was a different matter, a pestilence whose genesis no man could fathom though many had their own opinions. The fever was a vomitous, tortured, noisome way of dying, a swift destroyer, but not swift enough for the stricken. It steamed out of the miasma of the swamps, some said. Others believed it was born in the heat of late summer and carried by the winds from unknown sources. None suspected a tiny mosquito. For more than 150 years yellow jack especially scourged the lower Mississippi valley until salvation from Cuba at the turn of the twentieth century, when brave volunteers proved its source.

Kindness, and confidence in the "salubrity" of Holly Springs' elevation as the highest point in Mississippi, brought yellow jack to Holly Springs in 1878. The community could have—and in view of what we know today should have—quarantined itself against refugees from the stricken lowlands.

The epidemic that year began in New Orleans and, racing northward to Grenada, bypassed elevated Holly Springs and struck Memphis with unparalleled ferocity. On August 12, Holly Springs set up a board of health with Dr. F. W. Dancy as its head. The revered Colonel Walter visited stricken Grenada and, believing the Holly Springs air to be safe because of the elevation, urged that the town be opened to refugees. Dr. Dancy and Dr. Compton, the one-time Republican leader, besought a quarantine. When the aldermen split on the issue, Mayor A. W. Goodrich broke the tie and the Grenadians were permitted to enter. Within a week the first of the refugees had died in the little brick building which had housed the original land office and yellow fever began ravaging Holly Springs. Before the epidemic had run its course 2,000 of the town's 3,500 population had fled. Of the 1,500 who remained—some 300 whites and 1,200 Negroes—1440 contracted the fever and 304 died. The first native to succumb was Mayor Goodrich who had joined Colonel Walter in opening the gates of the town. Within a week, Colonel Walter and his three college-age sons were also dead. The colonel had sent his wife and younger children to Nashville and had opened his stately home to the ill.

Trainmen refused to bring their locomotives through the town and halted their trains at what they considered a safe three miles from the station. The Howard Association of New Orleans, a relief organization, sent doctors and nurses, a telegraph operator, a druggist, and others who could help. From the nation came medical supplies, clothing, even champagne, for the sick and convalescent. The courthouse was converted into a hospital. Some of the volunteer doctors were immune because of having previously survived attacks of the fever, but two Texas physicians died during their first week as good Samaritans. So did Dr. Compton who had pleaded for the quarantine. The white patients, under the best medical treatment then known, deprived of water so the fever might burn itself out, almost all died. Most of the Negroes, untreated, managed to survive. Of the epidemic a contemporary historian records: "In the streets there was no sound save perhaps the frantic clatter of horses' hooves as someone rode in from the country to implore the attendance of a doctor or the rapid roll of the hearse's wheels as a corpse, followed by no mourners, was borne to the grave."

Sherwood Bonner hurried home to help her doctor father nurse the sick. Her father and brother both died. Father Oberti and the six Sisters of Mercy from Bethlehem Academy, the Catholic school which had been opened after the war, turned nurses for white and black victims alike who lay in the courthouse hospital. One by one the Sisters and the Father were stricken until all died. Home from Jackson came Editor Kinloch Falconer, now Secretary of State, to aid in caring for the sick. He too died.

Colonel W.J.L. Holland, editor of the *Reporter*, who knew telegraphy, remained and kept the telegraph lines open. In one issue of his newspaper he reported that the doctors said it would be safe for those who had fled the fever to return home after the second killing frost. On November 5, Holland tapped out a message, saying that it would probably be his last. The first frost had come, he said, during the night, but he had contracted the fever. He was dead before the second frost.

The epidemic broke every merchant on the square except one: he was the druggist who supplied the medications. One merchant, Brodie Crump, who had been worth $150,000 and had that much more coming to him from planters and others, was wiped out.

The town survived, but what was left would never be quite the same again. War, Reconstruction, and finally yellow fever, drained the economic and spiritual resources of the people. In desperate reaction, the very morals of the town deteriorated along with its material well-being. As John Mickle was to describe it in the *South Reporter* in 1930:

This epoch in 1878 changed the life as the war had changed the old life, and was followed by even a greater relaxation of high standards. Night life was lurid and lasted much of the night. . . . Ladies seldom ventured on the square at night unless there was something on at "the Hall". Saloons were more openly operated; the front doors were dutifully locked on Sundays, but open in the rear. One occupying the entire M. and F. Building operated its poker games upstairs and bar below day and night. Excursion trains of ten or twelve packed coaches were often run here from Memphis on Sundays and when the saloons were over-crowded, porters with waiters of whiskey would be sent out to peddle them on the square.

It was the extreme revulsion of taut nerves from the horrors of the epidemic that follows all disasters. . . .

Now began the years of Lethe.

BERN KEATING

*A modern generation at the old depot, Negro youngsters, in an afternoon's play, race down the street. Fifty-five per cent of the town's population today is Negro.*

As the nineteenth century gave way to the even more dramatic and menacing twentieth, Holly Springs fell further behind her sister communities of Mississippi, even as Mississippi fell further behind her sister states. Life went on and children were born and people died and many, not only the young, moved away, so that the population during this period never came close to reaching its prewar or pre-yellow fever figure. The young men went away to war in 1898 and again in 1917, but save for the temporary cotton prosperity in the World War I period, nothing much changed. To the past belonged the conquest of the wilderness and the building of a community of culture and the golden dreams; to the past also belonged the war, the political and racial disputations and the pestilence which so quickly had turned the gold into dross. Remembering the past, listening with quickened pulse to the old warriors until the last man died, a bemused community slept on, cushioned and blanketed in its recollections. Some believed it was the sleep of death. Even the rich soil of the tableland and river bottoms began to surrender to poor farming practices, to low agricultural prices, to soil erosion, to neglect, to abandonment, as some still prospered and some still dreamed. The building of the east-west railroad in the 1880's brought no prosperity; there was not much to ship except the everlasting, underpriced cotton and little income with which to buy. The new, and generally far more modest, homes did not even replace the older ones which vanished. The courthouse and the square remained the center of the community's outward life. The young people married and old names persisted. Few were the newcomers, for there was nothing much to attract them; gone were the glittering and the stormy and the dreadful days.

Then something, created at the beginning out of adversity itself, began happening again to Holly Springs, not all at once but rather from the time of the great Depression of the 30's to the years of World War II and those which came after. To the farmer was extended from the Federal Government an unfamiliar helping hand that offered assistance in the salvation of the soil and support of farm prices. Also through the Federal Government was created the then controversial Tennessee Valley Authority which has changed, and indisputably for the better, the face of much of the South.

And in the middle of the Depression came also the beginnings of a state-sponsored self-help, a then revolutionary plan to balance agriculture with industry, the author of which was Hugh White, a well-to-do south Mississippi lumberman who was educated in Holly Springs and who twice served as governor of the state. Under this plan, the towns or other political subdivisions, could float bond issues to finance the building of industrial plants for approved industries, which would then amortize the bonds through long-term rentals and which would enjoy certain state and local approved tax exemptions. The plan was opposed at first by most of the cotton-centered towns where cheap manual labor was believed to be a mandatory requirement for production. Holly Springs was one of these. It did not turn vigorously to Governor White's Balance Agriculture with Industry program, called BAWI, program until most of the rest of the state was already pointing pridefully to the results from the new industries.

But turn Holly Springs did. Today new industries afford 1,500 jobs in a rising, relatively prosperous community of more than 5,000, nearly double the population of thirty years ago and almost equal to that of the pre-Civil War years. Men and women work in the modernized brickyards and in streamlined industrial plants, turning out electric irons, rotisseries, sandpaper, abrasives, pianos, television parts. Many of the workers live in their farm homes and drive into town to their jobs and to spend their pay checks. From the managerial group which has moved to Holly Springs can come the potentially leavening influence of men of new horizons.

Harris Gholson is president of the Bank of Holly Springs and a historian of parts, a man unbelievably young for his years. His bank, a marble-faced structure and one of the town's oldest, faces the square. In its foyer portraits of George Washington and Robert E. Lee look down on the customers, but all the bank's literature is as much concerned with the present as with the past. One brochure reads: "The town of Holly Springs is one of the best-managed towns in the state. It is one of the few . . . that owns all of its utilities from which . . . it has a net income of over $100,000 a year. Since the town was organized 132 years ago it has never been . . . late in paying a bond or coupon. In fact, it recently paid off $75,000 of bonds before maturity. Holly Springs gained 71 per cent in population in the past ten years."

In this material renascence, the presence of the government which was once the enemy is pervasive: in the power lines of the TVA; in the 8,000 soil-preserving farm ponds and lakes; in the great Sardis dam which in times of flood impounds the river waters that otherwise would imperil the lowlands and add to the menace, farther south, of a Mississippi River swollen in springtime; in the 80 million pine trees the government has distributed in Marshall County for private planting; in the acres not planted to cotton but employed again for diverse crops; in the financial rewards for progressive farm practices; in the local offices of a dozen Federal agencies; in the 122,000 acres of the verdant Holly Springs National Forest.

But forward-looking people are needed to take advantage of such assets as the four gas pipelines that pass eastward near the town, the two railroads which cross it, the TVA power, the BAWI plan, the recreational potential of Sardis lake and the national forest within five miles of the city. Such people now live again in Holly Springs.

*Founded during the Reconstruction era, Mississippi Industrial College where these students are studying is one of the town's two Negro colleges. The other is Rust College.*

Join now in an unabashedly sentimental journey.

In Holly Springs one soon becomes aware of a curiously perceptible interlocking of life and death, of past and present. Only latterly has pride in the present begun to match pride in the past. So it is fitting to go first to Hill Crest Cemetery.

On this quiet knoll where the soft thud of falling hickory nuts has the muffled sound of a requiem drum is reflected the history of Holly Springs. The first white child born in the settlement lies here, as do members of many a pre-Civil War family: Claytons, Humphreys, Bradfords, Chambers, Chalmers, Clapps, McCorkles, Govans, Watsons, Trotters, Crafts, Forts.

Here can be found the tomb of Roger Barton, ardent states righter who for the twenty years before his death in 1855 was one of the most able leaders of the South's Jeffersonian Democrats; of Lieutenant Colonel James Autry, slain in defense of the Confederacy, a son of Micajah Autry who fell with William Travis, Dave Crockett, and Jim Bowie at the Alamo. Beneath this dedicated earth are the remains of nine of Marshall County's thirteen Confederate generals who represent nearly half of Mississippi's top officers in the War Between the States. Among them are the intrepid Major General Edward Carey Walthall, the Virginia-born cavalier and a foremost officer of the Confederacy who attended St. Thomas Hall and practiced law in Holly Springs; General Absalom West who re-established the Mississippi Central after the Civil War; and Christopher Mott, jurist, statesman, Mexican war vol-

unteer and a general of Mississippi state troops, who fell at Williamsburg while his commission as a general in the Confederate army was on its way.

Nearby, with no apparent separation because of race, lies Hiram R. Revels, the Negro who became a United States Senator from Mississippi; and in the plot of the white family whom she served long and lovingly rest the remains of another, humbler Negro on whose tombstone is inscribed: "Mammy, Faithful Unto Death."

Here are the mortal remains of the six Catholic Sisters and Father Oberti who died in the yellow-fever epidemic, their memorial erected by people of every religious persuasion. Another monument honors six Mississippi newspapermen, including Kinloch Falconer and Colonel Holland of Holly Springs who died in the same epidemic. Colonel Walter and his three sons are buried here, as are scores of other yellow-fever victims.

Two Confederate monuments rise among the soughing shade trees and tended shrubbery of Hill Crest and here rest side by side unidentified Union and Confederate soldiers.

Here, too, are the mortal remains of the parents of the late Edward Crump, a born and bred son of Holly Springs, who, as the longtime indisputable sovereign of Memphis, was one of the nation's most absolute and personally honest political bosses.

Here are reminders alike of sorrow and pride and a remembrance of achievement a century and more old, and mingled with them the fresh mourning of today.

*The Gothic architecture that rose along with the Greek Revival in the late 1850's is handsomely preserved at Cedarhurst, now owned by Mrs. Fred M. Belk (above).*

Come next to the enduring homes in which some of the living dwell by inheritance from the dead and others by acquisition. Some sixty ante-bellum dwellings survive in Holly Springs. Of these, a number are open to the casual visitor who attends the annual spring pilgrimage of the Holly Springs Garden Club; the doors of others will swing wide for the stranger with such credentials as friendships in common or introductions or a mutuality of interest.

Older homes survive in America, and larger than the most imposing mansions of Holly Springs. Many are far more commercially and continuously displayed, for a cause or for the gain of the resident, both of which reasons are tenable. In Holly Springs the visits which are paid for are restricted to the three days of the spring pilgrimage and these are worth whatever time is expended. Even seeing the old houses from the outside is a worth-while experience.

The roll call can be but partial:

*The Walter Place.* This is perhaps the grandest, combining Georgian pillars with turreted wings in the Sir Walter Scott tradition. Here lived Mrs. Grant at the time of Van Dorn's raid. A daughter of the heroic Colonel Walter left this house to become a medical missionary in China for forty years and returned to write her memoirs, *My Days of Strength.* An eight-hundred-year-old Chinese screen, rare porcelains and a magnificent silver service are among the treasures she brought back.

*Airliewood.* Built in the great days of the 1850's as a copy of a Swiss chalet. All of its materials save for the native brick were imported. It served as military headquarters for General Grant and legend has it that his soldiers' target practice removed the tops of many of the ornamental rails in the Jones and McElwain iron fence surrounding the grounds. Gracing the double parlor of this home of Mrs. Charles Dean and her lawyer-planter son, Charles, is a well-cared-for Steinway brought in by oxcart before the war.

*Montrose.* Home of the Holly Springs Garden Club, it has been leased by the club from the city since it was presented to Holly Springs by the children of Mrs. Jackson Johnson of St. Louis. A daughter of Holly Springs, she married the young local man who became president of the International Shoe Company. The house was built by Alfred Brooks in 1858 as a wedding present for his daughter, Mrs. Robert McGowan. Its spiral staircase, statuary niches, elegant cornices, and ceiling rosettes suggest his sensitivity.

*The Strickland Place.* The first two-story house in Marshall County, it was built by Dr. James Thompson whose daughter became the wife of Major William M. Strickland. He was a close friend of Jefferson Davis, who frequently visited here. The house is now the property of St. Joseph Catholic School.

*Cedarhurst.* Owned today by the widow of Fred M. Belk, a Holly Springs lawyer, this was Sherwood Bonner's home.

Additionally, the French Gothic style of the thrice-peaked front and the rich iron ornamentation from the Jones and McElwain foundry make this a house of distinction.

*The Magnolias.* Delicate iron grillwork give a New Orleans aspect to this ante-bellum home. Antique furnishings collected by Mrs. Everett Slayden are particularly interesting.

And *Herndon. The Crump Place. The Mimosas. Grey Gables. Cuffawa. Linden Terrace. The Featherston Place. Colonsay Cottage.* And *The Fort-Daniel Place* and *The McCarroll Place,* the only two homes in Holly Springs that have been lived in continuously by members of the same family since their reconstruction.

It is notable that in a region where women have traditionally been placed on a pedestal but have also been relegated to "a woman's place," the two most creative folk of Holly Springs have been members of the weaker sex. One was Sherwood Bonner. The other was Kate Freeman Clark, honored in Holly Springs' unique art museum. The museum, built with funds Kate Clark bequeathed for the purpose, houses more than a thousand paintings she executed in her lifetime. The walls of the attractive, one-story brick art gallery are covered with her oils and scores more are stacked in air-conditioned storage rooms. An artist's entire production of a lifetime is here to be studied for, as her mother said, "It would be like selling a baby to sell one of Kate's paintings." So, in Holly Springs, may be seen again pictures once exhibited in Chicago, Pittsburgh, Boston, Philadelphia and New York then stored, in 1923, in a New York warehouse until their housing some forty years later in the town of Miss Kate's birth.

Kate Freeman Clark, a great-niece of General Walthall, was born in Holly Springs in 1877, and taken by her mother to New York when she was sixteen because of her precocity as an artist. There she studied under some of the best teachers, but she neither sold nor tried to sell a painting. She pursued her intensely personal artistic career in New York until her mother died in 1923 and then returned to her home town where she added a studio to the Walthall house she restored. She was only in her forties then, but until her death in 1957 she never painted again.

She willed the City of Holly Springs the Walthall home, her painting and the money to build the gallery. Long and unpleasant litigation reduced the monetary bequest; but today the muted still lifes, bright landscapes and represen-

BERN KEATING

*Classic grace and traditional hospitality come together at Montrose, built in 1858 and currently the home of the garden club, whose president, Mrs. Hubert McAlexander, is at the gate.*

tational portraits by Kate Freeman Clark attract the curious and the connoisseur alike.

The place of the town's beginning, the courthouse square, commands the town. All highways lead to it and impell the traveler toward it. The cupola-domed brick courthouse is flanked on two diagonal corners by gazebos which serve as bandstands and political rostrums. Almost as devastating as the Civil War to the buildings that face the courthouse across the broad paved streets was the 1951 fire which gutted two-thirds of the east side. But despite the new buildings, the general aspect of the square and of the people who trade there and have their shops and offices on the four sides give rise to the conviction that little has been changed. Small Negroes scuffle along the roofed sidewalks and peer into shop windows. Many of the law offices are here, just as they were more than a century ago. So are the banks and the stores whose modernity reflects the nearness of the competition of Memphis. But over and above the harmony of past and present stands the courthouse itself, symbol of the orderliness which the first Anglo-Saxons and Scots-Irish settlers deemed paramount.

There is more among the people today than the hypnotic impact of the past or of quiet gentility. Whatever the reason—and in part it would come from being to the manor born and possessing an ancient sense of noblesse oblige—Holly Springs and its people are blessed with a tranquility not usual in their state. The Federal Government has found no reason to delve into civil deprivations nor has a disturbed white minority been able to establish a Citizens' Council in the town. There exists at this writing a rare rapport between the Negro students of Rust and Mississippi Industrial College and the white citizens of Holly Springs, though it is undeniable that this relationship can be destroyed if the extremists of either side so will it.

But such is not the burden of this story.

Instead, in the manner of Holly Springs, let us thank at least some among those who made real for us this town of the lived-in homes. Charles Dean, the heir of Airliewood, a witty, brilliant Harvardian; comely Mrs. Hubert McAlexander, not a native daughter but president of the garden club and a person immersed in the traditions of her adopted town; Glenn Fant, scholar and lawyer, descendant of those who were locally among the first of these callings; Mrs. Augustus Smith who, one believes, could defend the whole of Holly Springs behind the ramparts her scrapbooks would make; Mr. and Mrs. Edgar Francisco, history lovers who live in what is indeed an historic treasure, the McCarroll Place, named for the man who built it in 1840 and who served Marshall County as sheriff for thirty-two years; young John Kennedy, one-time state legislator while he was still a law student, challenger of politics and politicians, and author of the statute which ended Mississippi's infamous no-questions-asked marriage mills; Hugh H. Rather, an imaginative architect who is a descendant of the equally imaginative Samuel McCorkle, the first land agent and developer of Chickasaw Cession territory; and Harris Gholson, the youngest 70-odd bank president in America, descendant of one of the earliest settlers, whose Bank of Holly Springs brochures are dedicated to extolling the past, present and future of his town.

So good-bye, folks, we love your town.

*The pastoral village, sturdily built by a religious sect, was a haven for Robert Owen's crusading intellectuals at the time a German traveler painted it in 1832.*

# Social Experiments on the Wabash

---

## *New Harmony, Indiana*

---

### BY WILLIAM E. WILSON

There is no other town in America quite like New Harmony, Indiana, in the history of Utopias. Here, a hundred and fifty years ago in a pioneer wilderness and within a span of a dozen years, groups of men and women put into practice not one, but two, of the major social concepts that flourished among American visionaries in the nineteenth century. First the town was the site of a religious community dedicated to the common ownership of property, and then it became the scene of Robert Owen's most ambitious experiment in the achievement of human perfection. Here, on the banks of the Wabash, these two notions so deeply rooted in American idealism and development were demonstrated for all the world to see. The first paralleled devout communities like those of the Shakers; the other foreshadowed such free-thinking ventures as Brook Farm and Oneida.

And all the world did see what was going on in New Harmony. Soon after the first community was founded, Lord Byron was writing from Italy about it in his *Don Juan*, satirically, but also with a grudging admission of its success:

> Why called he 'Harmony' a state sans wedlock?
> Now there I've got the preacher at a deadlock.
> Because he either meant to sneer at Harmony
> Or marriage, by divorcing them thus oddly.
> But whether Reverend Rapp learned this in Germany
> Or no, 'tis said this sect is rich and godly.

European travelers made the hard journey through the forests to see the pious members of the first community at work, and after Robert Owen moved in with his Community of Equality, the number of visitors increased. Owen's experiment was debated in Congress and studied with varying degrees of approval and disapproval by governments abroad. What is more, New Harmony remained a cultural center in America after its Utopianism became a matter of history, with notable scientists and philosophers and at least one President of the United States among its guests. Today, artists and theologians from all over the world convene in the town from time to time because there are still people there who are convinced that the world can be made into a better place.

Called the Harmony Society, the first community venture was based, like those of the Shakers, on a belief in the imminent Second Coming of Christ, though no violent physical manifestations of spiritual ecstasy shook the stolid peasants who poled their boats up the Wabash from the Ohio in the spring of 1814 and camped their first night at what is now the corner of Church and Main streets. These German founders of New Harmony, some five or six hundred strong, came from Pennsylvania to the southwest corner of Indiana to await the millennium. Indiana was still a territory then, and the nearest town of any size was Vincennes, forty miles upstream, with a population of 3,000; the rest was wilderness. Before the Harmonists came to Indiana, they had awaited the millennium for eleven years on the banks of Connoquenessing Creek, near Pittsburgh, after emigrating from Württemberg in 1803. But the Pennsylvania land, was "too brocken & too cold for to raise Vine," and vine-growing was the special skill they had brought from Germany. Their hearts had been set on an estate in the fertile Wabash valley for a long time before they were able to buy 24,734 acres there from the government for $61,050. In New Harmony, which they called Harmonie, they waited eleven years more; then they returned to Pennsylvania to wait again. They continued to wait until 1905, when there were only two of them left and one of these pronounced the vigil over and became the executor of the vast fortune they had accumulated in their century of existence.

The Harmonists' spiritual leader, George Rapp, was fifty-six years old when he came to Indiana, six feet tall, robust, somewhat heavy-featured, blue-eyed, white-bearded, and strong of will. In Germany, he had been a Separatist, formally breaking away from the established church in his thirtieth year and beginning to preach in his own house. He preached the basic principles of Lutheranism, but he believed that the Lutheran Church in Ger-

*This village scene shows the celebrated church of a celibate faith with a bandstand around the dome. The sketch is by the notable Owenite naturalist, Charles-Alexandre Lesueur.*

*The first Harmonist church, The Steeple House, was used by the Owenites for lectures.*
*Lesueur's 1831 sketch showed it intact, though lightning had earlier demolished the steeple.*

many had lost sight of these principles in the luxury and confusion of its ceremonies. Ultimately he became convinced that the First Resurrection, promised in the Book of Revelation, would come in his own lifetime. He remained so firmly convinced of this that, on the day of his death in his ninetieth year, he said, "If I did not believe that the Lord intended me to present my people to Him on the last day, I would think I was dying."

Father Rapp thought that "the last day," when Satan would be shut up in the bottomless pit and Christ would begin his reign of a thousand years on earth, was an event not simply to wait for but also to prepare for. He believed the Lord helps those who help themselves, but expects them to help each other as well. On the basis of a verse in The Acts—neither said any of them that aught of the things which he possessed was his own, but they had all things in common—he persuaded his followers to surrender to him and his "associates" all their worldly goods and the products of their labors and to ask in return only meat, clothing, lodging, "and all such instruction in church and school as may be reasonably required."

George Rapp married young and had two children of his own, a son and a daughter, but in his middle age he adopted a young man, who was known afterward as Frederick Rapp, and Frederick became the chief of his "associates," his business manager. Frederick managed shrewdly and wisely and, while the Harmonists were in Indiana, was elected as a delegate to the state's first constitutional convention and appointed as a member of the commission that later chose the site of the capital. By the time the Harmonists brought their religious communism to Indiana, Frederick Rapp's management had made them rich. After they had paid for the Indiana land and before they sold their Pennsylvania holdings they still had $12,000 left on deposit in a Pittsburgh bank.

Shortly before they came to the Wabash country, the Harmonists began to practice celibacy, for which Father Rapp also found authorization in the Bible, not only from Saint Paul, who urged Christians to "abide," but from Genesis, too. He interpreted the story of the Creation and of Adam's Fall as meaning that Adam was originally bisexual, capable of reproduction without assistance from a woman. "So God created man in his own image," says the Bible; "in the image of God created he him; male and female created he them." Rapp argued that the "them" referred to Adam alone and that the statement, made in Genesis before the female element was taken from Adam to create Eve, made Adam a male-and-female creature. The ultimate creation of Eve from Adam's rib took place, Rapp said, to satisfy Adam's restlessness and loneliness after he had named all the animals in Eden and noticed that, unlike himself, their male and female elements were in separate bodies. Curiously, Rapp believed that if man abjured the

*In this view through a fanlight door, the graces of nature and the artisanship of Father Rapp were fused by Lesueur's skillful pen. The door from the second church, built by the founder, is now preserved in a local school.*

sexual relationship, he would someday return to the pristine, bisexual, self-reproductive state in which God had first designed Adam.

Marriages in the Harmony Society were not dissolved when the rule of celibacy was adopted. Husbands and wives continued to live together, but were expected to "abide," as Saint Paul put it. A few children were born in the years that followed, but only a very few. The parents were not banished or even punished, except by patriarchal and communal disapproval, which must have been hard to bear in such a small society. No new marriages were performed, of course, and among the first buildings the Harmonists began to construct in New Harmony, after they had finished their steepled frame church, were dormitories for men and dormitories for women.

Everything the Württembergers built at New Harmony was substantial and strong: four dormitories of brick, each large enough to house about sixty people, each with kitchens and community rooms; a fine house for Father Rapp and his family; two granaries of brick and stone; a water mill and dam; a textile mill; a dye house; two sawmills; a hemp and oil mill; two large distilleries; a brewery, in which the pump was operated by a large dog walking on a treadmill; forty two-story brick and frame dwellings and eighty-six log dwellings, all with fences, stables, and gardens.

The buildings were a triumph of construction. The brick-and-stone granary, the dam, the dye house, part of Father Rapp's house, a score of the other houses, and two of the dormitories are still standing after a century and a half. The houses and dormitories were insulated against heat and cold with soft bricks and with slabs of wood wrapped in clay and straw, and known as "Dutch biscuits." The same stove heated the first and second floors by means of a flue on the second floor, and the buildings were rudimentarily air-conditioned by tunnels into the cellars. They were so firmly mortised and tenoned by square pegs driven into round holes that they could not sag or lean. The timbers that went into the houses were cut in standard sizes at a central sawmill and numbered with an adz, so that they were interchangeable, and by this convenient uniformity of materials the Harmonists pointed the way toward modern prefabrication.

By 1822, the Harmonists had all but created a paradise on the banks of the Wabash in advance of the millennium. A hundred and thirty new members had come from Württemberg in 1817 and joined the original group, signing away not only their property but also the right to claim any wages or compensation should they choose to quit the society. Delegates had gone back to Germany and returned with 20,000 gulden in inheritances due the emigrants. Flatboats were leaving regularly for New Orleans loaded to capacity with agricultural products and whiskey, which the Harmonists never drank, limiting themselves to the small rations of beer and wine that Father Rapp doled out

to them; and the factories of the town were turning out about $100,000 worth of goods a year—woolens, silks, wagons, hats, rope, and leatherwork. The homes the workers lived in were a striking contrast to the Hoosier backwoodsmen's pitiful, dark "log-holes," as one early traveler called the pioneers' cabins; their streets were broad and clean, shaded by lombardy poplars and mulberries; the hillsides surrounding their village were covered with vineyards and orchards; and great flocks of Merino sheep grazed in their pastures.

They led a quiet, well-ordered life. Each morning they were wakened to the day's labor by the mellow tones of French horns. After the community milk wagon had made its rounds, and the chickens, the only domestic creatures that refused to adapt to community ownership, had been fed, the workers marched singing to their allotted tasks in the fields and shops. At nine o'clock they paused for lunch, at noon for dinner, at four for *vesperbrot,* and at sunset they came home for supper. Sometimes the band played while they worked in the fields, and in the shops fresh flowers decorated their workbenches. At night, the shepherds slept under the stars in a house on wheels known as "Noah's Ark," while in the village the slumbering Harmonists were secure in the knowledge that the watchman was crying the hours: "Again a day is past, and a step made nearer to our end. Our time runs away and the joys of heaven are our reward."

Yet over this bucolic paradise there lay a solemn air. Travelers who passed through New Harmony between the years 1814 and 1825 repeated over and over the same observations. The Harmonists, they said, seldom conversed in the streets, and they never laughed. They loved music, but music seemed to be the only sound that ever broke the silence of the town. They refused to discuss their religion and were not cordial to strangers. In fact, most of them could not speak English.

By 1822, the town now built, their labors were so light that the only occasion when they were all called out was "in the event of sudden bad weather, when the hay or corn is cut, but not carried."

Perhaps it was the increase of the Harmonists' leisure that brought an angel to Father Rapp in a dream in 1822. This angel gave him the specifications for a new church that would require great labor in the building. Rapp told his people about the dream and the construction of the church began under his supervision. Made of brick and in the shape of a cross, the transept and the nave were each one hundred and twenty feet long; twenty-eight columns of cherry, walnut, and sassafras supported the roof, each column hand-turned and polished from a single tree butt. Atop the church was a dome encircled by a railed balcony where the community band could play on summer evenings. Frederick Rapp, who was something of an artist as well as a shrewd businessman, carved and gilded a rose on the stone lintel of the main door. Today, this door and lintel, which are all that remain of the church, form the west entrance to New Harmony's schoolhouse, built on the church site in 1913. The church, after being partially dismantled, was torn down about a hundred years ago and the bricks were used to build a wall around the Harmonists' cemetery. An English traveler, seeing the imposing church before it was finished, wrote in his journal: "I could scarcely imagine myself to be in the woods of Indiana . . . while pacing the resounding aisle and surveying the stately colonnades."

But the church was finished sooner than the angel and Father Rapp had planned, and Harmonist hands were once more idle. They continued to build dormitories and acquire land, but even so there was not enough work to keep them busy all the time. George Rapp and his associates decided to sell their little Zion on the Wabash, at a sacrifice if necessary, and begin another community elsewhere. They had other reasons for moving, too: New Harmony was a profitable agricultural colony, but they had visions of an industrial enterprise that would be more profitable in the East; and Frederick Rapp was beginning to dream of high finance. The West was not altogether what they had expected.

When finally the Harmonists left New Harmony, the long-awaited angels of Judgment Day had not yet appeared, but by that time gossip about Father Rapp and an angel other than the one in his dream was troubling the Harmonists much more than the Lord's delay. The story concerned a slab of limestone that Frederick Rapp had bought as a curiosity in St. Louis in 1819. The stone was marked with the delicate tracing of naked human footprints, which, said the Harmonists' Hoosier neighbors, Father Rapp used to deceive his people. According to the gossips, Rapp told the Harmonists that Gabriel had come down out of Heaven to advise him to lead them out of New Harmony against their will and Gabriel had left his footprints on the stone where he alighted.

The story was apocryphal. Frederick Rapp was showing the stone to visitors soon after he brought it to New Harmony and describing it merely as a curiosity. But the slander haunted the Harmonists the rest of their days; as late as 1914, their executor, John S. Duss, was referring to it in his letters as "this damphoolishness," and today's tourist in the town is still occasionally shown the old footprint rock and told the libelous tale.

The man who bought New Harmony, lock, stock, barrel, and alleged angel tracks, was Robert Owen, the British industrialist and reformer who had made a fortune in the

*Sailing for Owen's paradise from Cincinnati, the passengers in this Lesueur sketch included teachers and feminists. The craft was dubbed "The Boatload of Knowledge."*

*Lesueur's sketch of supper below decks suggests the close quarters of the vessel. Frequent layovers allowed passengers to explore the river-side and stretch their legs.*

textile business. His model community of textile workers at New Lanark, Scotland, was famous. Owen was a worldly idealist and where Rapp waited for a Second Coming, Owen announced that he was bringing a social millennium to Indiana himself. At New Lanark, he had established a school to reform the character of the working class and had long preached his doctrine that man is not responsible for his acts and can be saved from ignorance and poverty only by the improvement of his surroundings. Owen had little faith in the Lord and regarded all religions as "superstitions." By 1825 his public attacks on religion had lost for him much of his influence and popularity in the British Isles, and he was ready to seek fresh fields for his utopian projects. When he was approached by George Rapp's agent in Scotland as a prospective buyer of the town on the Wabash, the agent was so astonished by Owen's immediate interest that he said to Owen's son, "Does your father *really* think of giving up a position like this, with every comfort and luxury, and taking his family to the wild life of the far west?" Owen came to America and in New Harmony closed the deal with Frederick Rapp on Sunday, January 2, 1825. Accounts of the price he paid vary from $50,000 to $190,000; whatever the figure, he got a bargain.

Robert Owen suffered all his life from an inability to stay on any job long enough to see it well done; he was always mistaking the word—his own word—for the deed. He had no more than signed the papers for New Harmony when he was off to Washington to tell America about his plans as if they were already a *fait accompli*. In two speeches before joint sessions of Congress, with the President of the United States and members of the Supreme Court in attendance, he exhibited a model of the town he planned to build at New Harmony and, with only a hazy explanation of its governmental structure, predicted the spread of communities like his all over the United States and a consequent release from ignorance and oppression such as mankind had never before witnessed. Immediately afterward, having set up no kind of organization in New Harmony whatsoever and with only his son William, just turned twenty-three, left there as his representative, he published a manifesto inviting any and all who dreamed of a socialist millennium to move to the town on the Wabash at once. The result was that by the time he returned to New Harmony three months later, about a thousand men and women had moved into the town before the last of the German Harmonists had moved out and people were living there two and three families to the house.

Undismayed, Owen dedicated the Harmonists' brick church to free thought and free speech, renaming it The Hall of New Harmony, and promptly made therein the first of the many speeches that were to be his substitute for action. "I am come to this country," he announced, "to introduce an entire new state of society, to change it from

*Built with brick and beams by the Harmonists, this communal dormitory had become
a prosperous dry goods store in 1898 and is one of two dormitories still standing.*

an ignorant, selfish system to an enlightened social system
which shall gradually unite all interests into one, and remove all causes for contests between individuals." He then
outlined, in general terms, a constitution for a Preliminary
Society, pointing out that for a while he would keep the
property in his own hands and the people must temporarily
accept "a certain degree of pecuniary inequality," although
thenceforth there would be no social inequality. Three
days later the community adopted his constitution.

This Constitution was mostly preamble, establishing
very little beyond the fact that "persons of color" were not
to be included in the social equality, that the society was
not answerable for its members' debts, that those who did
not want to work could buy credit at the community store
by paying cash quarterly in advance, and that everyone
must try to be "temperate, regular, and orderly" and set a
good example for everybody else in order to achieve the
goal of "universal happiness." The actual government of
the society was to be by a committee which Robert Owen
would appoint, but neither its size nor its function was defined, unless the statement that it "would conduct the
affairs of the society" can be regarded as a definition. As

soon as the Constitution was adopted, Owen appointed
four members to the governing committee and allowed the
society to elect three more "by ballot among themselves";
and then he was off again, to the East, to spread the news
of New Harmony further, and to Scotland, to settle his
financial affairs. This time he was gone seven months.

During the first month of his absence, the Preliminary
Society ran well enough on the momentum of its first enthusiasm. In accordance with the program Owen left
behind for them, the members danced on Tuesday nights
in The Hall of New Harmony, the committee held a business meeting on Wednesday nights, there was a concert on
Thursday nights, and on Sundays there were lectures in
the Harmonists' old frame church, which the newcomers
called "The Steeple House." "Here there are no brawling
braggarts and intemperate idlers," one Owenite wrote back
home to his son. He described how well the postmaster
lived with his wife and several sons on the $1.54 a week
that he earned in credit at the community store by being
not only postmaster but also a committeeman, Superintendent of the Farms, and a selling agent for the store. But

by midsummer, discontent and dissension had set in. "The idle and industrious are neither of them satisfied," one member wrote to a friend, "the one contending that they do enough for their allowance, the other thinking themselves entitled to more." At the same time, this letter-writer's wife was telling her aunt in Pittsburgh, "The hogs have been our Lords and Masters this year in field and garden. We are now . . . without vegetables, except what we buy; and I believe we shall go without potatoes, turnips, or cabbages this winter, unless they are purchased."

Her prediction came true, and by the time Owen returned, in January, 1826, the society was in chaos and splinter groups were in the process of forming both within and on the periphery of the town. Owen, however, was so delighted by what he thought he saw that he announced the time had come, a year in advance of his original plan, for the formation of a permanent "Community of Equality." Another constitution was drawn up, not greatly different from the first. In a short time the threatened splinter groups were a reality, one of them calling itself Feiba Peveli. Pledged to a scheme of nomenclature, devised by an English architect, in which letters were substituted for

the numerals in latitudes and longitudes of places, the group suggests the eccentric spirit of Owen's New Harmony. The architect proposed the renaming of Pittsburgh as Otfu Veitoup, New York as Otke Notive, and New Harmony itself as Ipba Venul.

It was at this point that William Maclure came on the scene at New Harmony as Owen's partner and a financial backer. Like Owen, Maclure was a wealthy man, a Scot who had accumulated a fortune in an English-American export business. Some twenty years before, he had made a geological survey of the United States, traveling alone, crossing and recrossing the country some fifty times. His primary interest in the New Harmony community was in its educational experiment, and he soon began to look upon his partner's social theories with a jaundiced eye. Before the year was out, Maclure and Owen quarreled and dissolved the partnership. But, happily for New Harmony, Maclure's practical, level-headed influence continued.

A remarkable boat had brought Maclure to New Harmony in January, 1826. A keelboat of his own purchasing,

DON BLAIR

*Horseless carriages had replaced steamboats and wagons, but this centennial parade in 1914*
*honored an idealistic and intellectual heritage carried on by the Owenite descendants.*

first named *The Philanthropist* but rechristened for posterity by Owen as *The Boatload of Knowledge,* it carried an astonishing intellectual cargo on one of the most hopeful and halting voyages in the history of the Ohio River, starting from Pittsburgh. Among the boat's passengers were Thomas Say, the American naturalist; Charles-Alexandre Lesueur, the French naturalist; Madame Marie Duclos Fretageot, a Pestalozzian schoolmistress from Paris via Philadelphia; Robert Dale Owen, Robert Owen's oldest son, the future founder of the Smithsonian Institution and crusader for women's rights; and a score or more of teachers and pupils for the school system that was to make New Harmony famous in the history of American education.

In New Harmony, these people and others of equal renown who followed them wrangled deplorably over the nature of universal happiness and the proper pursuit of it. They were required by Owen to wear a ludicrous costume —white pantaloons buttoned over a boy's jacket without a collar, compared by one observer to "a feather-bed tied in the middle." But in spite of their inability to manage their everyday lives, there was a persistent charm and an initial enthusiasm for the New Moral World that Owen dreamed of. Most of the Owenites were not designed by nature or experience for the work they needed to do to keep the community going, but they tried at first to do their share of the harsher chores. Thomas Say developed such blisters that he could hardly shake hands with the Duke of Saxe-Weimar Eisenach when the the Duke visited the town. Robert Dale Owen spent a day sowing wheat and got a sore arm and, after that, lent a hand in the community bakery and spoiled the bread. Charles-Alexandre Lesueur preferred zoological expeditions into the woods to teaching school. Plaiting his beard and tucking it into his waistcoat, he fled as often as possible with his three dogs— Penny, Snap, and Butcher—to collect specimens. One of these was a skunk, which his French biographer, a hundred years later, described as the first "pool-cat" ever to be sent alive to Europe. Joseph Neef, a pupil of the Swiss educational reformer, Pestalozzi, struggled to control his old soldier's profanity in the schoolroom, but had a hard time of it, because not all the children of New Harmony were as phenomenally shy as Sir Charles Lyell, the British geologist, observed them to be when he visited the town. Old man Greenwood, discouraged by the handicap of advanced age, marched about town carrying a twelve-foot iron rod every time there was a thunderstorm; he wanted to die, but thought it was God's duty, not his, to do the job.

Meanwhile, everybody read and thought and wrote and wrote and talked and talked and talked, when they were not attending lectures in The Steeple House or dancing the night away in The Hall of New Harmony. Lovers wandered in the mystic labyrinth that the Harmonists had designed with tailored hedgerows and a small temple at the center and which the Owenites allowed to grow into a jungle. Picnickers gathered in the neglected vineyards and boating parties drifted on the river. One day the picnickers took axes with them and chopped down several trees as preparation for the new town Owen planned to build; but they ended by listening as Mr. Owen made another speech and by singing a song, which began:

> "Ah, soon will come the glorious day,
>   Inscribed on Mercy's brow,
> When truth shall rend the veil away
>   That blinds the nations now."

A duel was fought in the Harmonist cemetery, but with no casualties, and two women engaged in fisticuffs in front of Community House No. 4 without serious damage to each other. Single gentlemen complained that their socks were stolen from community-house washlines, and Madame Fretageot told the Duke of Saxe-Weimar Eisenach, in German, that Mr. Owen's democracy was harmful to the manners of the young. The schoolchildren played tricks on their mathematics instructor, Monsieur Guillaume Sylvan Casimir Phiquepal d'Arusmont, and Monsieur Guillaume Sylvan Casimir Phiquepal d'Arusmont eventually gave up in despair and married Frances Wright, the feminist. A group of dissenters built a coffin and would have buried "Owenism" if the coffin had not been smashed by unidentified persons the night before the funeral. It is little wonder that the Harmonists' factories stood idle, the Harmonist mill wheels no longer turned, the Harmonist fences broke down, hogs had the run of fields and gardens, and there weren't even cabbages to store when the second winter came.

Owen's experiment at New Harmony lasted altogether about two years and ended in chaos, but with Owen and Maclure still owning most of the property. Owen tried to save his dream by frequent reorganizations and, toward the last, by offering land for lease or sale to anyone who would attempt to establish a community according to his design. On July 4, 1826, once more mistaking the word for the deed, he sought to free the community of all its troubles by making a "Declaration of Mental Independence." On this date, the fiftieth anniversary of American political independence, he announced, "I have calmly and deliberately determined upon this eventful and auspicious occasion, to break asunder the remaining mental bonds which for so many ages have grievously afflicted our nature and, by so doing, to give forever FULL FREEDOM TO THE HUMAN MIND." (The capitals are Owen's.) Less than a year later, he delivered two successive farewell addresses in New Harmony, on May 26 and 27, 1827. Thereafter, deeding his property over to his sons, he left the community to its own devices and took off in pursuit of a new dream: he would ask the government of Mexico to give him Coahuila

*Farm prosperity was reflected at a local grain elevator in 1913 as farmers brought
in wagonloads of corn. Today's farms, fewer and larger, raise much wheat.*

and Texas for his next "experiment" in the expectation that the United States and Great Britain would support his sovereignty in that vast borderland. Owen died in 1858, at the age of eighty-seven, a spiritualist, on familiar terms with Napoleon, Shakespeare, and Benjamin Franklin.

Where George Rapp, believing that the "last day" was at hand, built New Harmony as if it were going to endure forever, Robert Owen, convinced that a new world was just beginning, erected nothing permanent. What one sees of old New Harmony today is the work of the Germans; there is not a single visible structure left that was created in Owenite days. And yet, with all the monuments to the Germans' industry, it is difficult to determine what went on in their minds and spirits as they worked, while the stamp of the Owenites' intellectual independence and cultural aspirations has shaped the history of the town throughout the intervening years and is still apparent. Owen was not a practical reformer, but he was a prophet and a catalytic agent among other dreamers. He created in

New Harmony a lasting spirit like his own by his sincere good will and his great personal magnetism, "gentle bore" though he was, according to Macaulay.

Specifically, Owen shaped New Harmony's future by the remarkable group of people he brought to Indiana, many of whom remained, and by leaving behind four remarkable sons and one remarkable daughter, who became the town's "first family." The people of New Harmony like to speak of the period immediately following Owen's community days as "the Golden Age." Certainly the town remained for a long time as lively and exciting a place to live in as it was when Robert Owen was proclaiming his miracles of Mental Independence and the New Moral World. Indeed, throughout most of the nineteenth century, the town was a cultural if not a celestial Zion unlike anything else in the vast, raw, and often ugly newness of the Middle West. Although the population has never much exceeded one thousand, it has supported a library,

*Plays were performed until 1912 at the Opera House built by the Harmonists, but now used as a garage. Owen's son started the theater group in 1828.*

a museum, an art gallery, several lecture series, a Thespian Society, a theater, two newspapers of national reputation and a half dozen of regional fame. As if such adornments were not enough, the first woman's club in America was organized in New Harmony in 1859. In fact, about the only civic virtue the town has failed to acquire in its seven score and ten years, either by its own initiative or by the generosity of its numerous benefactors, is a public sewage system. With a millennium of one sort or another always just around the corner, such a preparation for permanence on this earth has perhaps seemed superfluous.

After Owen's departure, Maclure became the first citizen and major patron. Like Owen, Maclure never spent more than a month or two at a time in the town; the climate was too much for him. But unlike Owen, he knew the value of able lieutenants in his absence: Madame Fretageot, who served the New Harmony school system until 1831; Thomas Say, who remained in the town until his death in 1834; and Maclure's brother, Alexander, who died in New Harmony in 1850 and is buried with Say in a vault on the lawn of the Maclure home that had formerly been George Rapp's. William Maclure did more for the community in outright gifts and, through his agents, gave it more guidance than it received from the man whose name is more often associated with its history. Under Maclure's direction, New Harmony had the first free-public-school system in America for boys and girls alike and the first trade school, supported by his generosity until finally the state of Indiana adopted a school system supported by taxation. Through Maclure's generosity also, the Workingmen's Institute was founded, a society of mutual self-improvement for the common man; and largely because of his spirit New Harmony's public library remains today remarkable for a town of its size—a large three-story brick building, housing 18,000 volumes available to a population of 1,121. When Maclure died in Mexico in 1840, he left a sum of about $80,000 that helped to establish 144 libraries in the state of Indiana and sixteen in Illinois.

Shortly before the German Harmonists left Indiana, they bought a printing press for the publication of George Rapp's *Thoughts on the Destiny of Man,* in German and English. When Robert Owen came, he purchased a new Stansbury press in Cincinnati and had it shipped to the town on the Wabash. On this press, *The New Harmony Gazette* was published regularly every week for three years, from 1825 until 1828, edited first by William Owen and Robert Jennings and later by Robert Dale Owen and Frances Wright, who finally took the journal to New York City and renamed it the *Free Enquirer.* The motto of the *Gazette* was, "If we cannot reconcile all opinions, let us endeavor to unite all hearts"; but it was, of course, primarily the organ of Owenism, and it published many of the speeches and treatises of the British reformer written before the New Harmony venture, as well as essays and editorials from the pens of two of his sons, Miss Wright, and William Maclure.

William Maclure sent a press from New Orleans in 1827 for the use of students in his School of Industry, and on it was printed the first issue of his *Disseminator of Useful Knowledge,* a bimonthly that, for the better part of a decade, was the official organ of the town. It had two mottoes: "Ignorance is the fruitful cause of human misery," and, later, "He who does his best, however little, is always to be distinguished from him who does nothing." In time, the *Disseminator's* press produced a number of books in New Harmony, among them Maclure's *Opinions on Various Subjects,* in three volumes; schoolbooks for use in Mexico; Michaux's *North American Sylva;* and Thomas Say's *American Conchology.* Mrs. Say and Charles-Alexandre Lesueur drew the sixty-eight illustrations for this beautiful book. The coloring was done by pupils in the New Harmony schools. Later, Josiah Warren, inventor of "the time store" and founder of The Village of Modern Times on Long Island, came to town and invented his speed press, the first to print a newspaper on a continuous sheet.

The inspiration of William Maclure and Gerard Troost, the Dutch geologist, and the presence in New Harmony of Maclure's large geological collection are indirectly responsible for the town's being the headquarters of the United States Geological Survey from 1839 until 1856. When young David Dale Owen joined his father in the community, he had already abandoned the career of an artist and was contemplating the practice of medicine, but the sight of physical suffering was so painful to him that he abandoned it and turned to a study of Maclure's collections. Ultimately he was appointed United States Geologist. The "laboratory" he built on Church Street in 1858 remains today one of the most distinguished and interesting houses in New Harmony and is the home of Kenneth Dale Owen, great-great-grandson of the reformer. David Dale in turn inspired his younger brother, Richard, to become a geologist, and he was for a while his brother's assistant. After distinguishing himself in the Civil War,

DON BLAIR

*Spring floods in 1913 did not deter carriages or pedestrians at a corner that*
*was always a good place to meet and chat, to sip pump water, or just sit.*

Richard became a professor of Natural History at Indiana University and later was chosen as the first president of Purdue, but he always maintained his residence in New Harmony and spent the last eleven years of his life there in retirement, dying in 1890. These two men were, in large part, responsible for the visits of many famous scientists to New Harmony, including John James Audubon, Sir Charles Lyell, and Prince Maximilian of Wied-Neuwied, who brought with him the young Swiss painter, Carl Bodmer.

The oldest Owen brother, Robert Dale Owen, was in and out of New Harmony all his life, sometimes maintaining a home there, sometimes paying his sister and brothers long visits. In the 1840's he served two terms in Congress as a Representative from Southern Indiana and, while in Washington, wrote and introduced the bill that created the Smithsonian Institution, which David Dale Owen helped to design. In 1850, New Harmony sent Robert Dale Owen to Indiana's second Constitutional convention, where he served in the vanguard of those fighting for the rights of women. From New Harmony, the oldest Owen son wrote the letter to President Lincoln that is said to have persuaded him to issue the Emancipation Proclamation. Owen died at Lake George, New York, in 1877, but sixty years later his remains were brought back to New Harmony.

Robert Owen's niece, Constance Fauntleroy, who had lived abroad with the Robert Dale Owens when Owen was American Chargé d'affaires in Naples, and who had been educated in Europe, organized the Minerva Society, a woman's literary club, in New Harmony. Uncle Robert Dale wrote its constitution. Before that, in 1825, Frances Wright had gathered a Female Social Society about herself in New Harmony; so whichever of these is "the first woman's club in America," New Harmony can claim it.

The tradition of the theater was perhaps the longest-lasting in New Harmony's story and was started by another Owen son, William, who did not live long enough to become as famous as Robert Dale, David Dale, and Richard, but locally he achieved greatness by founding the Thespian Society in 1828 while still a bachelor. His spirit inspired New Harmony's theater for almost a century thereafter.

The Thespians used The Hall of New Harmony as their first theater and, after that, the upstairs ballroom of the Harmonists' Community House No. 1. On one occasion Charles-Alexandre Lesueur designed magpies that soared down out of the flies and stole objects from the stage in such realistic fashion that backwoodsmen in the audience informed the actors of the birds' mischief. Lesueur's beautiful backdrops would have been ornaments to New York productions, for he was a first-rate artist as well as naturalist. The scenery he made for *William Tell* was used over and over for fifty years.

The Thespians eventually built a theater in Community House No. 4, tearing out the interior walls and partitions, constructing a large stage, and installing removable seats in orchestra and gallery. Peter Duclos, a passenger on *The Boatload of Knowledge* in his boyhood, designed the scenery, having previously helped to decorate the St. Charles Theatre in New Orleans. Called Union Hall, New Harmony's theater became the second largest in Indiana, a rank that it held until its demise in 1912.

The local theater was a permanent attraction that brought people to New Harmony from miles around and drew outstanding actors, including the Joe Jeffersons and the Goldens, who made New Harmony their home and the headquarters for their traveling troup. Showboats, in their heyday, tied up at the New Harmony wharf and the Thespians themselves at one point briefly tried the river life.

The last plays in Union Hall were produced by the Lilley Stock Company; after that the building was sold and became a garage. It still stands on Church Street, owing half its fame to the fact that it was built almost a hundred and fifty years ago by George Rapp's Harmonists. The words "Opera House" are inscribed over its door and the outlines of the old stage are still visible inside.

The inherited wealth that preserved the gracious living and culture of New Harmony well into the present century and that is still in evidence was shored up against depletion by the fertility of Posey County land. However, during the town's long history, fortunes have also been made from small beginnings; one, for example, by an Irishman named Edward Murphy, another by a Frenchman named John Ribeyre. Murphy wandered into New Harmony in 1826 at the age of thirteen—a runaway from a harsh man in Louisville, Kentucky, who professed to be his uncle—and the town adopted him. He tried various trades in his youth, finally became a doctor, increased his income by putting it out at interest, and when he died, in 1900, had repaid New Harmony with gifts to the Workingmen's Institute totaling $155,000. The other self-made man, Ribeyre, came from Severac, Aveyron, France, in 1848, and is said to have acquired property in Posey County worth over a half million dollars. His son, Alfred, inherited the father's shrewdness in land-dealing and soon owned what seemed like half of the Posey County countryside. Painting all his farmhouses and outbuildings an unmistakable ugly yellow, he advertised on their barns that he was "The Corn King."

By 1900, most of the famous citizens of New Harmony had either died or departed, but many of their kin and the descendants of other Owenites still lived in the village— Fretageots, Elliotts, Fords, Coopers, Schnees, Pelhams, Fauntleroys, and others. These people, residing in the old Harmonist houses, carried on the social and intellectual traditions of the past and talked about the "Owenites" and "Rappites" as if they were contemporaries. They made lively use of the library of the Workingmen's Institute, supported an annual lecture program in a new and handsome auditorium named for Dr. Murphy, had revived the woman's club, and knew how to entertain a former President of the United States, William Howard Taft, when he came to help them celebrate their Centennial in 1914.

By the 1920's, however, New Harmony, like most small towns in America, began to suffer from the prosperity and magnetism of the cities, and in the 1930's the Depression dealt a blow that was only partially tempered by the discovery of oil in Posey County. Many of the town's children went off to college in those years and did not return; and the automobile, the metropolitan movie palaces, radio and then television, city banks and city supermarkets destroyed the old community life for those who were left behind. By the 1950's the town had become a derelict, too far from any city to become a suburb, too near to have a life of its own. The children who passed in and out of the schoolhouse door that Frederick Rapp had made for Father Rapp's church in 1822 were still told about their remarkable past, but they no longer felt that they were a part of it.

But now, in the 1960's, after several decades of decay and despair, New Harmony is once more awake. The revival of its cultural life is modern and different from anything in its past, and yet by that very difference it is in the New Harmony tradition. The wife of Kenneth Dale Owen has come up from Texas with a new dream for New Harmony. She has bought and refurbished some of the old Harmonist houses and buildings, even moving them to different locations when it suits her convenience. Setting up a trust, she has erected a "Roofless Church," of vast proportions designed by Philip Johnson, and adorned it with a bronze madonna by Jacques Lipchitz. At the edge of the Wabash River bottoms, where tall corn grows, she has created a small park and named it for Paul Tillich and, in June of 1963, imported Dr. Tillich himself to dedicate its "Cave of the New Being." To ensure a continuity of this new culture when she was not on the scene, she employed for a while a clergyman in residence to act as her agent, and she houses aspiring poets and artists in her various properties to work at their crafts in a kind of Yaddo-like seclusion. Still more recently, the townspeople themselves have formed an organization to supervise their cultural life.

A century and a half ago, a backwoodsmen who came into New Harmony to stare at the Owenites and try to figure out what they were up to was quoted as saying, as he scratched his head and spat in bewilderment, "I thinks and thinks about it." Today's visitors in the little town on the Wabash—Posey County farmers and American and European tourists alike—have new food for thought as they watch the solemn ceremonies and gay festivities of the "foreigners" gathered by the town's new benefactress from the world of art, music, religion, and philosophy. The conclusions they draw as to the intention of it all may vary, but there can be no doubt that angels' wings are once more a-flutter in the balmy Southern Indiana air. The celestial presence plagues a few of the townspeople, who protest that they would prefer to be left alone with the quieter and less disturbing echoes of past visitations, but New Harmony is once more prospering and, in one sense at least, being saved.

DON BLAIR

*A bygone landmark, this covered bridge outside the town was razed in 1926 to make way for steel. But urbanization has bypassed the town where Owenite descendants still live.*

*The town of this 1880 lithograph had a distinctive New England look, given by its New England settlers, and a steamboat gaiety resulting from a logging prosperity.*

# Gentility in a *New* New England

---

## *Marine on St. Croix, Minnesota*

---

### BY JAMES GRAY

The town of Marine on St. Croix stands on the banks of the river from which it derives its surname. So peaceful, so almost somnolent is its present mood a casual observer might be tempted to suggest that it *loiters* there. On a day in winter, when the current of the old logging stream flows along the shore under a crust of ice; on a summer day, when water skiers flash like silvery explosions past the green curtain of pines, even the forces of energy seem to be under the control of a placid, unthreatening temper.

Marine, unaffected by the challenge of change, survives and persists with a special kind of resolution. It looks much as it did when it was one of the first settlements of the valley and the heart of the oldest industry of the region a century and a quarter ago. Staunchly—though only on particular occasions articulately—proud of its past, it accepts the present with indulgent dignity. To paraphrase a comment of Sigrid Undset, the town brings an abiding concern with "the timeless things of human nature" to an urban and scientific age.

From the river bank where the sawmills and the flour mills once throbbed the town makes its way by gradual stages up the terraces of the ravine. The walls were cut deep and sheer by a glacial stream as it escaped in the dawn of time from the ice sheets that once covered a vast area to the north. Weirdly picturesque formations of jagged rock, lining the impressive canyon, give the natural scene a look of pageantry on a stupendous scale. Remembering with a touch of ironic humor all the dark fears of the race, admirers of the river have seen it as a sort of wild research center of evolution. Rocks farther up are called the Devil's Chair, the Devil's Pulpit, and the Devil's Oven. In certain stretches the river boils through rapids and gives swimmers a workout if they choose to challenge its four-mile-an-hour current.

The river served the lumber industry well for more than half a century, offering a highway for the delivery to mills of the vast wealth of white pine that stood on the banks of the St. Croix and its contributory streams. The river makes its way from one Lake St. Croix in northern Wisconsin to its outlet in another Lake St. Croix in southern Minnesota, marking the boundary between the two states with its lower stretch. (A ferry from Marine once linked the shores; it continued its daily operation until a few years ago.) At Prescott the waters of the St. Croix join the Mississippi.

All the way the sheer cliffs on both sides of the St. Croix are covered with pine, oak, maple, and birch. The scene achieves an awesomeness in fall with its stunning variety of natural color—flame, yellow, bronze, purple—amid the year-round green. In spring the banks are strewn with the unobtrusive abundance of hepaticas, anemones, bloodroots, trilliums, jack-in-the-pulpits, and even the rare moccasin flowers; birds of some three hundred species make the river valley a favorite northern meeting place; deer swim the river and clamber en masse up the banks to nibble at the fresh shoots of small trees, and red foxes make their angry-woman clamor in the nearby woods.

The land lives in uninterrupted intimacy with the record of the years. To a man who has left his car in a public gathering place (William O'Brien State Park lies just two miles north of Marine) and has launched himself on the river in a rented canoe, the scene cannot look very different from the way it looked to seventeenth-century explorers or to the rampageous voyageurs who used the St. Croix as a channel of commerce nearly three centuries ago. All of these visitors were impressed by what they saw. Daniel Greysolon, Sieur Du Lhut, who helped to establish French forts on the soil of North America, described the river as "very fine." A century and a half later the first native American explorer, Henry Schoolcraft, saw the scene as one that should tempt enterprising exploiters with the riches of its physical resources and also as a place of startling beauty. "The banks are high," he wrote; "[they] afford series of picturesque views which keep the eye constantly on the stretch."

When another two decades had passed, the pioneer editor, James M. Goodhue, in 1849, made a trip up the St. Croix to see for himself what the first settlers had made of their opportunities. He was gratified by evidences of brisk industrial advancement and at the same time beguiled by the inviolable natural charm of the setting. "The country," he wrote, "is surpassingly beautiful."

Marine cherishes its serenity. The suggestion was recently made that the town should vie with other communities for the privilege of becoming the site of a new county courthouse. But the proponents of the gospel of getting-on found little encouragement—only a kind of bafflingly benign apathy. Who wanted all that bustle and for the love of what advantage not already available?

From the water line the town climbs up the first level of the all but "perpendicular wall" (as an early visitor described it) to the center of commerce. Here is the general store built in 1870, still the direct successor to the first mercantile establishment that was destroyed by fire. Next to it is the firehouse for which Marine had to wait until 1888, but which in its exact original form continues to be part of the safety system of the community. Across the street is the bank, a white stucco building decorously disguised as a Greek temple. (What right-thinking banker of a century ago would have dreamed of conducting business in any other sort of structure?) It is complete with toy, nonfunctional Doric pillars. In a miniature park nearby the huge round stones of the first flour mill are enshrined as monuments along with the bell from an old river boat.

The old highway leading to Minnesota's famous north country cuts straight through the village, but it serves only local activity now. A few hundred feet away a new thoroughfare carries modern traffic by. Sturdy reminders of the old pioneer village dot the old road—the blacksmith shop and a completely indestructible log cabin built more than a century and a quarter ago. The latter has been incorporated into the operations of a garage, blending past and present with the casual adaptability that is characteristic of Marine's sense of continuity.

As the old road starts to climb the hill to meet the new highway one encounters the periphery of the present day —filling station, barbershop, post office, lumber yard. It is perhaps appropriate that the post office should represent a sprightly concession to modernity. An unknown genius was inspired with the thought that dwellers in the "land of the sky blue waters" should have a sky-blue center for the distribution of mail and he bravely gave one to the residents of Marine. The barbershop is a kind of halfway house between present and past. Men with no immediate need of the barber's professional services stop in passing and go in to learn "what's new." The barbershop is as much a clearing house of male gossip as the general store is a gathering place for co-educational exchange.

And that is Marine in the totality of its existence as a mart of trade.

From this center the town wanders up the hill . . . past the old schoolhouse (a giddily modern one is discreetly hidden away on the edge of the community and its predecessor has become a dwelling place) . . . past Dr. Gaskill's drugstore (now the office of the real-estate man, but still a kind of informal museum of pharmaceutical lore, equipped with the cases which were once filled with the awful mysteries of the healing art) . . . past a scattering of frame houses . . . past—or rather across—the old mill pond . . . past the cemetery . . . over the railroad tracks (the station was closed a few years ago, but freight trains still make their way along the route to Duluth) . . . and finally over the last rise of land to "the dump," set characteristically in a fine stand of pines. It should be mentioned that the dump has become accepted, quite without waggish self-consciousness, as a tete-à-tete corner for those who have happened not to meet during any day at the post office, barbershop, store, or garage.

It is a comment made often by latter-day discoverers of Marine that the town looks like a bit of New England, dropped down in this unlikely place. The same impulse of thrift that prompted the New Englanders to build their houses of wood inevitably suggested itself to the settlers of Marine. Lumber was available in seemingly endless supply and it was cheap. So there are the tidy frame dwellings painted white, each set on a reasonably spacious piece of land. Experts in such matters say that the similarity in appearance between Marine and a village of Maine, Massachusetts, or Connecticut is by no means as close as it seems. Marine lacks the focal center of a town green which gives the older New England villages their unity of mood.

An observer who has been admired for the photographic accuracy of his eye as revealed in his travels—Sinclair Lewis—always caught the shadow of Vermont in his personal impressions of Marine. He visited the town often for periods of a day, a week, or months on end. In the diary of his 1942 return to Minnesota he wrote: "Marine on St. Croix, hilly farms like New England," adding a little tartly: "One comes from New England to Minnesota in 1942 as one did in 1872 and seeks hills and houses as much as possible like the New England one has left in disgust."

New England, in fact, sent its first delegations of restless men into the Midwest many years earlier than 1872. "Old Stock Yankee" had been exploring opportunities in the wilderness from the time when the century was in its teens. Typical was the group of men who created Marine on St. Croix in 1838. They migrated from Vermont, Connecticut, and New York state and came together in Madison County, Illinois, at a village called Marine. These men had had experience at various trades, as tanners, brickmakers, storekeepers and tavern keepers and most of them a background of farming. But, after a few years as apprentice pioneers, they became restless again and turned this time toward the north. The fields there did not look greener, perhaps, but the pine trees did. After earnest consultations

in the tavern of one of their number they sent out two emissaries to find a site for a prospective lumbering organization. The scouts traveled up the Mississippi River in September of 1838; later by steamer and flatboat they explored the St. Croix, penetrating by these far-from-easy means to a distance forty miles north of its mouth. They were not quite the first to think of waking the river from its long sleep and putting it to the service of industry. Just a year before, in 1837, treaties with the Sioux and Chippewa had opened up the delta between the St. Croix and Mississippi rivers. This tract was rich not only in pineries but in fertile soil excellent for growing wheat. Settlers had begun to avail themselves of these resources. A sawmill was already in process of construction at the falls of the St. Croix when the two men from Illinois made their trip of investigation. Encouraged by the confidence of these predecessors the scouts decided on a site approximately halfway between the falls and Lake St. Croix where a stream raced down the west bank with a fine show of power. They staked a claim by blazing the trees with the individual mark of what was to be their company and returned to Illinois to report to their principals.

The land lay in what was then officially Iowa Territory. (Minnesota Territory was not created until 1849 and statehood was not achieved until another nine years had passed.) The tract had still to be surveyed by the national government and parcels of it could not actually be purchased at a land sale until this had been done. It was possible, in these circumstances, for claim jumpers to move on the tract and three of them did after the two explorers had left. Seizing the same site, they arranged for one of their number to put up a cabin, clear a few acres, and assume physical possession.

The Illinois group, ignorant of what had happened, went forward with their own plans. Eight of them set out from St. Louis on a chartered steamer which carried complete equipment for a sawmill. They had with them millwrights, blacksmiths and the first white woman to reach the area, the wife of one of the partners. Mixing equal parts of audacity and imagination with her loyalty, she had agreed to cook for the entire company.

At the millsite the party was greeted, in May, 1839, by the cheerful effrontery of the claim jumpers who refused to give over until they had been bought off for a substantial amount, three hundred dollars. But having survived, however ruefully, this "moment of last suspense," the original claimants took firm possession of their rights and set actively to work on their project. By late August it had become a going concern. Two of the partners were by then in the woods cutting logs along the banks of the Kettle, the Snake, and the Namekagon rivers and preparing to float them down the St. Croix; the others directed the activities of the mill itself. The first winter's work was less than satisfying to its participants. Their muley saw earned its name by being stubborn and inadequate. Driven by an overshot

**WALKER, JUDD & VEAZIE.**

WHOLESALE DEALERS IN ALL KINDS AND QUALITIES OF PINE LUMBER LOGS, LATH, SHINGLES.

*The local sawmill bore the name of the settlers who had founded it. Soon after*
*this 1874 print, the boom moved west, leaving the town impoverished.*

wheel, equipped with buckets, it could not be disciplined into cutting more than 5,000 board feet a day. The entire output of the mill for its first season was 800,000 feet cut from the 2,000 logs that reached Marine.

But at least the creative effort had been justified. Something existed that had not existed before. A significant contribution had been made toward the establishment of an industry which, during the next phase of Midwestern history, was to support some 75 per cent of all workers in the region. More dramatically still, it was to build many of the great cities which were springing up all along the route of the westward march across the continent. Eight men, one woman and two small sons had set up an outpost of progress. They lived in minute log dwellings and endured weather which, if the unverified stories of the time may be believed, took the thermometer down—at least once—to 58° below zero. These pioneers probably had no very rewarding sense of serving destiny. But unobtrusively and resolutely they did.

So, there they were—the Walker brothers (Orange and Lewis), Asa Parker, George Judd, Hiram Berkey, Samuel Burkleo, David Hone and William Dribble—in business. Lawrence Taliafero, Indian agent at Fort Snelling, visited them at the very start of their effort and recorded in his journal the impression that "these Eastern men" were all ones of "character and capacity."

In their group picture Orange Walker stands forth commandingly. He was in poor health when he arrived in Minnesota and this may have been one of the reasons why he wished to move north. Minnesota enjoyed the reputation of being a health resort long before it had become a vacation land and the home of the Mayo Clinic. Eastern and Southern states dispatched their invalids to enjoy its somewhat austere benignity and to be cured of tuberculosis. In the instance of Orange Walker's personal history Minnesota's reputation seems to have been justified. The pioneer lived halfway through his eighties and was irrepressibly busy through all his years. During the half century of his life at Marine he was a kind of grand seigneur to the whole community. He created its industry; through the company store he served all of its daily needs for food and clothing; as operator of company steamers and teams he provided communication with the outside world; he accepted every kind of public office from postmaster to representative in the state legislature. When Indians swooped down on the village, frightening women and sending men in search of their guns, it was Orange Walker who provided a modest but successful distraction by offering the unwanted visitors a feast of sour crackers from his store. He even held an official post, Overseer of the Poor, and he occupied it with consummate tact. It was his custom to deposit baskets of provisions anonymously on the doorsteps of the needy and he did so at night when the gift could not be observed by the neighbors.

The founders of the village called their new home after the old one—Marine. When a flour mill was added to its industrial establishments everyone fell into the habit of referring to the community as Marine Mills.

Adjustment to the condition of living in the midst of a wilderness seems from the records to have been surprisingly unmarred by major threats from the Indians. The place called Cedar Bend, eight miles north of Marine, is traditionally supposed to have marked a kind of No Man's Land between the territory of the Chippewa and that of the Sioux. The tribes, of course, surged into and across it often, challenging one another to battle and killing one another with such enthusiasm that various spots were identified by the historians of the time as "the valley of the bones" and the Golgotha of the warriors. But it would appear that the Indians exhausted their hostilities on one another. In the annals of Marine there is no scarlet page concerned with massacre. Instead the white men bartered frequently with their Indian neighbors and profited by the exchange. The Spartan rigor of their diet was relieved by the Sybaritic delight of eating the partridges and the wild rice brought by the Indians in abundance to the local markets and to the lumber camps. Among other products made available by the industry of a people—who were never as idle as their detractors assumed—were blueberries (in season they could be bought virtually by the hillock for trifling amounts) and the Indians' special kind of maple syrup, black, granular, and strong with the memory of smoke.

It was, however, no idyllic pastoral that the white man and the red enacted together. The settlers did not think of the Indian as the "noble savage." Complaints against him were numerous; these had to do with acts of gleeful spite like burning haystacks, with minor thefts involving the loss of traps and game, and with the waste of wild life. Destruction of deer at the rate of twelve hundred animals a week threatened the region, it was said, with the total loss of this resource of food and clothing. After a public meeting, held at Marine on December 20, 1856, an appeal was sent to Governor Willis Gorman, demanding relief. The spirited but injudicious document even suggested that if the citizens did not get help from the government, they might be forced to drive the Indians out of the neighborhood at the point of their own guns. The governor's response, addressed to Orange Walker, said, in effect, "Forget it!" and, a little shamefacedly, the settlers did. In the end the problem was solved when the Indians simply moved on.

When Marine had been in existence for a decade and a half, the growing success of the lumber company seemed to promise that prosperity would be permanent and highly contagious. More settlers from New England—Maine, Vermont, and Rhode Island—joined the original group. Names like Lyman, Otis, and Moore appeared on the register of citizens. In a January issue of 1856 the St. Croix *Union* reported that Marine had a population of some "two hundred souls—chiefly Yankees."

But men of other backgrounds began also to appear, asking for shares in the bounty of the forest, the soil, and the energy of village life. These men of German, French, and Swiss derivation added the wealth of many cultures to the service of the crafts—Rudolphus Lehmicke as cabinetmaker, Mathias Welshons and Hans Boock as carpenters. Amable Bruette, a logger later turned farmer, established a family line which has continued into the present day.

In even greater numbers came the immigrants from the Scandinavian countries. To the Swedes and Norwegians there seemed to be an affinity between the look of their homeland and the rough, hilly tracts surrounded by forests. The Scandinavians adapted rapidly to the new setting. However, they had psychological battles to wage and endure. The "greenhorns" were not always accepted either gratefully or graciously by the ex-Vermonters who retained much of the New England reserve. Children of the first settlers were even admonished not to speak to the newcomers sitting in the seats at right and left in school. But the Scandinavians, ruggedly self-sufficient, survived well—so well, in fact, that today, with all the names of the "old stock Americans" gone from the public registers, the names of the first Swedish and Norwegian settlers are everywhere in evidence, as they are throughout Minnesota and in the councils of the state. Many latter-day natives of Marine, earning advanced academic degrees, have gone out to serve the nation in conspicuous posts in the sciences and the arts.

The Scandinavians settled in the northern part of the town of Marine and maintained their group integrity by marrying among their own kind. There were a few exceptions. An Olson was once carried away by the inescapable attractions of a Mermond from Switzerland. And a Peterson found the person of a late arrival from Italy so much to her liking that she agreed to become Mrs. John Copas. But the Scandinavian influence most emphatically prevailed in the household of this mixed marriage. Once when the son of John Copas was an old man he was asked if he had ever learned to speak his father's native tongue. His tart answer indicated at least where the loyalties of this Swedish-Italian-American did *not* lie. "Say!" he exclaimed with an air of comic reproach. "I wouldn't talk that Wop talk."

The Scandinavian-Americans became farmers and good ones. The sandy loam, mixed with clay, grew excellent wheat and conditions in those early seasons of Marine history were so favorable that crop failures were happily unknown. The emigrants prospered and, with characteristic resourcefulness, many augmented the family income by working in the sawmills during periods when the demands of the farm itself were slack.

The ever-increasing demand for lumber, happily matched by what seemed to be the inexhaustible supply of highly desirable white pine, gave Marine a comfortable way of life. In the mid years of the nineteenth century the logging industry boomed along the St. Croix River. A visitor wrote that on a sight-seeing trip to Taylor's Falls he had never been "out of sight of rafts and strings of logs." He added that it required "no great stretch of fancy to imagine oneself passing through a country in military possession of Queen Victoria so often do we pass detachments of stout hardy men dressed in red." He referred to the red shirts and red flannel trousers of the lumberjacks, which were almost an official uniform.

The lumberjack seemed to belong to a breed of men like no others known to the human race. Many of them came out of New England following the westward course of the logging industry. When logging declined in Minnesota, they pushed on like true nomads, all the way to the forests of the Pacific coast. A few turned to farming; their first interest was tilling the soil and they "went into the woods" only to augment their earnings during the winter months. But the prototype was a rootless creature whose mistress was the river. He did not marry or establish any sort of base on land. Devoted as he was to A. E. Housman's famous trio of gratifications, "liquor, love, or fights," the lumberjack was triumphant in youthful possession of his freedom, his brawn, and his special skills; but the end of his life was forlorn. During the 1920's the last survivors of the species—those who had never left Minnesota or who had returned to it—often wandered the highway between river towns, without employment, without destination, looking aimlessly for rides, for handouts and for brief moments of conviviality with anyone who would listen to stories of the old days.

But in his interval of fulfillment the lumberjack was superb. Shaggy and indomitable as his own legendary hero, Paul Bunyan, and seeming often as huge, he was enormously colorful in all his activities. One of his dramatic talents was that of birling—the unique art of riding a log through the turbulent water of the river while standing upright on its slippery surface. He could make this unlikely mount spin under his feet, change direction under his guidance, stop dead in an instant at his will.

The lumberjacks managed to be dramatic and sometimes overwhelming when they took over the two hotels and six saloons in Marine. Their appetites were prodigious." Among the memories of a St. Croix boyhood cherished by the historian and crusading editor, Ray Stannard Baker, was that of seeing one of the river giants breeze through a light luncheon which consisted of six hard-boiled eggs, half a loaf of bread, two raw onions, a quart of coffee, a huge wedge of cheese and half a mince pie.

Not all the energy of this pioneer community went into the service of the logging industry. There were resourceful townsmen who knew how to satisfy public needs with profit to themselves as well as to their neighbors.

In the early days of the settlement farmers were obliged to carry their grain twenty-five or thirty miles over a virtually impassable road to reach a mill where it could be ground. A bitter critic of the only available thoroughfare said of it in an eloquent crisis of resentment, "Jupiter! What a road! The goats upon a mountain could not have engineered a worse!"

Isolation imposed on the farmer the hardships of an almost primitive pattern of agricultural labor. He had to thresh his grain by hand, often operating his flail on frozen ground. Then at last a modest hero of enterprise came forward to solve the problem. Dr. James Gaskill deserves to be reclaimed from the ranks of the anonymous great for the variety and quality of his contributions to the well-being of the town. In addition to being its physician, one of its storekeepers and its representative in the first state legislature, he seized opportunities to improve Marine's prospects—and his own—wherever he saw them. In the summer of 1857 he opened a gristmill which the *St. Paul Advertiser* described as unexcelled by any "in the valley of the Mississippi." So ended one phase of slavery to outmoded practice.

A later benefactor to the farmer was another typical pioneer, John Gabrielson Rose. Born Gabrielson, this son of a Swedish-American emigrant had suffered certain indignities at school for what seemed to his classmates to be the oddity of his name. In the casual way of the time he adopted as his own the name Rose, carved on his desk by the boy who had occupied it before him. Rose he became and Roses his descendants continue to be.

This adaptable man represented the kind of pioneer whose success may be attributed to the fact that he made highly exacting intellectual demands of himself. Finding about him few opportunities to become educated he rigorously educated himself. For a time he taught school and the love of learning became a part of family discipline; several of his descendants became teachers and scientists.

Rose doubled as benefactor and shrewd man of affairs by introducing farm machinery into the community. Early in the 1880's he operated two stores facing each other across the main street; in one he sold everything for the housewife, from thread and needles to cabbages; the other dealt in heavy equipment for harvesting grain. With this boost the Marine farmers virtually leaped out of primitivism into the modern world.

The next step in the logic of service was for Rose to take over a flour mill, expand and operate it. The county historian of the 1880's seems to have been impressed chiefly by the fact that the mill stood four stories high. What seizes the interest of a later-day follower of the town's progress is the ingenuity with which power was provided. The seventeen springs of the hillside were dammed and their waters conveyed a thousand feet to the mill by an elevated wooden flume. As picturesque as a Roman aqueduct, this structure was really spectacular when winter decorated its supports with huge, intricately molded icicles.

Even before the Civil War, Marine Mills had become a solid, self-sufficient civic entity—a community greatly admired by others for its thrift and perhaps envied for its prosperity. Observers were generous. As one said of its citizens: "They are all workers—no idlers here!" Wrote another: "To the invalid, the pleasure seeker, as well as the sportsman, no place affords more ample inducements for sojourn and recreation; to the emigrant, the farmer, mechanic, artist, merchant and banker, no place in the Territory can be found offering superior inducements for permanent settlement."

And the town was gay. As early as February, 1855, Adam Lightner had established a reputation among all the people of the valley for his art in "raising a ball." In the slang of the time a cotillion party given at the Lightner House in that year was described as having been "*some affair.*"

For nearly thirty years thereafter success exercised its benign influence and encouraged exuberance under the auspices of one group or another. There were balls, hops, cotillions, house-warming parties, excursions up the river (on "floating palaces" as enthusiastic reporters always called the old side-wheel steamers), picnics to celebrate the Fourth of July, sleigh rides into the depths of the surrounding woods with "sumptuous suppers" afterward.

MINNESOTA HISTORICAL SOCIETY

*Steamboats like these at Marine on July 4, 1887, not only linked the river towns but also made the village the major port of call. Visitors came from as far away as St. Paul.*

There can be no doubt that the citizens of Marine Mills offered a spirited kind of hospitality. To the boys and girls of Stillwater (Marine's neighbor ten miles to the south), to the enterprising youth of Taylor's Falls (upriver), and even to urban-center sophisticates of St. Paul, the glamor of Marine had exactly the effect on the imagination that the lights of a pleasure resort always have had for those who live a few miles—or hundreds of miles—away.

Even after the Civil War had begun the people of the valley continued to be drawn together around the "lights of Marine." In January, 1862, sixty pairs of partners danced at an occasion so successful that it drew from the *Taylor's Falls Reporter* a glowing tribute: "Three cheers for the Marine boys! Their style is good!" For a time, in the midst of the war, the social gatherings of men seem to have concentrated appropriately on gathering funds to be sent to Union soldiers and those of women on sewing for the armies.

By Washington's birthday in 1866 the impulse toward fun had recovered its full drive. "Our Marine friends," the Stillwater *Messenger* reported, "do not propose to let the anniversary pass without a proper observance. No other fellows know how to get up a big thing in better style than the Marine boys." A "grand civic ball" also in celebration of Washington's birthday was organized in 1872. Stillwater neighbors came virtually en masse. To make the pilgrimage they commanded all the resources of the community's livery stable. Again the Stillwater *Messenger* was happily impressed. With the modest deference owed to masters, the editor observed: "The reputation that the people of Marine have achieved for their ability in getting up tip-top times is too well known to need any comments."

The rewards of attending festivities at Marine must have seemed promising, indeed, to the young people of neighboring towns, for they were willing to endure a trip through sub-zero weather. Perhaps these indestructible creatures were gratefully aware of how different their situation was from that of many teen-agers living on the frontier. An often bleak, sometimes ferocious, boredom enclosed their existence. A curious document on the shelves of the Minnesota Historical Society is concerned, in part, with a description of the social life of the Midwest wilderness in the nineteenth century. One section is headed "Entertainment." In it, after a brief introduction of his subject, the writer turns, without apparent awareness of indulging in savage, Swiftian satire, to his first illustrative item: *Lynching of an Indian.* It is pleasant, by way of contrast, to dwell on the evocative charm of a line from another historical pamphlet describing a husking bee which inaugurated the season of 1882 at Marine: "The boys and girls husked corn all day and danced all night."

A taste for worldly pastime also characterized the town's routine. The "sport of kings" was none too good for these sturdy democrats who knew what they wanted. Horse racing was a popular activity all up and down the St. Croix valley during the 1870's. An unverifiable report that Marine once had a race track of its own may not be true. But it is a well-established fact that "Foxie V" owned by William Veazie of the lumber company Walker, Judd and Veazie was one of the great horses of the time. Foxie V's speed and stamina were admired by all the experts who wrote for national magazines of sport. No horse, bred, trained, and owned in the Midwest, with the possible exception of the great Dan Patch, ever was given such attention.

The prosperity of the community was easily able to support this spectacular extravagance throughout the whole decade of the 1870's. In February, 1880, the horses were still running strong. After a contest held in Stillwater there was so little doubt about local pre-eminence that the Stillwater *Messenger* reported: "The little town of Marine possesses the fastest horses in the country."

The Minnesota essayist, Charles Flandrau, once offered the suggestion that civilization is spread in a thin veneer over the surface of the globe and that it is no more remarkable when an aptitude for living pleasantly is found in a Midwestern town or on a Southwestern desert than when it is found in a great capital of the world. Perhaps the benevolent influences are spread in an equally thin veneer over the centuries, so that one period is quite as likely as another to value the gracious and elegant. It seems certainly to have been true that the tiny frontier town of Marine Mills displayed, during the 1870's, a modest command of the resources that can make living an art. The significant trifles that make this clear are in evidence on every page of the record. The women ordered from local dressmakers costumes as intricately contrived of ribbons and laces and cascades of silk as were to be seen anywhere in the United States. Patent-leather shoes, to be worn at all those hops and cotillions, were on sale in Orange Walker's store, which was never without a stock of "hair oil" to put a sheen on the heads of men who perhaps did not think of themselves as beaux, but who were nonetheless glossy.

One thing that helped to give flavor to the social life of Marine was that Adam Lightner and Mathias Welchons kept hotels of surprising excellence. Mr. Lightner's Marine House in particular received remarkable endorsements from travelers. The editor of the *St. Croix Union,* after a trip made in March, 1855, testified that "the establishment served edibles in a style that made it a favorite resort for those who acknowledge the value of a good meal." This, too, was different from the rule of the long, rough road that led through the wilderness. Standards in places where a casual wayfarer could find supper and a bed were abysmally low. One unhappy man, making a tour of the Midwest to describe its progress for an Eastern journal, complained with understandable bitterness that in a grim hovel where he was obliged to stop the only available nourishment consisted of "corn bread, a mess of rutabagas and a kind of tea made of wild grasses." But Mr. Lightner's and Mr. Welchons' ideas of how visitors should be treated were of another kind entirely. The "sumptuous suppers" for which their hotels were noted might well begin with oysters taken from one of the barrels which were shipped west regularly and buried in the snow outside the back door. A diner of experimental taste might have bear meat as *pièce de résistance.* But there was no need to settle for that. The local butcher could supply steak; the Indians, venison; the local sportsmen, game.

Many witnesses remain today to testify to the fact that the citizens of Marine built solidly for the future. Even their places of business prove it. The old store testifies to its history of endurance in the look of solidity that it presents today. Before he began to build it Orange Walker took account of the circumstances under which he must operate. Before the coming of the railroad there was no way of receiving supplies except by steamboats and these could not move up the river in winter. In the full basement which Mr. Walker designed there was room for great quantities of goods and the range of selection was wide. The superstructure of the building is correspondingly commodious and durable. Made entirely of wood, it is massive, with huge timbers and heavy joists. The foundation is on solid rock.

In constructing their private houses the leading citizens were equally concerned with solidity, but they were more willing to acknowledge the claims of charm. When Asa Parker built a house for the bride he was to bring from Virginia, it is said he hoped to remind her reassuringly of her original home. The house stands today and it is easy to believe that Asa Parker was trying to beguile a homesick girl. There is a family feeling between its architecture and that of a plantation house, even without the traditional gallery. The portico is there and so are the splendid columns towering up two stories to the hip roof. Scattered throughout Marine there are several houses which reflect the tastes of the original settlers—Samuel Burkleo, George Judd, and others. Most have been extensively remodeled by later owners, but here and there wide floor boards and curious staircases testify to their era. The charm of Marine as a place in which to live is still that of being old.

As the prosperity of Marine increased year by year through the 1860's and the 1870's the turbulence of the outside world seemed to affect it very little. The outbreak of the Civil War prompted a proper proportion of its young men to enlist. Minnesota, at the time, had been a state for only two years, but it was among the first to report officially for duty. Governor Alexander Ramsey went immediately to Washington with an offer to raise regiments of volunteers. But the struggle must have seemed both remote and perverse to a young community which was busy making a new world. The score or so of volunteers included the not-so-young Dr. Gaskill, and the town was without any kind of medical guidance for the duration of the war. Some of these men marched with Sherman to the sea and one was severely wounded. But none was killed and when the fighting was over, all returned to their farming, their storekeeping and, above all, to their familiar friend, the river. Their proper business was that of living the creative life unobtrusively; the gift of their community experience had been a simple, satisfying wholeness.

With a consistency so spontaneous that it seems to be at once dramatic, impressive, and droll, these self-made men came together in their polling places to present a solid Republican front, even before the Civil War. It was inconceivable to all but a few of them that a ballot *could* be cast for a Democratic candidate. . . . A wise, humorous, totally unimposed-upon woman of present day Marine remembers well the political temper of the old times. Still clear in her mind is the recollection of a certain crisis that occurred in her childhood some seventy years ago. A rumor raced across the playground at school that the father of Sara So-and-so was a Democrat. The little girl was not abused for being the victim of so appalling a taint; she was not ostracized or even treated with semihostility. The other children "just felt sorry for her."

These convictions did not keep Marine from listening to the other side. They must, indeed, have heard it expounded with pyrotechnical brilliance, for the great Populist, Ignatius Donnelly, often visited to speak at political rallies. From Marine's standpoint, being a Democrat was the oddest of Donnelly's whims, but it was by no means the only one. His corpulent person was stuffed with intellectual passions, liberal convictions, heretical judgments, original ideas, and fantastic speculations. At various times Donnelly presented himself to the public as lieutenant-governor of Minnesota, legislator in St. Paul and in Washington, founder of the Populist movement and author of its platform. He was also a poet and author of strange, brilliant, prophetic novels, several of which achieved wide popularity in America, England, and France. In addition to all else he claimed attention as discoverer—so he believed!—of what he called *The Great Cryptogram,* a decoding system that proved—chiefly to his own satisfaction—that Bacon had acknowledged authorship of all the plays of Shakespeare. When this comet, Donnelly, shot across Marine's sky in the course of a political campaign the citizens would watch with neither superstitious awe nor unbecoming levity. They simply withheld judgment and then voted as they had intended to vote in the first place.

It should not be made to seem that Marine, even in its moment of happiest adjustment to the conditions of an expanding society, was an entity to be labeled Friendship Village, or Eden of the Frontier. There was a dark side to

*One of two local inns, the Marine House was renowned for its suppers and cotillions. Its sumptuous fare and colorful society were wonders along the bleak frontier of the time.*

its existence. The inevitable matching of negatives with positives, of destructive with creative forces, was not magically set aside as a principle of nature in Marine's favor. Two words—fire and madness—identify the themes of violence that give lurid moments to the town's history. Each of these sprang out of the conditions of life to which the town was committed.

The fires were inevitable. A mill town built of wood was threatened by every kind of danger, from the forces of nature to the faults of inadequate machinery. The sawmill burned to the ground in 1863 with a staggering loss of all equipment. Three years were required to replace it and during the interval the town's prosperity waned. There were many unemployed and Orange Walker, while he worked to reorganize his company, had a preoccupying second job as overseer of the poor.

The Marine schoolhouse was completely destroyed by fire in 1856, fortunately at an hour when classes were not in session. Rebuilt the following year, the successor managed to survive for a decade. Then, in 1866, another night fire consumed it in a cruel blaze, the light of which could be seen as far away as Stillwater. Mathias Welchons' hotel, which had seen so much gaiety, went up in flames in 1882 during an off-season when the few guests could escape unharmed.

A particularly vindictive set of furies seemed to attack the ventures of William Veazie. He had arrived in the valley in 1855 to work as a logger. Later he settled in Marine and became a junior partner in the lumber company which, in 1868, took the name Walker, Judd, and Veazie. Three different houses were destroyed about Mr. Veazie's head in the course of a decade—the first in 1876, the second in 1882, and the third—valued at the comparatively fabulous price of $9,000—in 1885.

Dr. Gaskill lost his store and most of his stock to fire in 1863. It was then that he decided to enlist for service as a surgeon, reporting to an Illinois regiment. In 1866 he was back attending the sick, "in his skilful manner," as the Polk County *Press* reported.

Samuel Judd's splendid house which, according to an awe-struck chronicler of the time, was equipped with "all modern luxuries and conveniences," including central heating, gas lighting and a bathroom burned to the ground in 1884.

Two breweries were lost, both in 1886. When the second of these became a total loss, as the result of a fire that broke out in a dry kiln in the basement, the citizens were at last roused to action. They had managed to be philosophical about the loss of their homes, but the threatened loss of their beer was another matter. They called a special meeting of the village council to look into the cost of buying a fire engine and a hundred feet of hose.

In all the years of Marine's greatest prosperity water from the seventeen springs, from the brook, from the river itself had not been made available to avert these catastrophes. The fire theme surged up again and again drowning out all the other sounds in the symphony of daily life: the throbbing rhythm of the mills, the cheerful blasts of whistles and clamor of bells from the side-wheelers on the river, the roaring laughter of the lumberjacks in the saloons, the hum of domesticity. It serves to emphasize the most grievous fault of the pioneer spirit—this dramatic evidence of how little the rugged philosophy of getting-on was concerned with the needs of others. It left danger always at the elbow of comfort and meagerness in the midst of abundance. Even in considering his individual advantage the pioneer seems to have had more fortitude than foresight. He was better able to endure losses than to prevent them.

Inadequacies of foresight and sympathy induced more personal disasters. There was crime in Marine and little of it due to furtive impulses, housebreaking, or pilfering of tills. It was of the passional variety, flaming up out of emotional tinderboxes. A man who got very drunk, instead of telling the sad story of his life to the bartender, armed himself with a rock and attacked the bartender's skull, or lunged with jaw a-gape for his ear. Where legend tells such tales, facts add up to actual histories. A habitual alcoholic shot his wife dead in the "lady's parlor" of her father's hotel and was carried away to an asylum where he hanged himself with his bedsheets. In such a circumstance the townspeople always assured each other that they had always known the poor creature was insane. But it was no part of the responsibility of the pioneer community to do anything about insanity.

Obviously insane also—so the neighbors said when it was too late to do anything about it—were the two women who set fire to other people's houses. The themes of fire and madness were combined more than once in Marine's history and, in one instance, the circumstances so seriously compromised the reputations of the "best people" that it seemed wise to forget about any possible arrest.

Isolation and unconcern on the part of the community aggravated the madness of other citizens and produced even more appalling results. Eugene O'Neill's discovery that the blood of New Englanders ran to the darker impulses finds dismal, though inconclusive, support in rumors that the "old stock Americans" who moved from New England were unprotected from tormenting desires under the Minnesota elms. Stories which no one wanted very much to investigate at the time and which cannot now be verified insist nonetheless that unlawful loves between close relatives took place behind the most circumspect-looking façades of village houses. And there was never

any explanation of the item printed in a Stillwater paper which told of the discovery of "bottled babies" in a dark corner of a Marine mill. They had come, said the discreet and indiscreet editor, from the office of an unamed local doctor.

These misfortunes in the town's history suggest both the timeless and the particular characteristic. The drama of human existence repeats all of its themes in any community that comes together anywhere, and Marine was no exception. Yet the pioneer community, preoccupied as it was with the building of a great new plant for industry, showed a reckless unconcern with the problem of building —or preserving—men. Orange Walker's efforts at philanthropy did not offset the community's apathy.

The peak of Marine's "tip-top" times was reached in the decade of the 1870's. During that period the sawmill was strenuously busy. In 1872 the company felt the need of expansion so acutely that the old mill was torn down and a much more impressive one constructed. It was equipped with the best machinery available and the combination of water and steam gave the operation a rating of 108 horse power. To the old saws were added an edger and trimmer. Other new facilities—a planer and siding machinery— gave the plant a new look. The capacity of the mill reached 75,000 feet a day. In usual circumstances the Walker, Judd and Veazie interests cut 9,000,000 feet of logs in the pineries each season, but in the winter of 1880–81 the cutting was nearly doubled. Always keeping step with the times the company established telephonic communication with Stillwater at the earliest possible date, 1879.

The future seemed more promising than ever, but actually the forces of change had begun to work to Marine's disadvantage. A severe business depression in 1884 embarrassed the Walker, Judd and Veazie firm critically. Nature gave the *coup de grace* to its already crippled condition. A tornado swept through the St. Croix valley injuring, in the course of its malign spree, nearly every building in Marine. The devil was doing a full job. The mill's stacked lumber was caught up and scattered; its smoke stack, mill dam and sluice were completely destroyed. The company never recovered, and in 1885 was forced into bankruptcy. Goods in the company yard—the steamship, wagons, horses, implements—everything that could be adapted to some other immediate use—was sold at auction to satisfy creditors.

Efforts were made, of course, to preserve the industry. New owners of the mill made a vigorous attempt to piece the enterprise together; they did succeed for a time in relieving the local distress, but the truth was that the center of logging activity already had moved out of the St. Croix valley. New treaties with the Indians had opened up the richer stands of timber in the northern part of Minnesota. The industry had marched on, taking with it capital, imaginative energy, and history itself. There was a long

*By 1890, the warring Indian tribes of the area had either moved westward or been reduced to such tame demonstrations as this Kick-apoo Medicine Show in Marine.*

journey still ahead for the lumber business—from northern Minnesota west to the Pacific and south deep into Florida. But the boom had left Marine finally and irrevocably. Indeed, the chapter was closing for the whole valley. The roistering lumberjacks were gone; teams no longer clattered up the lumber highway; the crowds of visitors who had filled the saloons dwindled to nothing. In 1895 the melancholy final scene was enacted with, perhaps, only a few curious small boys going out of their way to watch. The sawmill was dismantled, its machinery sold to mills in St. Paul and Minneapolis, the buildings themselves torn down.

Spring was not actually silent in the St. Croix valley. There was a trace of activity among loggers for many years after 1895; the last products of its pineries were floated down the river in the teens of this century. But the city mills were well able to care for the needs of the region and were, in fact, determined to have the business. Similarly, competition exercised ever-increasing pressure on small-flour-mill operators. The flour mill at Marine had to give up the struggle, and there were no longer any mills at all to justify the town's name. Time contrived solutions for the private problems of owners. George Judd died in 1872, well before the debacle of Walker, Judd and Veazie. William Veazie, after the loss, during 1885, of both home and business, followed the march of the industry all the way to Tacoma. Orange Walker died in his house at Marine in 1887. John Gabrielson Rose, when his flour mill had to be closed, simply concentrated on the other activities of his busy routine, continuing to farm and to manage his general store until the day of his death.

In the last years before the turn of the century Marine, following its population explosion, shrank once more to approximately 150 inhabitants. Its way of life was now that of a marketing center for the farmers who lived in the immediate neighborhood. Descendants of the Scandinavian settlers had taken over as the dominant figures and their number constituted a conspicuous majority. Names of the "old stock Americans"—Walker, Judd, and Parker —were to be found only on the tombstones in the cemetery.

Life became ultimately simple. Prices for foodstuffs dropped in acknowledgment of the changes that had taken place in what was now a far from affluent society. A barrel of flour cost $3 instead of the $15 charged in the old days. The range in price for a dozen eggs was between fifteen and twenty cents. One of the pastors of the town bought beef (amount unspecified) for twenty-two cents, a head of cabbage for five and had, apparently, the basis of a substantial meal. A comparatively luxurious dinner could be provided with "steak and bone" which cost sixty cents. Coffee— essential to the well-being of citizens of Scandinavian extraction, who always had a pot ready to be warmed at the back of the stove—sold for twenty-eight cents a pound. It is pleasant to think of the probably deft and certainly frugal woman who provided herself with these materials for a costume: "musslin" bought for a dollar, lace for forty-eight cents, and thread for ten cents. The records indicate that the pastor, whose appetite was hearty and his account long, sometimes worked out a part of his debt by contributing labor. At one point a credit of $1.32 for service is entered in his favor.

The years of the century moved forward into the teens, reflecting other significant changes in the social climate. If saloons did not completely disappear, their number must have dwindled. Purchases of cider indicate what the taste of the community had become. Two-fisted drinkers no doubt made their way to Stillwater on Saturday nights. But for their sessions of gossip, their matching of stories about the old logging days and other racy exchanges, the men of the community seem to have gathered in—of all places— a candy store. The two pretty, discreet, and superbly self-disciplined little Holmstrom girls, who were often left in charge of this establishment had to become psychologically deaf to the startling expletives that exploded through the talk of their customers.

There were surprising moments to punctuate the generally uneventful record, but these were of a kind in which the town could share without experiencing any subservient fluttering of the heart. It was during the late teens of the new century that Sinclair Lewis first became a temporary resident. He took a house and lived there during a part of the time when he was writing *Main Street*. No one believes that any of the townsmen were used as models for any of the characters in the novel. Presumably there were more appropriate inspirations to be taken, for landscape and for figures, from Sinclair Lewis's native place, Sauk Center, Minnesota. The neighbors were friendly to the visitor while he lived among them in Marine; one, at least, became a daily companion. But even if they had known that the intellectuals of their homeland, sitting in a session of the Swedish Academy, would one day award "Red" the Nobel prize for literature, they would probably have felt less excitement than was engendered by the creation of their own annual Fourth of July parade. Staunch local pride was not to be lightly stirred by the appearance of a celebrity in its barbershop.

A major change began to take place in the life of Marine. This amounted to a new migration, a resettling on sites along the river. The impulse came from the people of the nearby cities who wanted two things in one: proximity to their daily work and weekend seclusion in the midst of serene natural beauty. These latter-day weekend settlers were business and professional people sympathetic to the idea of recapturing something of the adventurous tradition of their forebears who had helped to build St. Paul and Minneapolis. They were bankers, railroad executives, doctors, lawyers, men of affairs who felt the need to refresh their lives with weekly returns to the rewarding simplicities of existence.

They did well with the values of re-creation as well as those of recreation. George Ingersoll and Dr. Burnside Foster bought old log cabins and remodeled them to their families' needs. Judge John Sanborn of the Federal bench developed a tract of land lying high above the river; he himself cut down the trees to release views for his cottages. Dr. Edward Daugherty became owner of the oldest house in the village, built in 1846 by Samuel Burkleo and later occupied by Hiram Berkey. (Local legend insists that Hiram stubbornly refused to acknowledge that the property was no longer his and, long after his death, continued to haunt his old home.) Dr. Daugherty transformed the wide boards of an old barn into beautiful paneling for his dining room.

The members of the resettlement movement kept faith as well with their responsibilities to the community. Fred Ingersoll, Alexander Peabody, and Samuel Strickland took up permanent residence in the village and became active participants in its affairs. So did William O'Brien, pioneer lumberman, whose return to the St. Croix valley was that of a native. Mrs. Strickland, a woman of fabulous charm and fastidious worldliness, made virtually a life work of helping her Marine neighbors to market the products of their handicraft.

After the first wave of twentieth-century pioneering, there came another migration. This time the new arrivals were chiefly young people who, though they had no intimacy—by way of tradition—with the scene, still knew it for their own. They rented whatever farmhouses they could acquire. They bought old frame dwellings and moved them close to the river's edge. (Farmers, in the old days, had avoided close proximity to the water believing that dampness caused rheumatism.) They built cottages on any bit of river property with which a villager could be persuaded to part.

The resettlement was accomplished with the kind of spontaneous tact always shown by genuine respecters of nature when they retreat into a wilderness. Indeed they drew what was left of the wilderness around them and obscured themselves in it, hiding their houses in the deep woods. They kept decent distances between neighbors. They preserved the tone, the temper, and the tempo of a spacious, uncluttered existence. Today it is only on weekends that boats, equipped with airplane motors, roar along the waters. For the rest of the time birdsong is well able

JOHN W. G. DUNN

*Once a log-way, the river that made Marine an active mill town is today a serene attraction, lending its atmosphere and drawing summer visitors.*

to dominate the sound of river life. Du Lhut would still be able to recognize his "very fine river."

Old Marine has accepted the new Marinites with aplomb. At first it seemed downright strange that there should be all that passion for marshy bits of property where nothing much grew except cardinal flowers. The land couldn't be tilled and had never even been available for pasturing cattle. But the townspeople were realistically pleased when real-estate values rose and taxes could be made to mount correspondingly. And after all it was no new thing to see great influxes of visitors for the summer. Kentucky colonels and their ladies had come often to Mr. Lightner's Marine House. It was pleasant to have the general store (the same old one) once more crowded on Saturday with summer residents and visitors.

Marine today has a voting population of some 350. Among its citizens are young men and their wives who, having come first as vacation visitors, have decided to make the town their permanent home. The men commute to jobs, thirty-five miles away in St. Paul, or forty-five to Minneapolis. The link of Marine to the strenuous world of the present becomes tighter and tighter as the cities grow and push the limits of suburbia farther into the environs.

And yet the town retains the flavor of its individuality. Parts of the past are preserved in the museum, housed in the old stone jail on the top of the hill. There a lover of old things will find spinning wheels, oxen yokes, family portraits, charming old primers, pieces of china from which the Walkers and the Judds and the Parkers, as well as the Roses and the Holmstroms, ate their meals. Nonetheless the attitude toward people who are less fortunate in their store of memories is indulgent and gracious. The newcomers are welcome to enjoy the valley, the river, and the town. They are not required, despite the oddities of their costumes, despite their too verbal, rather naïve enthusiasm for everything old, to think of themselves as different. Marine receives them and accepts them.

There is, by way of illustration, the story of a summer resident from St. Paul who once received an endorsement as significant of good will as it was casual in the offering. She might be described appropriately as a grande dame; at least, far advanced into her fifties, she had acquired the dignity to support her years. Her devotion to children and her success with them on the tennis court and in water games had encouraged the widespread use of a nickname. Once as she stood watching the annual Fourth of July parade in the village, she felt a blow on her back, so unguardedly emphatic that it almost toppled her forward on her face. At the same moment she heard the cry, "Hi, Georgie!" Recovering her equilibrium, she turned to face a man, some twenty years her junior, whom she did not recognize but knew must be the father of children from a nearby farm, guests at one or another of her many picnics. She had the presence of mind to respond, "Hi, neighbor!" Linking her arm in his she drew him into the rhythm of the band and together they marched to the end of the street.

Of like triviality—and significance—is the anecdote of a delightful boy from Marine who knew exactly how to reassure his elders in a moment of trial. A man and wife in their sixties were planning to end their vacation on the river earlier than usual and they worried for fear of what neglect would do to their lawn when they had closed their cottage. They appealed to a young man who had worked for them from time to time during the summer. "Forget it," the boy said sunnily. "I'll take care of you kids!"

So, there is Marine, a fragment of society which encloses and preserves the old values of human experience. It had a good life in the mid years of the 1800's. It has one still.

ADLAI T. MAST, JR.

*The 1890 market town with farm wagons and orderly stores had sprung from
a tumultuous past, out of Spanish conquest and an American drive for land.*

# A Gateway of a Gaining Nation

## *Nacogdoches, Texas*

### BY JOHN EDWARD WEEMS

Ahead tower hundreds of cool black pine trees, quiet sil-
houettes reaching for the infinite silence of a violet
evening sky. Only the straight, deep scar left by the men
who hacked out the highway serves as a reminder that a
modern era has usurped the claims of the past. Glimpses
through the rear-view mirror as one approaches Nacogdoches, Texas, show more of the patient monsters, eerie
watchers that join arms and block a visual retreat.

Texas has many faces, and a nonresident isn't likely to
recognize this one. Those who have become acquainted
with the state only through the cursory glances of motion
pictures and television probably envision a land that is
clear and ranging. But that would be West Texas, where
stubby, spiny mesquites grow—and not many other trees.
Now the pines thin out, foretelling a settlement ahead,
baring the red soil, which many outsiders and some East
Texans consider ugly and poor. The road curves leisurely
across Banita Creek, down to the uneven floor of a little
valley and, abruptly, into a small town with a bland appearance that belies its momentous role in Texas history.

Except for the natural beauty of Nacogdoches—the
neat lawns summer-luxuriant from the usually abundant
rainfall, moonlit in an enfolding night—the community
seems as commonplace, as drowsy and resigned as many
a bypassed Southern town. In the entire four-block
"downtown" area along Main Street perhaps a dozen

window-shoppers stroll—slowly, to make it last. Most of the buildings are turn-of-the-century brick, uninteresting and fraudulent with new fronts. From inside the neon-red façade of the only business still open, a drugstore, recorded music shrieks, but not for the benefit of dancers. Inside, seated around small, shaky tables and in booths, students from the state college nobly attempt merrymaking over Cokes—and they succeed, as only students could.

A few cars crawl down the brick-paved street, their rubbery pit-a-pats futilely striving to add gaiety to the night. But the cars pass on, and the window-shoppers vanish. Drooping Main Street collapses, an ordinary lane in an early-sleeping, early-rising, sin-hating Texas town.

Look again, eastward up Main Street. To the left, on the corner of Main and Fredonia—where Smith's pharmacy now does business—once stood the Old Stone Fort, a thick-walled building erected in 1779 as a Spanish trading post and later used as a military installation in the many campaigns that blazed across this country. Across the street to the right, where, in the center of darkened Post Office Square, a boxlike brick building awaits the morning bustle, lay the old Plaza Principal, with a well that served inhabitants for perhaps two centuries.

And look again at Main Street itself, dismal and empty even at such an early-evening hour. This is the Old San Antonio Road—now State Highway 21, but in the misty days of more than two centuries ago El Camino Real, or The King's Highway, one of several roads with such designations that were blazed in the Spanish New World.

Look eastward the length of that drab street, as people do every day. Only in the distance does it assume any character, undulating over La Nana Creek, up a hill, and out of sight. The brick paving of Main Street, the dull store fronts, and jukebox music have replaced the colorfulness of two centuries, have in fact erased all evidence of the previous eras. Along that thoroughfare once traveled naked Indian runners and dazzling ceremonial processions, robed Spanish missionaries and merciless royal soldiers, rapacious freebooters of many nationalities and dauntless Anglo-American colonists.

This El Camino Real was laid out in 1691 by Domingo Terán de los Rios, the first provincial governor of Texas, to link his capital at Monclova—in Coahuila, Mexico—with missions established among the Indians of this area. Apparently the road followed an old Indian trail, possibly the same one that La Salle had traveled a few years earlier, during the period 1685–87, and had found "as well beaten a road as that from Paris to Orléans."

This Indian trail came into being during those nebulous days before the arrival of the first Europeans, when tribal history could be recorded only orally, passed down from father to son. One interesting but romanticized legend says that countless centuries ago there lived on the banks of the Sabine, the river of the cypress trees, a Caddo chief who fathered two sons. One of them grew up to be a swarthy, black-haired man whose dark eyes could sear one's soul. The other was light-complexioned, yellow-haired, blue-eyed.

As the old chief approached the end of his life he told the two sons that after his death the dark one should take his wife and children, travel in the direction of the rising sun, and make his home wherever he might find himself at the end of three days. He told the other son to travel in the opposite direction and to make his home in a similar manner.

So it was that the tribes of the Nacogdoche and Natchitoch Indians were founded, roughly one hundred miles apart, and the fair-complexioned son became the father of the friendly Tejas Indians of East Texas. Distance sufficient to prevent friction separated the two tribes; in fact, they came to engage in friendly trading, and for this reason they tramped out through their domain a broad highway extending from Natchez through Nacogdoches to the Trinity River. The road was in time to become part of El Camino Real.

More authoritative are certain documentable statements. Both the Natchitoch and Nacogdoche Indians were members of the Caddo confederacies, made up of agrarian tribes that long ago achieved an exceptionally high level of cultural development in the area that is now, generally, East Texas. The light-complexioned, friendly Indians known as the Tejas, from which word evolved "Texas," were actually Indians of the Hasinai confederation of Caddoes. The Nacogdoche, who were in the Hasinai group, called each other "taychas," meaning "friends"—a name with which they also greeted adventuring Spaniards, beginning with those who were led into the region by Hernando de Soto in 1541–42.

It was unfortunate for the prospering and friendly Hasinai that they happened to occupy strategic territory. The area around what is now Nacogdoches, Texas—near the Louisiana line—became a bone of contention between Spain, which claimed Texas, and France, which held Louisiana; later between Spain and the United States; and, still later, between Mexico and the United States. Naturally friendly toward the nearby French, the Indians were thus doubly courted yet distrusted by the Spaniards, who began building missions in East Texas for the dual purpose of baptizing the reluctant natives into Catholicism, an endeavor which failed, and of fending off unwanted foreign traders, like the presumptuous Frenchman Louis Juchereau de Saint Denis. One of the missions founded, in June of 1716, was Nuestra Señora de Guadalupe de los Nacogdoches. Its walls long ago crumbled into eternity, but its general site is known from old Spanish documents in the Nacogdoches Archives: near the present North Street, one of the oldest streets in Texas, overlooking the same stream that the highway now crosses.

From the date of this founding Nacogdoches can trace its history with greater accuracy. The mission was deserted occasionally—but it was never permanently abandoned. The Spanish withdrawal from Nacogdoches after their acquisition of Louisiana, oddly enough, resulted in the permanent settlement of the town. France ceded Louisiana to Spain, rather than see it fall into English hands along with Canada and the American Midwest at the close of the French and Indian War. With no border to watch and with some official sentiment anyway for centralizing Spanish forces in the Southwest, the missions in and near Nacogdoches were abandoned; the Spaniards there were ordered to retire to the vicinity of San Antonio, which had become the capital of Texas.

Among the Nacogdoches inhabitants thus ordered out was a man named Gil Antonio Ybarbo, a ranchman and trader whose financial stake in the new country was deep-driven. With the urgency that money can inspire, Ybarbo's first activity at San Antonio was aimed at getting permission for himself and the other evacuees to return. Governor Juan María Vincencio de Ripperdá, wary of the Anglo-American threat from across the Mississippi River, favored frontier outposts, and in 1774 he helped Ybarbo and the others to return at least some distance eastward—to an officially approved location on the Trinity River, where they lived for five years. Without specific approval for another move Ybarbo herded his small colony back to Nacogdoches, in April of 1779, to "the site of the Tejas Indians," as he wrote in a letter, "and three leagues beyond, the old mission of Nacogdoches, where there was a small chapel, where the reverend father may perform the holy sacraments and a house where he may live, as well as plenty of water, lands, and materials for houses." From this date may be traced the continuous existence of Nacogdoches, and Ybarbo is considered the founder of the town.

Probably that same year, 1779, he built the Old Stone Fort, with walls a yard thick. The building was originally intended as a commissary for storing merchandise, not as a military installation at all. But Ybarbo's penchant for shrewd trading led to his downfall. Appointed lieutenant governor, civil and military captain of militia, and judge of contraband, Ybarbo's power in this isolated district apparently ran away with his self-control. In 1791 he was accused of smuggling contraband goods into Nacogdoches and of trading, with the Indians, for horses stolen from his fellow Spaniards. Although Ybarbo was cleared of these charges, superiors doubted his integrity after that to such a degree that he was banished from the town for a number of years.

The stone house he had built indeed became a fort; through its thick front door walked most of the important persons of the day—and many of the leaders of various gun-backed causes that swept through the pine woods: the Gutiérrez-Magee Expedition, an unsuccessful venture launched in 1812 to support the Mexican revolt; the James Long Expedition, financed by Natchez residents angry about the 1819 Adams-Oñis Treaty, in which the United States renounced its Louisiana Purchase claim to Texas; and the Fredonian Rebellion, a brief flare-up resulting from an 1826 controversy between Mexican authorities and an Anglo-American *empresario*. The flags of those three lost causes waved over Nacogdoches, as did the colors of France, Spain, Mexico, the Republic of Texas, the Confederacy, and the United States.

Near the Stone Fort, in 1832, raged the Battle of Nacogdoches, a short, bantamlike fight that was to have giant reverberations. A band of Anglo-American colonists, supporting a liberal Mexican faction, defeated a centralist faction quartered in the town and forced it out, leaving a large area free of Mexican troops. Their absence helped to make possible the organization of the Texas Revolution three years later. Contributing to the instability which left Nacogdoches vulnerable to these waves of violence was its isolated position: in the horseback era authority was days, even weeks, away. Its absence gave birth to a spirit of independence that is noticeable in the town even today.

But Nacogdoches was scarcely isolated in another respect. Located on El Camino Real—and near a paralleling Smugglers' Road, a well-used thoroughfare which avoided clearings—it became a gateway for land-hungry immigrants from the United States. At first the Spanish authorities—and later the Mexicans—tried to dam the flow of these Anglo-Americans, but without much success. Many of the newcomers were undesirable. One present-day Nacogdoches resident tells a story of an ancestor's arrival many years ago. Although his kinsman wasn't known as an undesirable, some of those who made the trip with him must have been.

"Crossing the Sabine on a flat boat," the man relates, "there were a number of men, who, as soon as they landed on the Texas side, stood in a group and, waving their hats over their heads, shouted, 'Hurrah! Our debts are paid—our debts are paid!' Wherever [they] stopped for the night, the first question asked . . . was, 'And what did you leave the States for?' "

Good men came, too; among them the *empresario* Stephen F. Austin, who brought a colony of Anglo-Americans into Texas with Spanish approval. Fifteen years before Texas won its war of independence, Austin visited Nacogdoches. At that time the town was in one of the economic slumps that have periodically gloomed its history. Austin wrote: "Nacogdoches is now the ruins of a once flourishing little village, the church and Seven Houses are still standing entire, one of them two story high built of soft Rock—it was the seat of the Indian trade and a great deal of business was formerly done here. The situation is a valley. A creek runs on each side of the town."

*A way west having become a way to town, an ox team hauled cotton bales in 1892.*
*The east Texas town was in a slump and many immigrants had already moved on.*

Other Anglo-Americans followed Austin, many of them wending through the pines along the red gash that was El Camino Real. When they reached Nacogdoches, they invariably remarked on the big stone house, as Austin had done.

One of the most intriguing of the adventurers who followed Austin had been held prisoner in that same stone house twenty-two years earlier. He was Peter Ellis Bean, who had first come to Texas in 1800 as a member of Philip Nolan's filibustering expedition. His life story seems almost to personify the turbulent history of Nacogdoches, and it deserves a brief telling here.

Even before 1800, Nolan, who is said to have been the first Anglo-American to visit Texas extensively, had led men into the area. His purpose had been to round up the wild horses that roamed the land and to drive them to New Orleans or Natchez, where they were sold. On Nolan's last expedition, the Spaniards, knowing that he had recently conferred with Thomas Jefferson, then Vice President, speculated that Nolan intended to map the country for conquest. Considering Jefferson's expansionist sentiments,

they were probably right. Some of Nolan's men recalled years afterward that he seemed to have been keeping an exceptionally detailed record of the journey.

On all but this last trip Nolan had moved with Spanish permission. With him were Ellis Bean, an excited Tennessee lad of seventeen, and twenty-six other men, all lured by talk of gold and other riches to be found in the Spanish domain. After crossing the Mississippi River they struck out westward, but on the second or third day they were surprised to encounter a Spanish cavalry force. The Spaniards "told us they were in pursuit of some Choctaw Indians that had stolen some horses," Bean later wrote. "This was false, for they were hunting for our party, although they were afraid to own it."

Horsemen continued to shadow Nolan, on orders from worried Spanish authorities, and on a March morning in 1801—when Nolan had made camp at a site not far north of the present location of Waco, Texas, and had begun corralling wild horses—they finally attacked.

The fight that followed is said to have been the first in the Anglo-American conquest of the West. But Nolan was killed—his ears were cut off as a trophy for the governor—

and the survivors, including Bean, were captured and escorted away. On April 3, 1801, they reached Nacogdoches and were led into the Old Stone Fort, where they were held.

"The Commandant told us he was waiting for orders from Chihuahua to set us at liberty and send us home," Bean wrote. "We waited in this hope."

Instead, Bean and his companions were taken into Mexico, where he began a fantastic prison experience that has become legend. For the next decade he was in a variety of jails, and in one of them, the star-shaped Castle of San Diego at Acapulco, he occupied himself and perhaps kept his sanity by cultivating the friendship of a white lizard. Bean's account is well known to most Texas schoolchildren:

One day, as I was lying on my mat, I saw [him], for the first time, on the wall. Watching him, I saw that he was trying to catch the flies that had come into the prison when the door was opened, to get out of the sun. I did not know whether he was poisonous or not, but I determined to feed him. So I caught some flies, and put them on the end of a straw I had pulled out of my mat; these I slipped up the wall to him, and found he would take them off the straw. This was my amusement for some days, when he became so gentle, that he would take the flies off my hand. Every morning, as he came down the wall, he would sing like a frog, by which means I had notice that he was coming. In about a week he was so gentle, that he did not leave me at night, but stayed with me all the time. Every day, when they would open the door to come and examine my irons, he would get frightened, and hide himself under my blanket. When the door was again shut, he would come out and stay with me. I found that he was sincerely my friend; in fact, he was my only companion and amusement.

But at times Bean enjoyed other companionships. He was a remarkable young man who could charm even his captors, and he was sometimes given the liberty of whatever village he happened to be in. During these periods he spent many intriguing hours with dark-eyed señoritas whom he also charmed effortlessly.

Nevertheless, Bean was rather a forgotten man. Many years later the writer Edward Everett Hale was to name the central character in his *The Man Without a Country* "Philip Nolan"—coincidentally, Hale said afterward—but in this situation Nolan's follower Ellis Bean actually was the man without a country.

"Our cases in this time had gone to Spain," Bean wrote, "and had also been sent to the United States, and laid before Mr. Jefferson, at that time president—who said he knew nothing of us. . . .

"What can a poor prisoner expect, when the leading men of his country fail to see justice done him? If I had been brought to my own country, I could have been happy under the severest punishment. . . . As Mr. Jefferson did not know us, and had no expectation of being benefited by us, it was less trouble to say, 'Hang them!' "

After several years Bean had almost forgotten his native language, through disuse.

Mexico's war for independence gave him his chance for freedom. Released from his cell at Acapulco to fight for Spain, he immediately deserted to the rebel forces under Morelos. Loyal service there won him favor and promotions, and when he finally returned to the United States, fifteen years after his departure, he came as an envoy of the embattled Mexican patriots, seeking aid for them.

But he was doomed to live out the rest of his years as a man without a country, torn between two loyalties, and thus firm in neither. Once in the United States he began yearning for Mexico; he returned and married a tender, dark-eyed woman. Then he left, alone, for the United States, where he again adapted quickly and married a Tennessee girl named Candace. In 1823 he took her to Nacogdoches and began still another life, not far from the Old Stone Fort, where he had once been held prisoner.

Predictably, the attraction didn't last; and Bean divided his time between Mexico and Texas. Before the Texas Revolution erupted he became a Mexican official stationed in Nacogdoches, a town that was to lead all Texas in financing the Revolution. Bean was trusted by neither the Anglo-American colonists nor his Mexican superiors, although he remained on friendly terms with both. His sole contribution during that turbulent period seems to have been helping to ward off Indian attacks.

At one time he was again jailed in the Old Stone Fort, detained there by the Anglo-Americans because he was a Mexican officer. After his release he returned to a citizen's life at Nacogdoches, but he died in Mexico in 1846 in the company of his Mexican wife.

During the years preceding the Civil War Nacogdoches enjoyed in Texas an importance it has never regained, although even then it was beginning to lose influence in political and social matters, and was losing population. Newcomers realized it was easier to move to prairie land farther west than to try to clear the forested areas of East Texas.

Frost Thorn, Texas' first millionaire, lived in Nacogdoches, as did Thomas Rusk and, at times, Sam Houston—Texas' first United States Senators. The first nonsectarian institution of higher learning in Texas, Nacogdoches University, was built by local people, who donated both money and labor. It was chartered in 1845, with the provisions that "no religious, sectarian tenets or doctrines shall be inculcated in the course of instruction, and that the institution shall be equally open to the education of the children of persons of all classes, without regard to

*This frontier kitchen, restored to its mid-nineteenth-century appearance, belonged to the Sterne family, in the tradition of Southwest affluence, and was a separate building.*

their religious belief." This was a paradoxical development for a town with a history of staunch denominationalism: Catholicism, by law, during the days of Spanish and Mexican rule, and after that, hard-shell brands of Protestantism, particularly Southern Baptist in the twentieth century.

During the years before the Civil War, Nacogdoches was a true Southern town, depending largely on money from cotton and other crops worked by slave labor. Local economy was coupled with slavery: A "prime field Negro" male was worth fifteen hundred dollars; the value of a woman was two or three hundred dollars less. A slave of either sex could be hired out at two or three hundred dollars a year, and many small East Texas farmers were forced to depend on such rentals for their seasonal labor. But there were also several large plantations. Not far from Nacogdoches was Julian Sidney Devereux's "Monti Verdi," an area show place of ten thousand acres worked by eighty slaves. Devereux's noble mansion, still used as a home, is as attractive today as it was then.

In those ante-bellum days Nacogdoches life was gay and gracious among the wealthy, and relatively comfortable for almost everyone. Society, though not extensive, was conspicuous. Grand balls planned by committees of leading citizens became gala social events attended by many people who came from miles around, stayed overnight, and returned home the next day. Nacogdoches and

a nearby town, San Augustine, exchanged hospitalities through the medium of these balls, and a Negro fiddler of Nacogdoches, known as Old Wiley, gained local fame by playing for them.

But Nacogdoches never was known for culture in the strictest sense of the word. Its people were isolated and much too busy hacking out a living amid the pines to be able to devote time to the arts. A leading citizen, Adolphus Sterne, complained of this in his diary entry for December 15, 1838.

"Commenced raining about 10 A.M. and continued all day," he wrote. "Streets muddy and unpleasant. No place to go to spend the time rationally—not a room where one could read or write and no company congenial to my habits."

The Civil War ushered in six dark decades. Before the war a good many persons identified with Nacogdoches had opposed the idea of secession. Sam Houston was one such man, and he never did agree to help with the breakup of the Union. When the inevitability of war became apparent, however, Nacogdoches supported the Southern cause fervently and witnessed the same events that were occurring across the country: recruitment, presentation of banners, sobbing farewells, knitting clothing for soldiers far away, weeping as heartbreaking dispatches arrived. At first food was plentiful: corn, pork, beef, mutton. Serving as a coffee substitute, however inadequate, were parched corn, chicory, and various berries. As the war ground to its inexorable climax, however, food became scarce. Nacogdoches starved with the rest of the South.

During Reconstruction, East Texas suffered more than the rest of the state, although it had been spared the ravages of actual fighting. The war left it inert; trade dwindled away to a trickle; railroads bypassed East Texas forests, which were difficult to slice through; immigration flocked to other localities; the pine forests, far removed from lumber markets, were considered useless commercially; and the financial possibilities of oil went unrecognized. While to the west, Texas was beginning to recover from the postwar paralysis with big cattle drives and other ventures, Nacogdoches and most of East Texas languished.

Moreover, violence roared across the land. Its large Negro population was now free and largely idle. To "keep them in line" the Ku Klux Klan rode on nightly missions, and many a Negro who was considered troublesome by the white citizenry was frightened to see eight or ten ghostly figures appear suddenly at his home from out of the darkness. They would surround him, drag him outside and flog him—in eerie, glimmering torchlight—until he promised to "reform."

Another minority was there: descendants of the early Spaniards. Unlike the Negroes, they were allowed to live in peace, but they were low-rated by their Anglo-American neighbors and never were able to hold up their heads as were the old Spanish families of California.

Descendants of Gil Antonio Ybarbo and other early Spaniards have resided in the area continually and are there today. They aren't easily recognized on the streets, however, because they are generally fair and without a noticeable accent.

Still, their background is different enough to have caused a few, in the past, to change their names. And even today the Spanish-Americans tend to keep to themselves, mainly because of religion. They have adhered to Catholicism, and most of their neighbors are Protestants.

Half a century after the immediate post-bellum years had passed, Giles Haltom, then editor of the Nacogdoches *Daily Sentinel,* reminisced about them in the fiftieth anniversary edition of his newspaper (December 8, 1928), which he had edited all that time. Nacogdoches was a small town isolated in the depth of the East Texas wilderness—Haltom recalled—without railroads, paved streets, electric lights and telephones, ice plants and water works. From every direction the pine forest encroached, but sawmills were few. A man built his house of logs, and he used split logs—puncheons—for flooring. He finished the walls with rough-hewn boards, which frequently had to be affixed without nails, scarce and expensive. The boards were held in place by split poles, their flat sides facing the boards and secured to the wall of the house by wooden pins. Even door hinges were sometimes made of wood, and when the door was opened it squawked loudly.

*The parlor, restored in the main house of the Sterne family, has ornate furnishings brought by settlers from the East or bought later in New Orleans.*

Although the finer building materials were expensive and hard to find, food was plentiful and close by. A farmer could walk a short distance from his clearing into the pine woods and shoot a deer, or he could call up a turkey and kill it. His wife "fixed" corn pone, cracklin' bread, chicken and dumplin's, lye hominy, corn dumplin's, potlicker, chittlin's, ham, sausage, boiled custard. Coffee was a popular drink. All day long a blackened pot sat close to the fireplace, to be instantly heated when a neighbor appeared or when members of the household ran out of energy. The East Texas climate, warm and humid, was also partly responsible for the habit: some people thought hot coffee could ward off the malaria that thrived there.

If coffee alone didn't work, people added quinine to it in a dose that every child and adult learned to despise. If the doctor had to be called—for malaria or any other reason—he drove up in a horse and buggy, entered the house unhurriedly, first looked at the patient's tongue, then felt the pulse, shook his head, clucked, and invariably called for a teaspoon and a glass of water. Finally, if the person died—and in those days of patent medicines getting him well wasn't easy—his neighbors helped to build a coffin and dig a grave, and they conducted the last rites at virtually no cost.

These were the leisurely days of the wild catbell, of the June bug with a string tied to one leg, of the old fluttermill by the water gap, and of persimmon thickets, stretchberries, maypop vines, and the first ripe plum of spring.

And they were the days of borrowing. People borrowed meal, the crosscut saw, the froe, a chunk of fire, a horse, anything; said, "Much obliged," and it was all right. In one locality only one person owned a crosscut saw, and it made the rounds of the neighborhood, each man taking his turn using it and keeping it sharp. They shared a grindstone the same way.

Camp meetings and logrollings were social gatherings remembered for long afterward. Camp meetings were austere—and especially in line with the after-work pursuits of that unsophisticated age. Under a dry brush arbor, seated on hard planks that warded off drowsiness, the congregation listened to impassioned sermons against drinking, dancing, and gambling. Sometimes the word came morning, afternoon, and night, but the sin never gave out. Sometimes, too, the congregation stayed for as long as a week, camped in tents or other temporary shelters always located near a spring of good cool water sufficient to slake mundane thirsts but hardly adequate to extinguish the flames fanned by Satan.

Logrollings were perhaps less severe, and with Nacogdoches surrounded by hills covered with pine, oak, elm, and hickory, they were popular and inescapable. When a man wanted to clear a field, he invited his neighbors to a logrolling, and few healthy ones had the gall—maybe not even the desire—to refuse, since most of them owned fields waiting to be cleared, too. A score of men could fell the trees quickly, chop off trunks, pile brush in heaps, and reduce trunks to rails for fencing the new field.

Men also helped each other at rail splittings, house raisings, and cotton choppings. For the women there were quilting bees, and an old-time East Texan, G. L. Crocket, now dead, once described one in his book, *Two Centuries in East Texas.*

After the lady of the house had pieced together, from dressmaking scraps, a number of fancy quilts, she invited her neighbors to help finish them. The embryonic quilt was stretched in frames to full size in such a way that it could be rolled up as work proceeded. The frame was suspended by its four corners from the ceiling. Cotton for filling had been deftly carded by hand into light, fluffy batts and laid on the lining. The pieced-up top was laid over all and properly secured; chairs for workers were placed at two- or three-foot intervals on both sides; and scissors, needles, thimbles, and thread were passed around. Work began in earnest, and heaven help the insensitive matron who allowed her tongue to move faster than her fingers as she finished her part under the critical gaze of her sisters.

Beforehand the hostess had prepared a big dinner—it wasn't "lunch." At noon came a break in the work. The quilters invited their menfolk to the meal as necessary adjuncts, more or less, and after dinner the men retired to the gallery, where they smoked and talked crops or politics while their women returned to quilting.

As the afternoon sun arced westward and the work inside progressed without interruption, the host often proposed a hunt. Events thereafter followed quickly; no persuasion was needed. Someone called up the hounds, and an expert "driver," on foot, set out with the pack to the known range of a wily buck.

Hunters stationed themselves at every spot the deer would likely pass in its effort to evade the driver and his dogs; and the master of the hunt, who was presumed to know the animal's likely route, stationed his guest of honor in the most strategic location of all.

Then the driver and the hounds broke into a yelping, hollering chorus and went after the deer. The experienced hunters in the crowd thrilled to the distant baying of the dogs and the mellow shouts of the driver, but this feeling wasn't universal. A few men were known to have become unnerved upon sighting the swift, delicate creature with the head held high, eyes peering this way and that, and they sent their shots crashing harmlessly into the treetops.

From these languid post-bellum days to the twentieth century was an easy transition for Nacogdoches, because the town changed little. Except for the usual improvements every town enjoyed—electric lights, municipal water works, and the like—Nacogdoches remained the sleepy Southern town it had become, depending on cotton and

*These mustached and bearded turn-of-the-century fiddlers, here posing with their instruments, played at local square dances and at rousing "Fiddlin' Contests."*

other crops grown on poor land that had been under cultivation for a century or more.

But there had been some interesting developments. In the mid-1860's, Lynis T. Barrett drilled Texas' first producing oil well in Nacogdoches County, then gave up the venture. Because of the absence of an oil market he couldn't find any backers. About that same time two other men began trying to market oil in the Nacogdoches area. They observed seepage from oil springs, gathered the crude as it collected, and sold it by the keg—for softening leather and greasing wagon axles.

A few local historians credit these men with discovering crude oil in Texas, but Spaniards had known of oil springs as early as 1543, and even before that East Texas Indians had been aware of other seepages. The Indians used crude mostly for medicinal purposes.

Another development, of great local renown, was an experiment with revolving fans—before the advent of electricity. In the early 1880's, W. U. and Sam Perkins, owners of a drugstore, hit upon a novel way of cooling their place of business during the muggy summer months. They built a small, slanted treadmill in an alley behind their store, connected this mechanism with a series of ceiling fans inside, and selected an especially energetic burro for

the power supply. When thermometers climbed to an uncomfortable degree, Perkins Brothers led their ambulatory power plant to the tilted treadmill, tied him there facing uphill, and cranked up the apparatus so that the floor began moving—downhill. This triggered the burro into action; he broke into a trot, revolving the fans above the comfortable, complacent customers inside.

The abused burro had one ally. Across the alley, in a stuffy newspaper office, the editor of the *Star News* quickly became unnerved by the continual clatter. He tried to close his window and to ignore the noise, but in the stifling summer heat this failed. He left the window open.

To everyone who came into his office the editor denied, in the most businesslike manner possible, that the loud contrivance was in any way connected with the *Star News*. Once, however, he lost the last vestige of self-control, leaped to his feet, damned Perkins Brothers generally, and shouted, "I wish Will Perkins was in that treadmill instead of the mule." Then his sanity returned; he quieted himself, and the office became normal again.

Like the burro—and like a good many other Southern towns of that turn-of-the-century period—Nacogdoches was on a treadmill, trying to keep up and getting nowhere. The town still depended largely on an economy governed

*A corner meeting place and a saloon, in 1900, the 1779 stone fort had been the scene of nineteenth-century battles. It was torn down by an unremembering town in 1902.*

by hand-labor farming of cotton, corn, and tomatoes by Negro tenants. In good years the red-sand roads leading into town were crowded on Saturdays with farmers coming in to sell, trade, or buy. But when the unpredictable Texas weather chose to play vicious tricks everyone suffered. Crops were short, money became scarce, and Saturday wasn't a big day at all.

The lumber industry helped to soften these blows, but not much. Lumber workers in those days were in a continual state of near-poverty themselves: They weren't paid much, and what money they did get was often owed in advance to the company store. Better pay wasn't needed to entice the workers to stay; they were already immobile because of their illiteracy and their fear of the unknown. They had been born, reared, and isolated in the East Texas pines. They knew no other life.

That was the picture until Franklin D. Roosevelt's administration gave the local economy two notable boosts: The farm program, directly administered from county seats like Nacogdoches, gave the town more money and greater importance; and the soil conservation programs helped to renew the worn-out land. Fields badly eroded by two centuries of weather and hard use were given new life by fertilizers and given protection by legume covers.

But the hills and the trees made the terrain unsuitable for mechanized farming, which had become necessary for profit-making. Even in cleared fields equipment was likely to smash against any one of the countless stumps. With hand-labor farming disappearing, most of the Negro tenants moved into cities and found jobs in prewar defense industries. Several years ago an insurance estimate showed 1,700 Negro families from Nacogdoches County living in Los Angeles County, California.

Today Nacogdoches is the center of lively cattle and poultry industries, both giving year-round incomes instead of meager seasonal profits. Cotton hasn't been king since before the Second World War, but the annual value of farm products in the county has shot upward from $1,241,556 in 1940 to $13,490,284 in 1959, an increase that certainly isn't all due to inflation.

And this is on poor land. Even the virgin soil isn't very productive; for any time the climate is warm—thus allowing a long growing season—and the rainfall high, the soil is poor. In a long growing season the vegetation uses up more of the soil.

Virtually all farmers and ranchmen around Nacogdoches now fertilize at least once a year—in the spring—and fertilize grasslands as many as three or four times a year.

"Using no fertilizer a stockman around here can produce one hundred pounds of beef to every acre each year," says County Agent George Rice, who knows the land better than anyone else. "By using two hundred pounds of fertilizer per acre—at four dollars a hundred pounds—he can double the beef produced per acre. But when he goes to six or eight hundred pounds it all depends on rainfall. He has to have a wet year to get the full value from it.

"The Nacogdoches area needs more rain anyway. Water soaks through the sandy soil easily—and the trees use up a lot of water too. A big pine tree can evaporate four to five hundred gallons a day through its leaves."

In contrast to the days of the burro-powered drugstore fans, Nacogdoches now has electricity, enabling two men to milk two hundred cows in a day, and one man to take care of as many as 80,000 chickens a day—by raising and lowering feed troughs for him, by transporting eggs to a central location, and by performing other chores.

The poultry business has been lively ever since the first broiler house was built in 1948. Now broilers can be raised for as little as thirteen cents a pound, and they can be ready for selling within nine weeks of hatching. In 1963, the United Arab Republic, seeing chickens as an easy answer to the protein need of its people, ordered 800,000 broilers from one Nacogdoches firm alone.

"Our town has changed a lot in my lifetime," says F. I. Tucker, a native. "Just before I started practicing law here in 1927 we had a Georgia stock-farm economy—a hungry cow-sow-and-hen subsistence thing. But you could give a man a gun and a fishing pole in those days, and he wouldn't starve.

"By the time I began observing closely we had a cotton economy. The town was small—we all knew each other—and everything was done on credit. Bills weren't even mailed out; you just paid up once a year.

"But then cotton went to hell, and the depression came. This county looked as if you were getting ready to give it back to the Indians, if you could have found an Indian to give it to. Fields were full of stumps and weeds. Houses were falling in. We lost substantially in population, but they were mostly submarginal farmers who would have created a labor problem if they had stayed.

"We got rid of the cattle tick [a parasite that had been plaguing East Texas stockmen] when the state passed a law requiring the animals to be dipped. Then came rural electrification and all the rest, and here we are. But until the 1930's Nacogdoches was a community sitting in the shade of its family tree, listening to the hardening of its arteries."

Another major factor in bringing Nacogdoches around was Stephen F. Austin State College, opened in 1923 primarily for training new teachers. The college now has more than three thousand students, a budget of four million dollars, the only forestry school in Texas, and a soil-analyzing service for farmers wanting to know what kind of fertilizer their land needs. But the college possibly exerts its deepest influence on the once-isolated, and still provincial, town by exposing its citizens to bits of culture.

Most programs on campus are open to townspeople as well as to students.

Still another factor in Nacogdoches' reawakening has been the construction of a gracious community hotel, the Fredonia. In the early 1950's a group of local businessmen met informally at midmorning coffee and asked themselves whom they could persuade to build a first-class hotel. Discussion convinced them that no outsider would be likely to sink his money into such a risky operation; so they decided to build the hotel with local money.

They sold more than half a million dollars' worth of stock and borrowed about the same amount. They paid off the loan after five years and borrowed half a million more for building cabanas. Meanwhile, stockholders had voluntarily given up their dividends, telling the company to put the money back into the hotel instead. The management of the 114-room Fredonia now boasts 97.5 per cent occupancy and a yearly income of $800,000, accounted for by conventions, averaging one a week, and by salesmen and tourists.

Nacogdoches today is a prosperous town of about 12,000 people with a growing tendency to forget the lean years. But it is conservative, having saved its money after hard farm work—in contrast to communities that have seen riches accumulate quickly in speculation or even in established industries. Although several residents have acquired fortunes in less than a lifetime through enterprises that are now world-wide, an easy attitude toward money is absent.

This conservatism evolves also from a stern religious background. Nacogdoches is known as the cradle of Texas Protestantism. Symbolic is Old North Church, four miles north of town on U. S. Highway 59. A sign in front proclaims it the "oldest living Baptist Church in Texas." The building, a boxlike white frame structure, dates from 1852, but the church was organized in 1838. In its yard stands an aged oak tree, under which the first Baptist prayer meeting in Texas was organized in 1835.

The doors of Old North Church still swing open to worshipers every Sunday. Inside, some thirty-five persons —counting children—listen to a quiet sermon delivered by the minister, a deep-voiced speaker—but no pulpit-pounder, as might be expected. "Man's greatest need today," he says, "is to forgive and to be forgiven."

On the austere front wall is tacked the Church Covenant. By squinting one can read it: ". . . avoid all tattling, backbiting, and excessive anger. Abstain from the sale and use of intoxicating drinks. . . ."

And that brings to mind a crack in the local Christian armor. Nacogdoches County was among the first in Texas to outlaw liquor under the current local option plan; yet it is "wet enough to suit the drinkers and dry enough to suit the church folks," as one resident says. The county line isn't far away, and package stores are available there. Law-abiding citizens, visiting the line, can bring back a reasonable amount of liquor. Bootleggers also go there frequently to pick up unreasonable amounts, and on return trips they expect cat-and-mouse play from the patrol cars. One bootlegger stowed away three gallons of hooch in a spare tire in his trunk compartment, so that it was almost invisible to the deputy sheriff who brought him in.

Still, the liquor paradox is understandable, if one listens to F. I. Tucker, the attorney:

"My father would walk a mile for a drink of good whisky, but he always voted dry. He hated saloons, and in the 'nineties downtown Nacogdoches had open saloons that a woman wouldn't walk past without an escort—and not at all on Saturday nights. Open saloons are still remembered here, and that's one reason they were voted out."

Also paradoxical, and less understandable to the history-minded, is an acute lack of local interest in the past. No comprehensive history of the town or county has been written, but state college President Ralph Steen, himself a historian, explains, "There's so much history here nobody has dared to tackle it." M. M. Stripling, a native who has had a close look at the town as mayor, finds another reason. "Our history is associated with a period that's vague," he says. "First the Spaniards, then the Mexicans, were here in those days. They aren't now, not in the same numbers." He feels that Anglo-Americans aren't much interested in studying a foreign-dominated past.

Certainly one reason for the lack of historical interest is the scarcity of landmarks. Nacogdoches has no distinctive heritage as does, say, Williamsburg, Virginia. In the early days structures were meant to be practical; they were for shelter and not for looks. Furthermore, comparatively few of them survived; most were built of unfinished wood, and they vanished years ago, rotted in the warm, wet climate. Notable landmarks remaining are the Old North Church; the Nacogdoches University building, which might have been transported directly from the University of Virginia campus; the 1828 Adolphus Sterne home, now a public library; the two-story Sidney Murray Orton home, which has a "strong room" on the second floor for the detention of prisoners; a solitary Indian mound, from which grows a giant oak two centuries old; some traces of Smugglers' Road, so compacted that even today when a farmer hits it his plow will occasionally "jump two feet in the air"; and a restoration of the Old Stone Fort.

But the Stone Fort itself attests to a lack of appreciation of history, at least as was evidenced half a century ago: In 1902 it was demolished to make way for a new building.

A few persons opposed its destruction. Among them was Miss Adina de Zavala, granddaughter of a close friend of Sam Houston, who visited Nacogdoches as a representative of the Daughters of the American Revolution with the hope of arousing support for preserving the Old Stone Fort. To local women, however, the building was nothing more than a dirty old saloon, and down it came. In 1936 the State of Texas built from the original stones a painstaking restoration, on the state college campus.

Even the old talk is dying out. Twenty or thirty years ago an East Texan was easily recognized by his vocabulary and by his pronunciation. "Bluejohn" was milk beginning to turn sour; "blinky" was milk too sour to drink. "Soda water" designated any carbonated soft drink. "Norther" meant—and to many Texans still means—a sudden, wintry wind from the north. Drink was pronounced "draink," "swing" was "swaing," can't was "cain't."

"Terrible things are happening to Texas talk," W. D. Bedell, an East Texan, wrote recently in *The Journal of Southern History*. "Some of the words are dying because the things they describe aren't around any more. Kitchens don't have safes these days. Singletrees are seldom used. . . .

"And on TV and radio and in the papers you learn new words for the old things. My son says 'cold front' instead of norther. Think of a Texan saying that!"

Many persons would make even more changes. "This little group of historians," one man says, "—they disgust the rest of us. They would rather see a rail fence than a modern chain link fence.

"San Augustine and Jefferson [two other old East Texas towns] hung on to their relics till that's all they've got. Let them have the relics, and give us the future."

There's much support nowadays for courting the tourist trade with new recreation offerings. Already there are horse shows and fox hunts; and Nacogdoches' vital statistics—a three-hundred-foot altitude, an annual rainfall of 45.5 inches, a mean temperature of 65.4 degrees—make the country ideal for the man who relishes boating, hunting, camping, and fishing.

East Texas rivers, unlike those of the arid West, run continually except during the worst droughts. The nearby Angelina, a crooked, winding stream of many deep holes, is known for its catfish, bass, crappie, and bream—and for alligators. The river was used commercially until the 1880's, and old-timers used to talk about the excitement of hearing boat whistles blast through the silence of the forest. Home-town boosters want to develop this and other possibilities, but if they include—or even leave alone—the historical it will be only for crass commercialism.

Still, a few things do remain unchanged: the graciousness of yesteryear, an independent attitude, a drawing-room society that recognizes, primarily, length of family residence rather than money.

Graciousness is obvious at once. Nacogdoches banks have coffee rooms where customers can enjoy quiet breaks from work, or talk business in a friendly atmosphere; and even the busiest citizens have time to talk with a stranger, especially if he is white and nonunion.

Less in evidence, perhaps, is the lingering attitude of independence, an unwillingness to concede anything. But in the past, when something has been needed for the public good, the municipality has usually been forced to take it through condemnation.

Obvious only to new residents is the restricted social circle. The phrase, "Born in Nacogdoches," and membership in a respected old family, even by marriage, frequently opens doors that money alone can't. One native recalls, "My wife was once asked how she got invited to dinner in my parents' home. 'Well,' she said, 'I just pulled up a chair, said, "Move over; I belong here now," and I've been there ever since.'" A "newcomer" is anyone who has lived in Nacogdoches less than twenty-five years, and one frustrated newcomer declares, "I can compare old Texas family trees with the best of them, but that doesn't affect them one bit."

Some persons scoff at the whole environment: the provincialism, the pettiness, the hypocrisy, the dullness—each of which is indeed present. A blonde visitor from California, a coed who loves to dance, says, "Nacogdoches is dead. There's nothing here." She has relatives in town and knows something of the history, but still she looks unseeing into two hundred years of human toil, frustration, despair, and triumph. Like Ellis Bean, the man without a country, Nacogdoches grew up and thrived in a wilderness—virtually unsupported, almost disowned, and sometimes even trampled on by the nations which demanded its early allegiance.

The late Texas poetess, Karle Wilson Baker, wrote, in "Nacogdoches Speaks:"

I was the Gateway. Here they came, and passed
The homespun centaurs with their arms of steel
And taut heart-strings: wild wills, who thought to deal
Bare-handed with jade Fortune, tracked at last
Out of her silken lairs into the vast
Of a man's world. They passed, but still I feel
The dint of hoof, the print of booted heel,
Like a prick of spurs—the shadows that they cast.
I do not vaunt their valors, or their crimes:
I tell my secrets only to some lover,
Some taster of spilled wine and scattered musk.
But I have not forgotten; and, sometimes,
The things that I remember rise, and hover,
A sharper perfume in some April dusk.

*A new-car rally, bound for a countryside tour in July, 1915, brought local drivers to the center of town where a crowd and a lone horseman looked on.*

*Along a valley settled by Spanish explorers in the early 1600's, the adobe buildings of Chimayo bask in uninterrupted solitude below a mesa and amid cottonwoods.*

# The Still Young Sunlight

—

## Chimayo, New Mexico

—

### BY WINFIELD TOWNLEY SCOTT

Chimayo, New Mexico—it is pronounced "chim-my-yo"—spreads in high country where immigrant settlers arrived in the late sixteenth century. It is a mountain town, 6,872 feet above sea level, and lies between two famous places: Santa Fe, twenty-eight miles to the south, and Taos, forty miles or so to the north. Rand McNally says that it has 700 inhabitants, but this is to count only the center—to the extent that it has a center. From boundary to boundary, Chimayo gently climbs for more than four miles up the Santa Cruz Valley, and altogether some 2,500 people live within it. It is thought that nearly half that many souls—though, of course, they were Indian souls—

lived on this land in the year A.D. 1000. And who knows how many and for how long before that?

Of the various approaches to Chimayo, the most amazing is the back way down from Taos. With the great Taos Mountains abruptly behind in the north, you quickly leave U.S. Highway 64 and proceed through Ranchos de Taos into a country that mingles mountainside and meadows, forests and wild open spaces, a string of far-scattered towns, watery places and desert places, at times incredible distances of vision, all this lifted high as it were in the thin air of the New Mexico sky. Near Penasco the land is deep and dark with evergreen, but of course the colors of the country alter with the seasons and on an autumn day the golden aspen spurt up like random fires in the forest.

Down a roadbed sometimes smoothly paved, sometimes rocky and dusty, on past Dixon toward Trampas and Truchas, suddenly the horse-drawn plow, cows and sheep in pasturage; shrub-bordered, vine-bordered, tidily fenced, the land is gentle as a byway in Vermont. A piercing sense of remoteness enters at Trampas—a cluster of adobe houses, slanted metallic roofs sullenly gleaming in the sun, fly-specked dogs in the empty plaza, all dominated by the massive ancient adobe church. That sense of being within a landscape has vanished. In its place grows a feeling of fright, of rushing toward an edge. At Truchas, tough, remote and inbred, the edge is there and it is the edge of the world.

Along the eastern sky lies the irregular stretch of the Sangre de Cristo Mountains, named by the conquistadors in memory of Christ's blood, because of their swift rose sunset color. These and the Jemez Range along the west are the southern reaches of the Rocky Mountains. Looming over the town is Truchas Peak, 13,300 feet high. It thrusts far above timberline in an awesome and untrodden baldness of rock, gray or brown or blue as the light affects it, but always cold.

As to its main street (there are farms off stage), the town of Truchas seems perched along a ledge of mountainside. One thinks of a foreign country, looking at this run of shops and houses, bars, hay-filled barns and pigpens, a dominant crucifix, poised over vast valleys down which the land falls in violent plunges. The way south toward Chimayo is a twisted hogback in the bright sky: leftward, on the east, deep canyons of green, and steeply far below the highway a town or two. On the right, westward, a mighty sweep of sand-colored earth, sometimes fantastically shaped by the weathers of centuries.

The near hills are pocked with piñon, that gray-green bushy growth that bears a tiny, hard-shell nut and that, more valuably, is the staple firewood. It gives off a burning fragrance which has become part of the character of this land—so much so that enamored visitors often pay a good deal to fetch a few logs as far away as New York, the better to remember this strangest part of the United States.

As you spiral down toward Chimayo the piñoned hills give way to occasional russet-colored thrusts of upright land that look like ruins of architecture. Far off in all seasons but winter the cottonwoods twist a green arterial trail that marks the southward course of the Rio Grande.

The towns glimpsed, close by but sharply down from the road, are Cordova and Cundiyo, places of fishing and farming. In Cordova there are fine woodcarvers, still turning out in a primitive purity the small figures of saints, the *santos*, in soft white cottonwood. Cundiyo is known as the town of the Vigils. No one not of this name may dwell there.

MUSEUM OF NEW MEXICO

*In the cool of a porch, Spanish Americans in the lineage of the first settlers are silhouetted against the outskirt buildings of the town, including an old Penitente Church.*

But this is not the route by which Chimayo's ancestral invaders arrived. They came up from the south, and nowadays there is a choice of southern routes. North of Santa Fe, you can turn in through Nambe and travel back country, passing at one point yet more of that melting architectural landscape, entering Chimayo through its easternmost rim, once known as Potrero, where the famous Santuario stands.

A long slap of macadam has just gone down cutting into Chimayo to the road up to Truchas, and speeding the way from Santa Fe. To any inhabitant of either coast, motor traffic on even these so-called improved roads in New Mexico is unimaginably sparse. There is no roaring through. Yet I must confess the look of the town bears a confusing wound—perhaps one that in time will seem to close over—and I am touched by the willful denial David Ortega makes, standing in his family's weaving shop nearby. "That road," he says impatiently, "has nothing to do with Chimayo." So let us, too, blot it out. In Chimayo the sounds one still most clearly hears are the wind in the cottonwoods, sheep bells and crowing roosters, running water in the *acequias,* and the calls of children across the way in the schoolyard, almost always under an untroubled sun.

My own preference is the oldest route: to drive farther north from Santa Fe on U.S. 64 and go in toward the mountains through the Santa Cruz Valley. The road winds and dips and rises; at first most densely it passes through orchards which in spring blow white with apple blossom, seemingly the more tender for the inhuman landscape just beyond. There are frequent fields of corn, and along the river bottom the bright green of alfalfa, the sharp pink of the peach blossom, and the delicate apricot, first to bloom in the windy, dusty spring. Everywhere are the cottonwoods, leaves twinkling pale green or in the autumn astonishing gold slowly fading to silver, and woodbine tossing along the staked wire fences and climbing into trees, where it makes tangles of fiery red. This is echoed fiercely in the same season by one of the main products of this country, the red *chili.* You see it spread on roofs, but more often hung along the sides of houses in cataracts of scarlet. It is picked green in September, and thus ripened and strung it is known as *ristras.*

The Santa Cruz River runs through the valley, coming down from Chimayo on its way to Española and the Rio Grande. Often it is dry. Little dusty side roads run left and right from the main route, which never ceases to dip and twist and rise. Some of these dips are extremely abrupt—in and out of them quickly—and after rains in the mountains the *arroyos* may pour water across the road; rarely but sometimes of dangerous force and volume.

On the left the post office certifies that you are in Chimayo. The houses on either side are small, adobe and stucco, and there are many flower gardens, and often in the lace-curtained windows rows of plants in old tin cans.

High in the sky to the left is a tiny family chapel: it looks like a toy church perched on its almost inaccessible peak. The taller land begins to emerge—Truchas Peak looming far off, and again those haunting battlements which Ruth Laughlin once described as "red castles in rock."

The road goes on up to Truchas and Trampas and finally Ranchos de Taos, but we take the bend right and are at once within Chimayo proper. Here is the central sense of the town, perhaps because here there is concentrated a silent sense of the past. "Chimayo," says one guidebook, "was the eastern boundary of the Province of New Mexico from 1598 to 1695, the frontier place of banishment for offenders, which in those days meant punishment greater than prison." Following the exploratory trails of their conquistadors from Florida to northern Mexico, then north again into this wild territory, the Spanish came here and gradually made a town where Indians dwelt for uncounted centuries. Here to begin with was the Indians' pueblo, their town.

About fifty years ago an authority in some of the arts, George Wharton James, penetrated to Chimayo. The verb is not too strong: it took him two and a half hours of a pitching and tossing buggy ride to get all the way up the Santa Cruz Valley. Once arrived, however, Mr. James admired the orchards, the whitewashed adobe houses surrounding the Plaza, the vegetable gardens in the Plaza, the native weaving.

"Here," he observed, "is no lazy, indifferent, drinking, gambling Mexican settlement, but the home of self-respecting, hard-working, thriving, law-abiding men and women, who," he added graciously, "could well set an example to many far more pretentious towns and villages in our eastern states." The precise time, by the way, was 1912, the year in which New Mexico became a state.

Half a century later Mr. James would find the Plaza mostly deserted and gone to weeds, would find the town more strung out; but the land not changed; the spirit of the town, which is to say the character of its people, unchanged. José Ramon Ortega of the weaving family speaks of the number of townsmen who commute to outside jobs, notably over to Los Alamos; and says, "They like it when there's a strike because then they can stay home and work on their own places. We would always be all right. Even if the eastern United States were destroyed and all industry paralyzed, we could always be safe and independent here."

Wool is now imported, so I said, "What about your weaving? Wouldn't you have to start sheep raising again?"

He shrugged easily. "Ah, we'd let other people raise the sheep."

That apparently is how it feels to be born and brought up and live in Chimayo. The town has many visitors from all over America and the world to see the weaving. But it is not a tourist town: there is no restaurant, no place to stay. For all the modern roads and cars, for all the com-

*The clear sun on the smooth stucco and a sombre shadow on the paneled door form*
*a serene pattern on a church front, defined by a glistening bell-tower rope.*

muting of job holders and the visitations of strangers, Chimayo still keeps its sense of isolation, in no way an inferior sense of being out of things, but rather the strong sense of locality and self-sufficiency.

The heart of the town begins at that right bend where the Ortegas' shop stands. A few steps farther on, but hidden, is the old Plaza. The dirt road winds gently down beneath cottonwoods and between lilacs and the yellow-orange Rose of Castille and cactus to a hillside cluttered with a tumble of crosses. Then over the little Rio Chiquito which hurries on to join the Rio Santa Cruz—now there is a feeling of old settlement with a small shop or two set among the close houses, a *tamale* stand, and then the church known as the Santuario which itself may mark a pre-Christian site once sacred to the Indians. All this within a few minutes' stroll.

The word "Chimayo" is an adaptation of "Tsimayo," which means flaking stone of superior quality. Geologists have declared there is no flaking stone, obsidian or other kind, in the area. But obsidian and flint arrowheads have been found here, from prehistoric times when perhaps all this was nameless and, again perhaps, the Indians living here were ancestors of the Tewas.

There is an Indian legend that anciently Chimayo was a place where fire and smoke belched forth. Nobody knows the source of this story, but along the Rio Grande route to Taos there is high black-rock country of volcanic origin, and west across the Rio Grande in the Jemez Mountains there is so vast a crater that scientists speculate it may be the remnant of the world's largest volcano.

Stephen F. de Borhegyi, to whose scholarly monographs I am unrepayably indebted, is my source for saying that perhaps as many as a thousand Indians lived in this area as early as A.D. 1000. Eight- to ten-room pueblos of stone and adobe were scattered along both banks of the Santa Cruz, and the inhabitants pursued the typical Rio Grande pueblo life of hunting and fishing and farming. From the thirteenth through the fifteenth centuries, Borhegyi's researches show that many of the earlier settlements along the river were abandoned for a greater concentration of population. The gold-seekers, the Christianity-spreaders —the Spanish—began to arrive: to harass the Indian way of life with goodness and cruelties, and, Indian lore aside, to write the first civilized pages of the history of the United States of America.

The Spanish began moving into New Mexico in the 1520's. In the 1540's the great Coronado vainly sought Cibola or the seven cities of gold. Conquistadors and friars

TODD WEBB

*A light snow—accenting the piñon on a hill, barely holding to the barn roofs—turns a decaying part of Chimayo into a scene of wordly desertion and elemental birth.*

explored hand in hand. And there were many deaths. At the very end of the century Don Juan de Oñate established the first Spanish settlement, San Juan, on the west bank of the Rio Grande (not far off from Chimayo). Roughly around the beginning of the seventeenth century a handful of settlers commenced moving into the Santa Cruz Valley.

There were at first far more Tewa Indians than Spanish in the neighborhood. The newcomers' ranch buildings "were actually small fortresses of adobe and stone. They consisted of four or five rooms, and some even had watch towers called *torreons.*" As the century progressed and the Spanish population kept increasing, there were pueblo revolts, occasional skirmishes, and peace-making. From the Spaniard the Indian got better agricultural methods, irrigation, horses, cattle, sheep, and goats; not wholly mitigating benefits, for the Indians were shoved farther and farther up-valley.

Thus, exactly in the midst of the 1690's, Diego José de Vargas allowed the Indians at San Cristobal (over near San Juan by the Rio Grande) to harvest their crops, but then he made them settle "farther up the canyon toward Chimayo." The very next year another Indian uprising was followed by more resettlement of the natives and eight years later the aforesaid De Vargas assumed the right to grant 44,000 acres "to all the Spanish settlers residing in the valley." This was in 1704.

So it went. In the mid-1770's the inhabitants of Quemado briefly took refuge in Chimayo in fear of Ute Indians, but the trend was incessant, ending with the disappearance of the Indian from this immediate region. There appears to have been no intermarriage, Spanish and Indian; certainly next to none. This is not mysterious when we consider that each of these groups was sternly proud of—jealous of—its own culture and, further, that when they lived adjacently, they lived on guard and often in a state of war. Chimayo today is as purely a Spanish town as any in the United States.

Many a visitor to Chimayo never sees the old Plaza because it is hidden behind houses on the right a few steps beyond the Ortegas' weaving shop. Its old name is Plaza del Cerro, "plaza of the hill." Of the string of little settlements which slowly coalesced as Chimayo, only one, La Puebla, is west of the Rio Santa Cruz; all the rest except Potrero, "the opening," to the east, run along the north side of the river: "Cuarteles, so called because a body of Mexican soldiers was once quartered there; La Puebla; Plaza Abajo, the lower plaza; Los Ranchos; La Cuchilla, so called because it is located on a small hill with a knife-like ridge; Rincon, the corner settlement; Los Ojuelos, the little springs; El Llano, the plain."

Only arbitrarily can one call any portion of Chimayo the center. Not unlike such huge American cities as Los Angeles, the evolution of modern Chimayo has been that of the linear type. It remains strung out. Yet one feels that the Plaza del Cerro is the heart of the village. Once the post office bearing the name Chimayo stood in this Plaza. Now ragged and worn it all sleeps in the sun almost like a tiny ghost town.

Nearly forty houses and shops surround the Plaza and only a few are not locked and empty. With but occasional interruptions the buildings are contiguous. For this kind of plaza—a combination of walled garden and town square—was made for defense, which also explains why time with its changes has brought about such abandonment. Access at the four corners, here and there wedged between houses a *calle jon*—"little street"—are classic, as here, but Chimayo's old plaza, almost perfectly square, is bisected by a road, and an *acequia* crosses with a long slant of gurgling water.

A dirt road boxes the center which is now mostly a tree-slanting, weed-jammed, fence-griddled wreck of all the gardens which once belonged individually to the adjacent householders. Here and there are catalpa trees, and some evergreen; over a fence some morning glories. Hollyhocks are known here as St. Joseph's Staff, for it is said that when a group of saints assembled to try to ascertain which one of them was to be the husband of Mary, St. Joseph's staff broke suddenly into flowers as they prayed. What was a general store now faces one side of the Plaza with big, amazingly thin panes of glass, beginning to buckle, and red-painted Victorian screen doors that are a bit of charming nostalgia. Indeed the entire Plaza is as though it were the past asleep and you, walking through it, merely its dream.

A friend unlocked a shuttered adobe house for me. In the dimness of empty rooms I got the sense of tidy substantiality: the small windows and doors, the low ceilings with the characteristic New Mexican *vigas*, "untrimmed beams"; the fireplaces raised and rounded, one in a corner of each room. Right behind the house stood its separate summer kitchen; and kitty-corner before it a small building called the dispenser—that is, a storeroom.

If you can find the right person, also with a key, you may view the second room on the north side, the Oratorio of San Buenaventura. Now in the custody of the Confraternity of Our Lady of Carmel, this little "church" was restored about a decade ago by the Spanish Colonial Arts Society. "The result," says E. Boyd, an expert in these matters, "with a remarkably well-preserved reredos, earth floor, hand-hewn furnishings, no electricity, and the characteristic feeling of proportion in space, is one of the rare survivals of the carefully kept, authentic, small private chapels of which once dozens existed in New Mexico."

Under a bell, up a steep step and through a narrow door, you enter to a bare simplicity of adobe floor and two windows with starched curtains. On the altar in front of the lovely primitive reredos are a mixture of plaster saints in

*A shrine to town and area, the 1816 Santuario heightens the region's architectural characteristics. The adobe is molded into an earthy entrance and rises to stately towers.*

the unlovely marzipan-like style of contemporary commercial-religious *objets-d'art,* but there is also one fine old *santo.* Once rosaries and novenas were said here. Such a chapel dates, of course, from the era when Chimayo was a mission, only now and then visited by a roving priest; hence the family places of worship of which this, as Miss Boyd says, is one of the very few left. Its date is unknown. The date scratched on a *viga*—1873—probably indicates the time of a reroofing. The chapel was long a possession of the Ortegas. They and the Martinez, Jaramillo, and Mascarenas families were all living here in 1730.

Such families, says Borhegyi, "already possessed relative wealth and ready cash" and they "brought in merchandise from Santa Fe and set up little shops in one room of their houses. They considered themselves the wealthy upper class of the town and as such exercised unquestioned political and even religious influence." The alteration of this concentrated life was begun through the Spanish custom of inheritance; the sons were willed strips of land adjoining the river. Often these were widely separated. Small ranch houses were built on the lands for use while the fields were worked, but in the early days the men returned each night to town, which was safer from Indian raids. As the decades passed and Indian menace became history, these houses gradually were enlarged into real residences. "The town nobility, the wealthy merchants and tavern keepers, whose shops and saloons had previously been located about the town plaza, found that they were losing customers" and they began a roadside scattering and left their plaza homes "to their poor relatives" who in time were themselves to leave them to nobody at all.

And as Borhegyi notes, this stringing out comes to an inevitable modern-day tendency of commuting to jobs out of town: to shops and gas stations in nearby Española or even down in Santa Fe; to jobs at Los Alamos where young men may be laboratory workers, technicians, warehouse foremen, or hold certain positions that are not divulged. The youngsters drive the same roads to movies and dances. Some church affairs constitute community activity as such. Otherwise there are the pleasures of small gardening and the fiercer pleasures—to these the Spanish-American is passionately committed—of politics.

But suppose, though strangers still, we had wakened here in the Plaza del Cerro one hundred years ago.

A summer morning, and the whole center of the square is massed with the gridded gardens: the corn, the beans, the *chili* all coming on toward ripeness. The stream in the *acequia,* of course, murmurs through the place as if everlastingly—at one corner it even flows beneath a house. There are brown-faced, beautifully dark-eyed children playing about in the road, the small ones wearing nothing but a little shirt.

In the still young sunlight a woman with a bright shawl comes out bearing a rather large earthen pot—of Indian make—and bends to the ditch to get water. Her shoes may be Indian moccasins or they may be a Spanish style of soft, heelless slipper. Her upper dress is a plain sort of chemise bound at the waist by a voluminous colored skirt that reaches to her ankles. Though small, she is rather stout, uncorseted, and she wears her dark hair in two braids over her shoulders.

Then another emerges to tend her bee-hive-shaped adobe oven, a few steps outside her house. She has been up much earlier and set a fire of sticks and twigs in the closed oven, so she approaches it with dough all ready on a plank she carries. The oven is now extremely hot. The woman rakes out the ash, shoves in her dough and re-fastens the metal door.

Many of the men who live in these houses are off overseeing their farms on the outskirts of town, and their orchards are nearing harvest time. But some shop-tenders are here; now in the quiet of midmorning they lean against the adobe whose strands of gold straw glint in the sun. There is throughout the Plaza an easy feeling of *poco-a-poco* —no hurry—and this attends the politeness, the soft run of Spanish speech, the air of formality with which neighbor greets neighbor. Their hatless, dark-haired heads bow with a civility that is one extreme of a people who can be hot-tempered and vengeful not short of murder.

The dress of the men like that of the women is standard: they are white-shirted and their wool trousers—blue or brown—fit tightly from waist to knee, but there flare, slitted open about the booted calf. On these trousers decorative silver buttons proclaim an economic superiority, even though they cannot match in number or splendor the costume of the real *caballero*. There are no great *haciendas* in Chimayo—wealth here is comparative and modest.

A swarthy little man in a broad Mexican hat and a heavy woolen *poncho*—despite the heightening summer day— with his dog drives a herd of sheep down the road bisecting the Plaza. In a nervous bleating and bumping together the flock humps and trots its way toward a field just beyond, where the *acequia* emerges and runs along under woodbine on the edge of pastureland.

Almost on the heels of the shepherd another rather small man comes round the corner of the dispensary, greets the nearest shopkeeper and they go inside. This is the village scribe. For—in the era to which we have gone back—less than half the people in Chimayo can read or write, and the scribe may set down anything from so small a matter as a bill of goods to so solemn a matter as a last will and testament. It is not impossible that he may even now be drafting a formal letter from Juan's father to Terecita's father just across the way: a letter adorned with gracious wishes and suggesting a meeting between the fathers and perhaps the

TODD WEBB

*Still inhabited, this row of tidy adobe houses on an overgrown plaza faced a community garden and were at the center of town life for two centuries.*

uncles of the two families to discuss Juan's desire to marry Terecita. A 1766 Spanish law "to prevent marriage between people of different social positions" may no longer be literally in effect, but it remains deep in the custom of the country.

The noon quiet of the Plaza is heaved open by a big horse-drawn cart, two men on the driver's seat, bearing goods for the shopkeepers. No doubt it left Santa Fe yesterday, has been overnight in Española and made a morning stop at Santa Cruz.

A black-shawled old lady, stooped, comes out of the house next to the Oratorio. There is sickness there. But since Chimayo has no doctor nor for that matter medical supplies, the old lady was sent for. She is expert in herbal doses and, perhaps, gifts of magic. There are those who whisper that she is a witch. She does not live within the Plaza and she shuffles out of sight down the road toward Potrero.

Here is a rarity: a priest. It is a good time of year for him to get by horseback into so remote a town. He is one of Bishop Lamy's young men—a Frenchman, not altogether at ease with these Spanish, nor they with him. But, of course, there is a carefulness on his part and a respectful civility on theirs, and he will be busy on errands of kindness: visiting the sick, saying rosaries, christening babies born since he was last in Chimayo.

He will be given a good meal and (let us suppose) we are invited, too. One of the several chests in the house serves as a table and we sit on the adobe floor around it. This is the house of the lady we saw early in the day putting her bread to bake—and it is excellent bread. The *señor* and half a dozen children are present. And we have both chicken and mutton, corn, beans, and those Mexican pancakes, the ubiquitous *tortillas.* There is some home-made wine.

The lady has done her cooking in the corner fireplace, for this is kitchen, dining room and living room combined. Two doorways lead to bedrooms and glimpses of bedsteads, which are fairly new luxuries; until recently, piled-up hides or blankets served as beds—as they still do in poorer parts of Chimayo.

At that, the furnishings of this central room are sparse and plain. The pine chests and the few chairs were made in the village, fashioned roughly with chisels, saws, and knives. They are knicked in decorative lines. The silver on the table is also of frontier manufacture and simple in its design. The walls of the room are very white and in one corner is a cupboard, a *trastero.* Here and there on the walls are sacred pictures, a shelf holding a row of *santos;* most charming, hung in another corner, a glass-sided tin box, garlanded with paper flowers and containing an image of the Virgin.

And so the day goes on. In the late afternoon a number of peons saunter into the various stores where the *patrón*

is their master; they are being paid in goods for working his farmlands. They seem in no hurry. And in the bright sunlight of early evening eight or ten of them squat in a ring at one edge of the Plaza and seriously watch a cock-fight.

And so the year goes on and (suppose once more) we see the harvest days, the fruit brought in, the augmenting of woodpiles as the air sharpens, the ranks of *ristras* red on the walls. Until at last it is Christmas Eve and we see the Plaza at its most lovely and touching. The whole Plaza is illuminated in the night by ancient custom: outlining the roofs and rowed along the ground are candles set in sand in paper bags, *farolitos;* and yet more brightly burning before each door three wood fires, *luminarias,* to light the Christ child in tonight through the slow fall of snow.

We return to the present and Ortegas' weaving shop, which fronts the little road and is lighted by big plate-glass store windows. The central room is large, piled and hung with many colored rugs and blankets, with smaller table covers and even with Chimayo jackets. Darkly down the rear there is a storeroom. At the left there is a smaller room where almost always one or more Ortega men are working the hand looms—José Ramon, his brother David; sometimes their venerable father Nicacio, his sallow old face lined with the years—working as their family has for unnumbered generations. All over Chimayo in small adobe homes there are other looms where weaving is also turned out for the Ortegas. It is a historic combination of enterprise, art, tradition, and a most successful demonstration of the principle of cottage industry. During my latest visit I glanced over the guest book on the window sill: within only two months people had dropped in from Colorado, North Dakota, Illinois, California, New Jersey, South Carolina, of course Texas—also England and the Congo.

When George Wharton James made his visit to Chimayo in 1912 he noted many close resemblances between Chimayo and Navajo blankets: the simple patterns of alternating belts or stripes of color crosswise. The reasons this should be so are historical, complicated, and they explain, for one thing, why most people get confused over which is which: a confusion abetted by vendors of so-called "Chimayo" and "Navajo" blankets which in neither case are genuine.

Indians were weaving long before the Spanish appeared on this continent. They wove with cotton, or kinds of fiber, sometimes with hair. Coronado's diarist, Pedro de Casteñeda, recorded the "fine robes woven from cotton" among the Zuñis and Hopis, and he also saw blankets of rabbit skin, loosely woven. As Ruth Laughlin says, "When Oñate and his colonists drove herds of sheep up the trail from Chihuahua in 1698 they started the sheep and wool industry in New Mexico. They soon taught the Indian slaves to pluck wool from the sheep by hand, spin and weave it."

It was the Pueblo Indians—the agricultural "town" Indians—not the Navajos who first performed this improved weaving. The roving Navajos raided the pueblos and stole blankets. An Indian tradition has it the Navajos agreed to cease the raids (a promise they did not keep) if Hopis and Zuñis would teach them to weave. Thus the origin of the Navajo blanket. It was, you might say, begotten by the Spanish on the Indians, and then continued over the years with resemblances to and variations by both races.

On through the eighteenth century most weaving was done by Indians. The women wove on upright looms, whereas the Spanish introduced the horizontal loom and the men did the weaving. The Indians often raveled out imported cloths or—pricelessly rare now—used the discarded red uniforms of conquistadors and made the rich "Bayeta" blankets.

By early nineteenth century the government decided it could profitably develop weaving among its own folk, and craftsmen were brought from Mexico City to teach the art. Don Ignacio Ricardo Bazan, for example, lived for six years in Santa Fe and taught weaving until presently the craft spread through many villages; annual fairs glowed with blankets and serapes. Everywhere it was a winter occupation: an indoor art between harvest-over and spring planting. In time the tradition of weaving lapsed in most places, but it was continued as a year-round occupation, in Chimayo.

In the old days, Ruth Laughlin says, "The wool was shaken thoroughly to free it from sand and dirt, washed in foamy suds made from pounded amole root and spread upon the sage brush to dry and bleach. Then it was carded with wooden combs, rolled into balls and spun with a distaff until the yarn was fine and closely twisted. This left the wool in the natural shades of white, black, brown and gray." The Indians made a blue dye from steeped Hopi beans, yellow from chamisa blossoms and yellow ochre, red from Tag Alder bark, red ochre and mountain mahogany—and, of course, combinations of these for other colors. In addition, the Spanish imported Brazil wood for mahogany color, and balls of anil for indigo. As for a design, it was carried in the head.

All this in times past; preparations long since outmoded by modern manufacturing. Now the skeins arrive at Chimayo from Midwestern mills. Nevertheless in design and method the tradition continues. If anything it is truer than at some periods of decline when, for instance, cotton was used as warp. Today the Ortegas use only a wool warp. And as the onlooker incredulously watches the weaver toss his shuttle in and out, back and forth, across the broad loom, he witnesses a beautiful art as it has been practiced for centuries.

The little dirt road goes down toward the Rio Chiquito between church and school buildings of the Presbyterian Mission. Such Protestant invasions—Protestantism is still a minor religion here—began ten years or so after the American Civil War. And just beyond, a bunch of small, weathered, wooden crosses thrust out of a thicket of cactus. They remind us of a very different religion, indeed, for this is Penitente country.

The Penitentes are not merely an order of flagellants, though, of course, it is for that spectacular display they are famous, not to say notorious. I think the Anglo—as we latter-day invaders are called in New Mexico (when we are not called Gringos)—is always struck by the bloodiness of the Spanish tradition within the Roman Catholic Church: the red-streaked crucifixes which so graphically insist upon the sufferings of Jesus. We incline perhaps to be less morbid and less realistic than the Spanish-American; he seems abler to bear in mind that in the midst of life we are in death. In any case the outsider must understand that the lashing processions of Holy Week are no more a "show" than are the dances of the Pueblo Indians; both are a deeply religious expression proceeding from ancient traditions. The Penitentes enact a kind of passion play and, as Alice Corbin Henderson said, "There is nothing at all mysterious about the Penitentes . . . they were never secret until the 'Anglos' came, and after the French priests attempted their suppression."

There is not an absolute certainty that the Penitentes stem from the Third Order of St. Francis. It seems likely, however, for there are European traditions of flagellation and the notion, sometimes put forward, that the heritage here comes from contact with American "savages" is nonsense. It is recorded that the Franciscan friars oversaw public penance during Holy Week as early as 1598 within this region.

After 1828, when there was a Mexican revolution, the friars were banished, but the Penitente cult persisted. It flourished in a terribly isolated era "when," Oliver La Farge pointed out, "that region was all but cut off from contact with the organized Roman Catholic Church." It is a true order, a Brotherhood, with elected leaders, and with a lodge building called the Morada. Throughout the year in mountain villages where priests were rarely seen, the members of the Penitente served the community—in sickness, in death—as a lay organization. This was the basic function, scarcely known in comparison to their days of public atonement for sin.

Their processions to various village shrines took place (I use, tentatively, the past tense) from time to time during the days of Holy Week. Leading the procession was the *Pitero* whistling through a *pito*—that is, a piper sounding a thin, high, eerie note; other leaders, often one of them chanting; then a straggling line of black-hooded men, bare to the waist, and wearing white cotton drawers. As they marched slowly along each lashed himself with a yucca whip. Sometimes a marcher was cactus-bound or rope-bound; sometimes a penitent hurled himself into a bed of

cactus. Often the procession was made the more frightful by the death cart.

The *Carreta del Muerto,* the death cart, is said to have been produced in superior fashion years ago in Chimayo. Now and then you may come upon one in a museum: a crude cart with solid, unturning wheels, and seated in it a figure of death, customarily a skull-faced image swathed in black and armed with an aimed bow and arrow. The man dragging this, harsh ropes around him, had no gentle task.

On the morning of Good Friday the flagellants marched alone to the Morada, without chanting or music, only the sullen thrash of the whips, over and over. In the afternoon a towering cross (probably seventeen feet high) was set in the ground in front of the Morada and a hooded man bound upon it. There he hung until the slumping of his body indicated unconsciousness and he was taken down and carried into the building. There have been rumors of actual crucifixion and of deaths, but these are unverified; and it is said that in recent time a shrouded figure has been bound on the cross, perhaps just a figure and not a man.

Even this re-enactment was surpassed by the frenzy of the services in chapel on Friday night. This is the *Tinieblas,* and Alice Corbin Henderson recounted her attendance at one such service. The chapel was lighted by thirteen candles. These were pinched out one by one as the *Hermanos Mayor*—the leading brother—read a ritual. There was then complete darkness and at once she could hear the flagellants entering the room:

"Shrieks, sobs, and howls, *metracas* rattling, chains clanking, the *pito* wailing; and through it all the swish, slap, swish, slap of the flagellants' whips. . . . This was the *Tinieblas,* the shadow, the earthquake—when the heavens were darkened and the earth gaped, and graves were burst asunder."

Now and then all the wild sounds ceased, prayers were said, then the whole cacophony resumed. And so on, through several sessions until Mrs. Henderson felt it unbearably terrifying. At last there came a silence and the chapel, its floor and walls blood-spattered, again was lighted. The leading brother made a short talk about the significance of the services and then all were released into the high starlit New Mexico night. This was thirty years ago.

Does this still go on?

There have been papal bulls against public penance. In New Mexico in the nineteenth century the church made attempts at suppression of the Penitentes; this was when the Right Reverend John B. Lamy was Archbishop. (He

*Carved in a niche of the Santuario, a bleeding Christ ornately robed suggests the suffering and splendor imbedded in Chimayo's religious belief.*

TODD WEBB

*The Santuario altar, painted with regional designs and fronted by a totem-pole rail, reflects the influence of an Indian heritage on a Catholic shrine.*

is now immortal in American literature as Father Latour in Willa Cather's *Death Comes for the Archbishop*.) The attempts relaxed into unhappy tolerance again. Some twenty years ago Archbishop Edwin V. Byrne offered the brotherhood "acceptance and church approval if it would bring its observances into line with church requirements," and it is said this mediation met with "real success."

But a lady in Santa Fe told me, "I've seen whiskey bottles tossed outside a Morada on Good Friday where evidently the liquor was being used to numb pain." A young Santa Fe writer exhibited a blood-spattered coat a few years ago which he was wearing as he hid under a bridge while a procession passed overhead. This was near the very same remote northern town where Mrs. Henderson attended the ceremonies three decades ago. A scientist at Los Alamos said to me, "Around Easter you should see the backs of some of those boys when they change clothes to go on the job in the lab." A lady in Chimayo said, "Well— if you just happen to be in the right place at the right time . . ." and she let it go at that. The real success in suppression of violent rites would seem to be a partial one; though now perhaps only in a very few places hidden in the high fastnesses of the New Mexico mountains, come Holy Week, the weird cry of the *pito* still summons that repetitive drench of yucca whips.

But now—to return to the sunlight of an ordinary day in Chimayo—after crossing the bright little river the road bends left and climbs around a blind curve into what again feels like a center. Among the houses there is on the left a plain building, the Medinas' family chapel which was built 1850–60. Larger than the old chapel in Plaza del Cerro, it contains the customary sacred pictures and objects, the paper flowers one so often finds as decoration in Spanish churches, and also, most importantly, the little image known as *Santo Niño*. His is the most charming legend in Chimayo, for this Holy Child is credited with running about the village in the night performing good deeds. He is rather fancily behatted and costumed, and once or twice a year new shoes are fitted on him, lest he wear out a pair on his errands.

A short way beyond, the road gives on an abrupt downslope of open land and there across an *acequia* and within a gated and walled graveyard stands the Santuario. This 150-year-old adobe church is Chimayo's famous building and in fact the only place of its kind in the United States. Nowhere else in our country is there a shrine of curative earth.

One survivor of two enormous cottonwood trees still looms above the water ditch where now and again a couple of ducks float along from a nearby farmyard. Behind the

Santuario the unkempt field slopes yet farther down to the river, whose convenient mud banks account for the pile of dried soil one can see—but who would prowl around behind a church?—beneath the window of the room containing the holy earth. Across the river the land flares high, rusty, smeared with moldy green streaks of clay. Far down the valley away from the town you can see across farmed fields and some wasteland the tall dam behind which lies the Santa Cruz lake. I remember a rare day when water ran over that dam—it was a shining June Sunday—and boys came galloping bareback from all directions just to watch.

Altogether this is the fairest spot in Chimayo, and perhaps it is the most ancient. Certainly there is an Indian belief that on the south side of the Rio Chiquito, where we have the Santuario, the Tewa Indians enshrined a pool because they believed its mud had healing properties. All through its modern or Catholic history, Indians have been among those visiting the shrine. There are Spanish legends —a crucifix was found near the site; or, a crucifix carried by a priest was buried with him here after he was killed by the Indians. All the stories, though they do not greatly differ anyway, have one particular feature in common: whether it was a crucifix or a *santo* whose discovery marked this area as sacred, once removed it always returned.

The Santuario is dedicated to Our Lord of Esquípulas, a name for the manifestation of Christ crucified. In 1813, Bernard Abeyta of Chimayo had a son, christened Tomás de Jesus de Esquípulas, and later that same year sought permission to build the Santuario. It is thought that he introduced the custom of dispensing little clay tablets, stamped, blessed, and sold as having curative power. The custom may have come from either Mexico or Guatemala and the cures were supposedly the work of the Black Christ on the crucifix.

A carved door between the narthex and the nave bears the date 1816. The Santuario is again in the records a decade later when the priest in Santa Cruz ordered all *santos* "painted on hides of animals and on rough boards" removed from the chapel. This foreshadowed the war upon the Spanish primitive art by the French priests in Archbishop Lamy's era. The *santos, retablos, bultos, reredos* they found so antipathetic and worked, with some success, to banish and destroy are now, whether originals or traditional copies, valued once again: as religious objects, as primitive art of such indigenous charm they are museum pieces and collectors' items.

In 1856, Bernard Abeyta died and was buried in the chapel. After that there developed complete confusion as to the "real reason" for the shrine; the Esquípulas tradition was mixed into and lost in the legend of *Santo Niño*. The fact that it became generally thought the Holy Child affected the cures undoubtedly was inspired by the Chavez family (heirs of Abeyta) placing a *Santo Niño* in the Santuario as a defiant rival to the Medina family's. Yet I must mention, with no conviction as to what light it throws on all our questions about traditions, that the crucifix in the Santuario is said to copy exactly the one in the Iglesia de Santo Niño at Esquípulas in Mexico.

Specifically Bernard's daughter, Señora Carmal Chavez, was heir to the chapel. Since she referred to it as her "only support" and since no money ever was charged for touching one's body with the sacred earth or taking bits away to be used medicinally in drinking water, there must have been a tradition of gifts of money left at the Santuario. So when, in the 1880's, a young priest "in charge of his first parish," says Earle R. Forrest, "was sent to Chimayo [and] demanded that Señora Chavez deed the Santuario chapel to the Catholic Church," the Señora waged a mighty battle. She held tight even while he excommunicated her and refused to baptize, marry, or bury any member of the Chavez family. Eventually she won. The bishop removed the priest. But she did not triumph forever.

The decades went on and the Santuario sat there—its two little belfries, its upper porch, its lovely carved doors, its wonderful paint-on-wood *reredos*, its images and its holy earth. In 1929 the Santa Fe artist Gustave Baumann heard that some kind of piecemeal sale of furnishings was under way because the Abeyta heirs had fallen on hard times. The famous *bulto* of Santiago, a man on horseback —his name was the Christians' cry in battle against the Moors, and many times his emanation has appeared, even in this hemisphere against the Aztecs—this most precious *bulto* in the chapel (where I hasten to interpolate it still is) was already in the hands of a curio dealer and someone was bargaining for the priceless carved doors.

The Santa Fe art colony was alerted. Baumann and Frank Applegate and newspaper editor Dana Johnson joined forces and one or another of them got in touch with Mary Austin. That indomitable writer, then living out her last years in Santa Fe, was at the moment lecturing in New Haven, Connecticut. Mrs. Austin got $6,000 from Olivia Murray Cutting, mother of New Mexico's famed Senator Bronson Cutting (the identity of the donor is here revealed for the first time) and she and her group bought the Santuario, restored it, and presented it to the Catholic Church.

In recent years a few changes have been made: pews fill the once vacant-floored chapel, a heater has been installed, to the left of the front door a room is used as a shop for religious articles, a priest serves the parish. The room of the sacred earth is through a little door to one side of the altar. There is the exposed, scooped ground near a simple window. The room is small and its walls are crowded with religious pictures, with abandoned crutches and testimonial notes of gratitude from those cured here.

Soon there will be a new church in Chimayo and the Santuario will be quieter again, but doubtless the pious will come pilgrimaging as always. It is unlikely, however, that it will ever enjoy a prouder day than April 28, 1946, when over five hundred people (its largest congregation) jammed the chapel.

The uniqueness of that day came out of the misfortunes of World War II. In August, 1941, the 200th Coast Guard Regiment was ordered to the Pacific on maneuvers augmenting General Douglas MacArthur's forces. Within a few months they were caught in actual war. As General E. P. King says, "When the decision was reached April 9, 1942, that there was no alternative but to surrender Bataan, the New Mexicans stood alone."

There followed then the dreadful Bataan death march and three and a half years' imprisonment. Indians, Spanish-Americans, Anglos, in all about 1,800 went from New Mexico. About 1,000 returned. About half that number may still be alive.

While they were imprisoned, many of these New Mexico boys vowed that if they got home they would make a pilgrimage by foot to the Santuario in Chimayo. And so, that April, 1946, twenty-three veterans and three women trudged the nearly thirty miles from Santa Fe up into the mountain country. Cars and buses jammed into the little town. A light rain fell.

The altar of the Santuario was festive with blue and gold streamers and rosettes. All the saints were freshly dressed. So densely did the people stand—men to one side, women to the other—that kneeling was scarcely possible. Outside, the crowd stretched back thickly another twenty-five feet. Many were families of the veterans and many had lost sons and brothers, dead in the Philippines and in Japanese prison camps.

At ten o'clock that morning High Mass began, sung by the priest from Santa Cruz. A Santa Fe choir sang. There was a sermon in Spanish. The services went on for an hour and a half. Then as the crowd dispersed a long line formed and moved slowly in and out of the Santuario, each person stooping to gather a handful of the sacred earth.

The spring night came on early. Quiet and lonesome again, Chimayo closed in on itself under the mighty lands surrounding it. If there were ghosts, they had to be Indian ghosts and Spanish ghosts. The old, still-living town closed in under the stars as though it were as self-sufficient as immortality. And—who knows?—perhaps all earth is sacred.

TODD WEBB

*Picket-fence graves, an old regional custom, and the wooden crosses of an ancient Catholicism stand in Chimayo's graveyard, next to a hillside of broken wagons.*

*Far below the mountainsides that once made it rich, the mining town that was a silver center presents a diminutive, orderly pattern of streets and houses.*

# A Rocky Mountain Fantasy

—

## *Telluride, Colorado*

—

### BY DAVID LAVENDER

"It *is* a fantasy spot," Theodora Kroeber said once while we were remembering Telluride, 8,800 feet high in the San Juan Mountains of southwestern Colorado, where both of us spent our childhoods. Not quite simultaneously, however. Theodora had left Telluride thirteen years ahead of me, when she was eighteen and I only five. Later she married Alfred Kroeber, one of the country's leading anthropologists, and after his death completed that marvelous book, *Ishi in Two Worlds,* a tale of the last surviving wild Indian in North America. But on this occasion we were remembering Telluride.

"In that thin, dry air," she went on, "life moved at a pace of almost terrible intensity. There were no neutral moments—the galloping brevity of spring and summer, the long months of winter with the threat of tragedy always hovering near. Colors were high—the reds in the soil, the fall gold of the aspens, the indescribable sky. Riding in summer and tobogganing in winter were fast and dangerous; the heights of the mountains and the depths of the canyons were beyond the human norm. One went about totally sensitized. No wonder recovery for the elders was a trip to the Coast, and for a youngster, introversion. Get on your horse and ride till you looked out and down, tremendously out and down. God was a pagan god, in the air, over the mountains, in the waterfalls. But how can I give the feeling-tone of my childhood in that high Alpine valley, which simply is one of the most beautiful spots in the world?"

How indeed? Helplessly one retreats to the matter-of-factness of geography and to that overwhelming rim of peaks, 13,000, even 14,000 feet high, which have always been and must continue to be the determining factor of Telluride's existence.

The camp—one never said "village," and "town" only on formal occasions— lies near the head of the San Miguel River, in the bottom of a profound, U-shaped trough. Similar deep-bowl settings are characteristic of most of the gold and silver camps of the Rocky Mountains. The mines themselves are high. "Ten times out of nine," a Colorado jingle says, "silver comes at timberline"—or above, in bleak glacial cirques where often there was not enough water or space to build mills that could start extracting the precious metals by grinding up the ore that came from the mines. Accordingly the reduction works sought gentler sites in the valleys two or three thousand feet lower. This, of course, meant shipping the ore down zigzag mule trails, breathless wagon roads, or, for those mines handling large volumes, in tram buckets swaying along dizzy cableways.

Inevitably the mill sites became transfer points for larger wagons and later for railroads that brought in supplies from the outside and took back concentrate, as the end-product of the mills was called. Even those few mills located beside the mines in the high country had to use the communal supply facilities. Soon a town was there, center of a web of trails and roads and aerial tramways that climbed to the smaller clusters of cabins and stores around the timberline workings.

Telluride was particularly fortunate in her valley. There was space enough so that the mills could be set apart from the homes and the town did not have to entwine itself with its industrial plants, as happened in some mining camps. Viewed from the approach through the canyon of the San Miguel River, the area took shape like this: First there is a steep climb past the cataracts at Keystone Hill into the spectacular horseshoe of cliffs and peaks that embrace the river's beginnings. At the top of Keystone Hill the valley widens into two miles of sunny meadow and marsh. Then comes the town. Though small mills were located in various pockets in all directions, the big ones were located on up the river. First came the steep-roofed, many-windowed

red hulk of the Liberty Bell and then, a mile and a half farther on, the great Smuggler-Union complex at Pandora.

Pandora was also the site of several other tram terminals and mine tunnels. It had barns, offices, boardinghouses. But it was not a town; it was a noisy gray sprawl of industry, run entirely by the companies located there. For town things—entertainment, business affairs, churches, shops, doctors, and homes in which to raise children—you went back down the river past the Liberty Bell to Telluride.

The steep mountain slope south of town, where snow lies deepest in winter, is thick with aspen and spruce. The slope to the north is banded with cliffs and punctuated at the very edge of the town by the plume of Cornet Falls, named after an early prospector.

Eastward, just beyond Pandora, the horseshoe closes in a high dead end of gray-brown cliffs. Above the cliffs tower conical peaktops, collared by green alpine grass and streaked with lingering snow. Streamlets sparkle through the deep V's between the peaks. At the very head of the valley, lifting the eye 3,000 feet above the level of the town, is the thin silver pinpoint of Ingram Falls. They too were named for a successful prospector, though ironically he did his work off to the left (north) in a different basin now named Marshall. One yarn about Ingram says that on reaching Marshall Basin in 1876, he found its most promising vein already claimed by a pair of earlier locators. He stepped off their lines. Deciding each was hogging more linear feet than the law allowed, he set up his own stakes in the middle of their contiguous holdings, called his claim, with dry humor, the Smuggler, and made the intrusion stick. In time the Smuggler absorbed its neighbors, renamed itself the Smuggler-Union, and became the district's leading producer. Spectacular aerial tramways carried its ore (and the concentrate milled at the Tomboy in an adjacent basin) from the cliff-hung mines down a resounding chasm to the nearest flat land, Pandora.

A more conventional legend than Ingram's, this one pure weeping romance, clings to misty Bridal Veil Falls, 365 feet high. The cataract, perhaps the loveliest in Colorado, pours over the cliffs southwest of Ingram Falls and opposite the Smuggler workings. Climax of Pandora's awesome scenery, Bridal Veil lies just out of sight of Telluride itself. Once, so the story goes, honeymooners visited the powerhouse (now abandoned) whose stone outer wall rises flush from the brink of the precipice over which the water plunges. As the new husband left the building and started boldly across a narrow plank bridge at the head of the falls, he slipped. For a moment he clung to a projection. Then, while his wife reached futilely to help, he lost his hold and fell over the Bridal Veil to the gigantic boulders below.

The tale may not be true, but there are times when, even for a historian, investigation seems like a twin brother to stuffiness. For example, consider the name Telluride. On formally incorporating the town in 1878 its twenty-

*An epic pack train, mules loaded with cable destined to electrify a mine, gathered in
1897 in a twenty-year-old town on imposing Colorado Avenue.*

eight voters named it Columbia. Because of confusion with
Columbia, California, postal authorities in 1881 asked the
Colorado town to change its name. This time the city
fathers selected Telluride, which is a gold ore that also
contains tellurium. Ever since then purists have been
pointing out that no telluride exists in the area. But to
miners the name rang golden and that was enough. Myths,
even obvious myths, are generally more satisfying than
statistics anyway.

In one sense all the mines of the San Juan Mountains,
where Telluride is located, were born in fable. The entire
western part of the state had been given to Ute Indians, in
the usual language of Indian treaties, "for as long as the
grass shall grow and the streams shall run." White pressures on the San Juans were irresistible, however. Colorado's first gold stampede had come in 1859. Prospectors
who had learned their business first in California and later
in Nevada poured in eagerly, bringing with them a steadily
increasing knowledge of deep-lying ore deposits. By the
early 1870's, gold had paled before Colorado's abundance
of silver. Silver camps were springing boisterously alive in
many sections, and enough illegal prospectors had slipped
over the edges of the Ute reservation to scent the heady
promise in the San Juan Mountains. Because the sweets
were forbidden, they took on a dazzling lure. Where noth-

ing is known, anything is possible. Extravagant yarns of
treasures of white metal began filtering back to credulous
ears.

Utes or no, miners were going to chase those rainbows
to the ground. To prevent clashes the government in 1873
asked the Indians to sell the United States a big block of
the empty mountain lands—absolutely no one was there,
not even Utes; the mountains were far too precipitous for
hunting. Sensing the inevitable, the savages agreed. But
they clung jealously to the foothills that surround the
cloud-scraping cession on its northern, southern, and
western sides. This meant that ingress could be only from
the east.

The east is not the logical direction from which to approach the upper San Miguel River. Logically one should
come in from the west, up its red canyon from the foothills,
as today's highway does. But in the 1870's the Indians said
no. The first prospectors had to work their way in from the
east across formidable gorges and vast ridges of colored
sliderock 12,000 to 13,000 feet in elevation. They paused
to search every basin and founded several other camps on
the way. As a result ore-seekers did not penetrate the San
Miguel valley—or rather the timberline basins above the
valley—until late summer 1875.

They found dazzling ore. The initial small shipment
from the Smuggler, packed on donkeys over the divide to

the east in 1877 or so, is said to have returned $10,000. Other easily tapped veins carried up to 150 ounces of silver per ton. But the figures walked the dark edges of mockery. One disgruntled miner put it this way to a reporter from the Denver *Tribune*. " 'The San Juan is the best and worst mining country I ever struck. It has more and better mineral . . . but, you see, it's no good. You can't get at it except over ranges like that' (sticking his arm up at an angle of eighty degrees) 'and when you're in, you see, you're corralled by the mountains, so you can't get your ore out.' "

Grudgingly a sprawl of log cabins not cohesive enough to be a real town grew up in the valley. No one at first seriously considered a town. The divide was traversable only in summer, and who wanted to live permanently in such rigorous isolation? Still, that dazzling silver was undeniable. There had to be a focus of energy somewhere, and more and more people kept coming, not only men to work the mines, but others to supply them with the services they needed. Columbia (later Telluride) was incorporated almost in spite of itself.

By 1880 six or seven hundred people lived in the area. Many immigrants from the mining sections of Europe were among them, bringing knowledge of their ancient trade—principally Cornishmen, called Cousin Jacks, and Scandi-navians. Irish and Italian laborers imported by the railroads which were building robustly in all directions also caught the fever and joined the hopeful.

Ophir Pass, the "easiest" of the eastern crossings, even yielded a wagon road of sorts to the invaders. My stepfather's long-time friend, Loren G. Dennison used to tell with delight how he loaded his bride and her trunks into a spring wagon and came across Ophir in September, 1882. As they started down the western side, the trunks slid forward and Nellie Dennison had to sit with her legs braced until the joints cracked to keep from being catapulted onto the horses' backs. When the newlyweds reached home—a 12-by-14-foot shanty of rough pine boards, its inner walls and ceiling covered with canvas to hide cracks and knotholes—the townspeople gave them the usual tumultuous midnight charivari (shivaree, they called it) of horns, bells, gunshots, and banging dishpans. Outraged, the bride refused to show herself. Embarrassed for her, Denny passed out the traditional cigars to the men, candy to the women and children. Then, sensing that feelings were still wounded, he invited the entire town to Pamperon's brewery in a log cabin by the post office, where all ended well. Happenings like that made people believe they really might have a permanent settlement taking shape around them, after all. It was in that same period that the first stone and brick buildings began to appear.

DENVER PUBLIC LIBRARY WESTERN COLLECTION

*A daily clatter, processions of mules like this in 1898 went through town dragging timber and bound for the mountains. The stakes were used as props in the mines.*

*In the heyday of small business, the hardware store in Telluride was a prospering enterprise,
selling items essential for mine and home in its forthright building.*

When the blockading Utes were finally herded out of
western Colorado in 1880, the narrow-gauge Denver &
Rio Grande Railroad began pushing tracks toward their
erstwhile reservation, and Telluride believed joyously that
its isolation soon would end. By 1882 the rails had reached
within forty-five miles of the town. There they stopped
and showed no indication of coming closer. Still, this was
better than fighting the timberline passes to the east. At
last the town could develop the logical approach up the
river. Diminutive Otto Mears, the prodigious pathmaker
of the San Juans, built one of his many toll roads up the
twisting red canyon. Stagecoaches rocked and raced; Dave
Woods' big draft horses and ox teams hauled in powder,
pipe, clothing, and groceries in high-wheeled freight
wagons. But it was still expensive and, as always happens
in a new mining camp, ore values dwindled steadily. Costs
had to be cut if Telluride was to survive.

Since transportation prices seemed fixed, the next search
was for ways to produce ore more economically. All sorts
of patent devices were proposed for, in the words of one
skeptic, "physicking" silver out of the rock. Not many of
the purges worked. Then a Telluride lawyer named Lucien
Lucius Nunn came up with a vision that altered not only
mining but industry everywhere—the world's first long-
distance transmission of alternating electric current for
industrial purposes.

Ninth of eleven children, L. L. Nunn had been born in
1853 on a prosperous farm near Cleveland. He was bright
but aimless. After graduating from Cleveland Academy he
drifted around Europe, then settled briefly in Germany
under pretense of studying law. Back in Massachusetts,
where he lived with an older brother, he read more law
desultorily in a Boston office and audited a few lectures at
Harvard.

He was five feet one inch tall and weighed 115 pounds.
He had abnormally long arms, pale blue eyes, a hair line
that receded early, wavy brown hair around his ears, a
wide forehead and a sharp, receding chin. He never married. He was aggressively religious. He also had a Napoleon
complex. He inserted N as the middle initial in the name
of his brother Paul, who was seven years younger than he.
He kept a picture of Napoleon on his wall and often declared, "The character of Napoleon I understand better
than do any of his biographers." He supposed that he and
the French emperor were the same height and was sorely
downcast on learning, in middle age, that Napoleon had
been four inches taller.

In spite of his Napoleonic drives, Nunn reached the age
of twenty-seven (in 1880) with no visible prospects ahead
of him. Disconsolately he drifted into Colorado and in
1881 landed in Telluride. His first home was a tent, his
first job shingling a roof. Because he knew a little law,

prospective litigants came to him for advice. He brushed up enough to be admitted to the Colorado bar and, inevitably, began specializing in mining matters.

By 1888 he controlled the only bank in San Miguel County, held an interest in several mines, and owned three or four of the fanciest store buildings on Telluride's main street. Although a bachelor, he built the town's biggest residence for himself, two guest houses for important visitors, a plush office, and a stable that held sixteen stalls. There he kept for his own use a pair of silky white carriage horses and two blooded saddle animals which he rode as expertly as a race-track jockey. Perhaps because he spent a great deal of money, he overlooked no opportunity of making more. When his house was new and contained one of the camp's few bathtubs, a zinc-lined affair standing grandly high on carved iron legs, he reputedly rented it to miners down from the hills for fifty cents per immersion.

One of the mines with which he was associated was the Gold King. It contained quantities of good ore, but like most of the properties in the district was floundering under exorbitant costs. It lay above timberline southwest of town, and coal packed to it by donkey train for running its machinery cost $2,500 a month. Nunn decided that this was the point at which to start his attack.

What about electricity? By that time (1890) Telluride had begun experimenting with a little electric plant that so far had lighted only a few street corners and saloons. Most householders were afraid of the stuff. Like all pioneer power plants in the United States, Telluride's produced direct current, which it generated by harnessing water power. Motors were not yet in general use, but Nunn saw no reason why they could not be. There was plenty of water available, wasn't there? Promptly, without really knowing what he was about, he began surveying a line from a fork of the river below town up a cliff-studded mountainside 3,000 feet high and across a storm-swept timberline flat to the Gold King, 2.6 miles away.

That kind of headlong confidence was typical of the mountain mining camps. Just coming into such areas, blandly assured of extracting its minerals no matter what the conditions, demanded so imperturbable a faith that from a distance it sometimes looks like recklessness. Nunn had it. For example, when bandits robbed his bank of $30,000 in 1889, he instantly joined the pursuing posse. His blooded horse soon put him ahead of the sheriff's men, but by then the quarry was in sight. On he tore. The bandits, somewhat nonplussed by his ringing but solitary command to halt, turned around, disarmed him, exchanged his fine mount for one of their scrubby animals, and galloped away with the loot.

He attacked electricity with the same precipitousness. After starting his surveys, he wrote his brother Paul, a high-school teacher, to investigate possibilities. Experts snickered. Electric motors in those days ran on direct current, and for various technical reasons direct current simply could not be transmitted as far as the Nunns planned.

Unaware of their folly, Paul went to Pittsburgh to consult George Westinghouse. By chance Westinghouse and engineer William Stanley had just managed to light a village or two in the east with alternating current, which can be transmitted long distances. So far no one had produced a successful alternating-current motor, but Westinghouse had one on the boards. The Nunns' proposal gave him an opportunity to put it to test. He built them a primitive single-phase generator to install in a log cabin beside the river at a place called Ames, and a matching motor to be erected at the mine. In June, 1891, after a winter of tests under abominable conditions, operations began on a six-day-a-week basis. The cost of operating the machinery at the Gold King promptly tumbled from $2,500 to $500 a month. An entirely new era of mining began, just because a cocky little Napoleon in a cocky little town did not know how foolish he was.

Town and Nunn soon clashed. In 1892 he acquired another mine and began building a second line from the Ames plant to energize it. En route the wires contoured the heavily timbered hill south of Telluride. Nunn had his roustabouts clear a broad swath directly down the slope to the edge of town. In the swath he erected a branch line, but left it dangling anticlimactically at the city limits. He then asked the company whose direct-current plant lighted the town whether he might share in their exclusive franchise. Backed by a friendly mayor, they told him, not very politely, to take his line back up the hill.

Anticipating refusal, Nunn already had acquired several vacant lots located at appropriate intervals between the city limits and his residence, guest houses, office, and stable. He erected poles on these lots, very close to the street. In fact, the mayor thought they were on the street in a bald-faced violation of the electric light company's charter. Seething, he ordered the local constabulary to chop the poles down.

Nunn called a mass meeting and harangued it with fiery eloquence. Was this the land of freedom? Could not a private citizen use his own real estate to bring his own power to his own home? The listeners, who considered lighting charges too high anyway, roared through resolutions of protest, conveniently prepared in advance, and stormed out to re-erect new poles quietly readied by Nunn's employees during the meeting.

After a resounding exchange of writs and injunctions, the beleaguered town capitulated. The chartered plant switched to alternating current and thereafter bought its power from the little Napoleon. Old-timers boast that for years Telluride was the best-lighted town in the land. This possibly is mere opinion, but it is a fact that the domestic-science classes in the fine new red high school studied and practiced in America's first fully electrified school kitchen.

Sunday-afternoon carriage and horseback rides from Telluride to Ames to see the plant start up after its Saturday night-Sabbath morning shutdown became a favorite excursion. Vicious arcs jumped six feet long when the switches were thrown. After the display some pop-eyed miner always asked how long it took the alternating current to rush up the hill to the Gold King, give the armature a twist, and return. When told they were invariably indignant: 186,000 miles a second? Whose leg are you trying to pull, Mister? Farmers from the low country were equally suspicious. So imperious a substance obviously was draining vital essences from the water and their crops would suffer during the next irrigation.

Professional knowledge was, relatively speaking, not much better. Trained electrical engineers did not exist. Nunn had to develop on the spot the men he needed. He assembled a library in the shack at Ames and persuaded promising young collegians to work for him for board, room, thirty dollars a month, and practical training in a promising new field. They had to do everything—cook their own meals, patch flumes, repair motors, shovel snow, string wire, and, above all, improvise ways to meet emergencies such as no man had ever faced before.

Locally the trainees were called Pinheads. They, too, bred legends. In September, 1909, for instance, a telephone rang at Ames and a frantic voice told the Pinhead who answered to run for his life; the dam at Trout Lake, a storage reservoir up the canyon, had broken and a mass of water bristling with timbers was boring down upon the plant. Instead of running, the Pinheads took out their slide rules, calculated the volume of water and the dimensions of the canyon. They then made a mark on a pole at the height they thought the water would reach. Deciding they were safe, they climbed onto the roof and waited. Sure enough, the waters reached within three inches of the mark and then subsided.

Maybe so. But if the facts of the yarn aren't strictly true, the spirit is. That was the kind of resourcefulness Nunn had set out to find. When he left Telluride to become one of the leading entrepreneurs of the infant power industry, a career which culminated in the vast Ontario works at Niagara Falls, he carried with him certain novel educational ideas he had developed at Ames. These grew into two unique institutions to which he devoted much of his energy and money during his later life—Deep Springs, a self-help college preparatory school for boys near the California-Nevada border, and the Telluride Association at Cornell University, Ithaca, New York.

In the fall of 1891, while Nunn was still proving that a gold mine could be run by electricity, a tight little narrow-gauge railroad, the Rio Grande Southern, at last reached Telluride. Freight rates plummeted almost as dramatically as power costs had at the Gold King. Heavy machinery arrived, lower-grade ores showed a profit, the mines dug deeper. Telluride was off on its quarter-century run of prosperity. The panic of 1893 and the collapse in the price of silver pinched the camp only briefly, for by then gold values were being developed and gold prices were unaffected by a depression which prostrated most of the rest of Colorado.

It was a level sort of prosperity. Telluride never boomed the way storybook mining camps sometimes did. Exact population figures are hard to come by. A mining society is fluid. Even after the major veins had been located, hopeful prospectors kept drifting through the hills. Tramp miners and tramp journeymen (including females) moved in and out—rootless souls who worked until they had a little stake and then drifted on to see the rest of the world. Adventure-seeking city youths dropped by to estimate opportunities. Some stayed; many went eagerly home. Although the percentage of such floaters was not high, it did give rein to the irresistible tendency of small newspapers to brag. They swelled their own population estimates in off years and each decade angrily challenged the more modest discoveries of the official census taker. Perhaps they were right to complain that the figures slighted the town. Still, it is not likely that the camp—which includes both the town proper and the twenty-five mines and mills—ever held 5,000 people in one year.

Physically Telluride was compact. The houses stood almost shoulder to shoulder along a steeply rising tier of streets. But it was not a homogeneous town. Humans being what they are, the camp's residents divided themselves into classes as rigidly stratified as the roadways along which they lived.

The main street, which ran east and west, was Colorado Avenue. The avenue's lower (western) end was one of the tonier residential areas. In the middle stood the bank, newspaper, assay shop, lawyers' offices, the principal hotel, stores, and so on. At the upper (eastern) end were the fancier shops. Scattered in between were frequent saloons and gambling parlors.

The river, muddied by mill waste, and the railroad tracks formed the southern border of the town. Between the tracks and Colorado Avenue sprawled a conglomeration whose only unity was its lack of social distinction. The largest ethnic group in town, the Scandinavians, congregated in the western part of this section, complete with their social halls and native baths. Finn Hall stood closest to the tracks. The Swede-Finn Hall (Swedes raised in Finland) was a little higher. Swede Hall stood closest to Colorado Avenue, a hierarchy echoing the stratification that prevailed north of the avenue.

East of the Scandinavians were the warehouses, blacksmith shops, and the teeming livery stables. Railroad spurs ran to the mines nearest town; otherwise all the chemicals,

*High life in the silver town in 1908 boomed at the gambling tables of the Cosmopolitan
Saloon below elk heads and nude paintings, in the presence of an amiable sheriff.*

wire, powder, tools and whatnot that arrived by train had
to be forwarded to their destinations in wagons or on mule
and donkey back. A regular morning alarm clock throughout town was the rasp made by the ends of mule-packed
planks or pipes being dragged along the gravelly streets.
Neighs, brays, crunching wheels, and clattering hoofs
resounded throughout the day. Ore returned in the afternoon.

Sometimes prodigies were performed. When Dave
Wood had to take nearly a mile of unbroken cable to the
Nellie Mine, he computed how many feet a single mule
could carry. He then stretched the cable out in a long U
down one side of a street and up the other side. He spent
two days winding it into a series of coils four feet in diameter, each weighing the specified amount, one coil for
each side of a mule, with the proper length of slack between. At dawn on the third day he led his mules between
the lines of the U—even coiled it stretched more than a
block—hired a few packers to help lash the coils to the
saddles, and went his way as if it were just one more ordinary load. Very picturesque—but the daily disposal of

mountains of manure was a continuing civic headache and
the black, humming clouds of bluebottle flies drove house-
wives to distraction.

East of the stables was the red-light district, rows of
cubicles, called "the line," for the girls and on the corners
fancy bordellos, the Silver Bell, the Pick and Gad, and so
on. The ground floor of each bordello housed a bar, a
gambling room, a restaurant run by the town's few Chinese, and a dance hall. Tiny bedrooms were crowded along
the hall upstairs. The orchestras were considered first-class
and were manned by alcoholic musicians who had drifted
in at the end of unhappy roads.

Since the husky male laborers of Telluride outnumbered
women three or four to one (some estimates run as high as
ten to one), prostitution was bound to exist. The city
fathers preferred it in the open, where it could be controlled by strict licensing and by the personal supervision
of the town marshals, one of whom was known as Snake-
Eye Tyler. One theory held that prostitution enabled decent women to live in the Colorado mining camps un-
molested. In theory, too, drunks were locked up before

*Miners like these at the Smuggler Mine boardinghouse in the 1890's lived under crowded conditions and worked for low pay. Violent strikes broke out in 1901.*

they could become public nuisances, and minors were sent home instantly, lest licenses be revoked.

Be all that as it may, the high spirits of the young men generally found release in robust and primitive gusto rather than in sophisticated wantonness. Rugged practical jokes were a favorite. For example: my friend Harry Johnson and a few cronies were taking a few days off from their mining early one winter while they spent the proceeds of a lucky streak at roulette. A big, round-headed Swede prospector arrived from the hills to buy a new stove. They toasted him in the Pastime until he was mellow, then accompanied him to a hardware store to help him select his equipment. After he had strapped the stove he wanted onto his back—it weighed an awkward seventy-five pounds—his friends suggested one for the road. They kept on suggesting, leading him from saloon to saloon, while the rumor ran through town and crowds of curious dropped by and laid bets about how long this could go on. It was a rough time. Harry and his fellow pranksters did not get to bed until they were broke, two days later. But it was worth it. That unsuspecting Swede did not get the stove off his back for two days, either.

Simple strength was universally admired. Another item: the strongest man in Telluride was Martin Oija, a Norwegian miner who stood six and a half feet tall and weighed 250 pounds. Whenever a car loaded with ore jumped the track in the mine where he worked, Martin took hold of the coupling bar and lifted it back. The time he broke his leg he climbed, a hop at a time, two hundred feet up a ladder from the mine and went, leg dangling, to the company doctor without mentioning the matter to anyone else. No use making a fuss about a bone.

Though amiable when sober, Martin could be difficult when drunk. Displeased one night at the Silver Bell, he slammed his fist clear through the barroom wall. Thinking to quiet him, the bartender hit him from behind with a stool. Martin picked the fellow up, sat him on the bar, and told him not to do that again. The marshal then interfered and rapped Martin across the head with a pistol barrel. Martin took the gun away and started up town, rubbing his bruises and grumbling to himself. The marshal recruited three or four helpers and after a wild melee they wrestled him down. But Martin wasn't ready to give up yet. He clung so tenaciously to the wooden sidewalk that his captors had to fetch an ax, chop out a section of the planks, and lug him and sidewalk off to jail together.

The yarn is, once again, useful more for what it suggests than what it tells. Although as real as breath, Martin Oija was also a symbol of what most old-timers of the Colorado mountains proudly felt was the essence of their camps. Tough, but not bad. Strong, like the mountains. The old epic: man against nature, where faith in strength is instinctive and right.

Mining was necessarily violent work, especially in those days before automation and carefully checked safety rules. The land outside the mines was violent, too. Just before spring the big avalanches began to run. Their courses were known and named; one would suppose, in hindsight, that men would have quickly learned to avoid them. But every year some slide buried trails, shattered bridges, uprooted a few shacks. Now and then, when circumstances coincided evilly, one would smother men.

The worst was the slide that swept away part of the Liberty Bell mine at seven thirty in the morning on February 28, 1902. As rescuers hurried up from the town a second avalanche dropped on them. And finally, after the rescue work had ended and the weary men were heading back to town, a third slide fired a parting shot. I cannot determine exactly how many were injured during the triple blows, but the count reaches at least eleven. And nineteen died, including my great-uncle. My stepfather saved himself by seizing a tree as he was being hurled down the hill; there he clung, deafened and almost suffocated by the powdery snow which packed like cement into his ears, mouth, and nostrils.

Floods, common disasters nearly everywhere, reserved special twists for Telluride. The bursting of the dam at Trout Lake in 1909—the cataract the Pinheads reputedly calculated—cleared out much of the railroad for sixteen miles and isolated the town for weeks. Overnight Telluride reverted to pioneer ways, bringing in supplies over the old trails by muleback and wagon just as though the intervening decades had never existed. There may even be significance in the fact that the first packtrain to reach the desolated camp was loaded with kegs of beer.

When Cornet Creek flooded five years later, it picked up a mill dump (waste rock crushed as fine as dust by the milling process) and rolled it in a syrupy wave, studded with boulders, through the exact center of town. One woman was drowned, several homes were crushed, the lobby of the Sheridan Hotel was filled with mud to within inches of the ceiling, and the streets were chest deep in ooze. But mud is no problem to a mining town. Modeling their handiwork after the sluice boxes used in placer operations, fifty carpenters built a long flume through the middle of the camp; other townsmen using fire hoses then washed the debris into the flume and off to the river.

Most of the mines and mills closed on Sunday; on Saturday nights, therefore, the town was thronged and noisy. Otherwise there were few holidays—the Fourth of July, Labor Day, Christmas. Everyone saved up to make the

HOMER E. REID

*The great orator on the hustings, William Jennings Bryan spoke in Telluride in 1903.*
*Roofs, windows, and street were filled with believers in his free-silver cause.*

most of them. Gold pieces bulged in the workers' pockets. (The mines all paid in coin; a paper bill was a distrusted curiosity; and my mother insists that a quarter was the smallest coin in circulation.) The first stop was the clothing stores. On the eve of celebrations, these stayed open until midnight. A single clerk could wait on three or four men at once. He'd gauge the build of a customer by eye, pull a six-dollar black clay worsted suit off a pile according to size, say, "This looks about right," and sell it for twenty-five dollars—no try-on, no alteration. Shoes, white shirt, and stiff collar went the same way. The store threw in a black tie and pair of suspenders free. A clerk I knew, Ed Pierce, boasted he often sold by himself, in a single evening, merchandise worth $2,000. Each miner rolled his part of the transactions into a bundle under his arm and went to the barbershop for a bath, haircut, shampoo, shave, and facial. Then he was ready for the dance halls.

The Fourth of July celebrations, as I remember them through a boy's eyes, were magnificent beyond telling. Parades in the morning—brass bands, marching miners, fire engines buried in crepe paper, fraternal orders in uniform, princesses on wagons piled with evergreens and festooned by blue-and-white columbines. Dogs and firecrackers. Everywhere the unabashed ripple of muscle. Rock-drilling teams struggled to punch, within a specified time, the deepest hole into a ten-ton block of granite set on a platform in the middle of Colorado Avenue: two men per team, bare-chested, grunting prodigiously, one swinging a massive sledge, the other on his knees holding the drill steel while the spectators whooped and bet fantastic sums. Footracers in spangled tights. Tug-of-war teams, heaving on either end of a rope. Hose teams blasting each other off their feet with heads of ice water that had dropped from the peaktops.

In the afternoon there were horse races and a baseball game at the park below town. You went down with picnic baskets, tingling so from expectancy you could hardly stand it. The special quality seemed a part of the very air. Literally. About halfway through the day you realized what it was—the profound stillness beneath the gaiety. The distant *brump-brump-brump* of the stamp mills up toward Pandora was gone—that dim insistent rhythm as pervading and vital and unnoticed as the pumping of your heart—today it was gone. And you let out another whoop, louder than ever, shouting back the silence.

A strong town, not bad. In a special close-of-the-century edition on December 30, 1899, editor Curry proclaimed in the *Journal,* which he ran and which my grandfather owned:

Telluride is as quiet, peaceful, orderly, self-contained a community as can be found in the United States. The few of the crude customs of the frontier mining camps that once found lodgment here have long since departed. It is probably the only mining camp in the Rocky Mountain region that has never

*In a winter paralysis, a team crossing the street in 1911 was stuck off the track while the sleigh rode the surface. Winter routes were eventually trampled down.*

*Winter-cleared, today's town with its old hotel still open has shrunk in population
because of automated mining. It hopes to revive as a ski center.*

had a lynching, and where mob law has never attempted to usurp the duties of the courts and peace officers. There has never been but two or three murders. This is a community of high grade schools, ample churches, numerous social, benevolent, and literary orders.

Eighteen months later neither Curry nor my grandfather would have written those words. The spasms of labor trouble which had been wracking several Colorado mining camps with bitter violence reached Telluride in July, 1901. The climax of a long series of disputes came when the camp's new labor unions called a strike to enforce demands that certain Cornish-style contract systems of payment be abolished in favor of straight wages. The Mine Owners Association retorted by employing "scabs" on terms very similar to those it had just refused to the union. Bitterness flared into bloodshed. Union strikers and non-union strikebreakers fought with guns at the Smuggler-Union on the cliffs near timberline. Three men were killed and five wounded before the scabs surrendered, were marched over a 13,000-foot pass without being able to see their families, and told to keep moving. In town a strike-breaking deputy sheriff named W. J. Barney was seized, taken up Boomerang Hill, ruthlessly shot eleven times, and tossed aside into the brush. Arthur Collins, superintendent of the Smuggler-Union, was murdered by a shotgun blast as he sat reading beside the window of his home at Pandora.

Outbreaks continued sporadically during the next several years. At various times a Citizens Alliance, an organization of non-mining employers working in close accord with the local Mine Owners Association, drove union agitators out of town at gunpoint. According to the confessions of Harry Orchard—a dynamiter who later achieved notoriety for blowing up the depot at Cripple Creek, Colorado, killing thirteen men and injuring twenty-six and who dispatched the governor of Idaho by wiring a bomb to his gate—he and the leaders of the Western Federation of Miners seriously discussed getting even with Telluride by (a) rolling barrels full of dynamite down the hill into town or (b) poisoning the municipal reservoir with cyanide. Neither threat materialized. But in 1903 the state militia was sent in to restore order, though estimates about the actual need for troops vary markedly with the accounts one listens to.

North of Colorado Avenue (to return to social stratifications) life was determinedly genteel. The churches were on the north side. Poor, eagerly respectable Italian and Irish families gathered in the east end of this upper level, between the Catholic Church and the cemetery. Toward the center on the first street—the first strata—many of the married gamblers made their homes. They were carefully quiet and carefully elegant: dark suits, dark stetsons, silk ties, diamond stickpins. The wives of many of them, it was whispered, had once been prostitutes, chosen by their husbands with care and discrimination. They were quiet and very mannerly. They lived in well-kept houses set back in quiet little gardens, attended by starched, quiet little maids. But those houses always struck Theodora Kroeber, she recalls, as "shuttered houses," and that short section of the street as a "shuttered street." The wives of the gamblers seldom acknowledged each other, and outsiders rarely called; even as a child, Theodora says, she sensed that those women in their reach for acceptance had achieved only a crushing loneliness.

Merchants, bankers, mine and mill executives lived farther up the hill. The view was better from those streets, and because the slope faced south it caught the spring sun; crusted snow did not cling there so stubbornly as it did nearer the river.

Winters were long and needed combating. There were no plows. After each storm the merchants on Colorado Avenue shoveled the snow off the board sidewalks onto the edge of the street. By March the ridge was man high, and shoppers moved in a kind of canyon along the store fronts. In midstreet was another canyon, tramped out by freight sleds and pack mules. On below-zero mornings the frosted planks in the walk cracked underfoot like pistol shots. When spring came, water and ribbons of mud oozed into the stores.

As long as snow permitted, skaters repaired to the flooded marshes below town. Tobogganing was the popular sport, however. Skiing was utilitarian. Scandinavians sometimes traveled that way from the mines, riding homemade boards much longer than those used today, their bindings only a leather strap across their boot toes. A more spectacular descent was to sit on a miner's broad scoop shovel, hold the short handle up between your legs, and flash down a course packed by a recent avalanche. You went so fast (if you didn't tumble first) that your shovel seat grew—this is solemn truth—too hot for comfort.

Each wife above the avenue held an afternoon "at home" once a month on her own unvarying date—the second Friday, say, or the last Tuesday. If a woman journeyed any distance on these occasions, it was quite proper to travel horseback and wear riding clothes. But evening receptions, dances and theater parties (the train brought in traveling troupes and even circuses of surprising caliber) were highly formal—white ties, long gowns, shoulder-length gloves. For a really lavish do, hostesses imported dream desserts from Bauer's in Denver, carefully preserved in blocks of ice. Society in general had a definite Anglo cast. Capital, engineers, and managers came largely from Boston, London, or Australia. Some of the sojourners even brought their polo ponies.

The great event was, in local vernacular, "going out"—to Denver, Chicago, San Francisco. This had an ineffable flavor, not a periodic brushing off of rustication so much as a slow unwinding from the intensities of Telluride. Men made business calls, women shopped, children saw the dentist. Everyone took in the theaters and the newest restaurants. One grew bored and came home buoyantly.

Of all Telluride, I think I remember those homecomings most poignantly. We boarded a broad-gauge sleeper in the evening in Denver and awoke very early the next morning in Salida. There we transferred to the narrow-gauge Denver & Rio Grande for the climb across the Continental Divide. How that little train roared and belched and shook . . . and crept! When there were girls to show off to, the boys dropped off the front of a coach, swooped up wildflowers in a handful of grass, swung aboard the rear of the train, and presented the prize in panting pride.

At Ridgway we switched to the Rio Grande Southern tracks for the long, looping climb past the magnificent gray ramparts of Mt. Sneffels. Then down the spirals of Leopard Creek into San Miguel Canyon, lovely with its terraces of deep red sandstone and its leaning evergreens. By then late afternoon had come—or evening, if the train was late, which it generally was. The oil lamps suffused a dim radiance. On cold fall nights a spot of hot metal glowed in the stove at the end of the aisle; the stale air grew brassy. Everyone sank lower into his seat—smell of coal smoke in worn plush. The wheel flanges shrilled against the rails, shadows leaned as we creaked around curves. And then, as we pulled off Keystone Hill onto the willow flats below town, speed quickened. Everyone stood up to reach for bundles on the rack overhead. The click of the wheels deepened as the conductor opened the door. Leaning through, he bawled out his invariable wit, "To Hell You Ride!" and we were home again.

It did not last. Most of the mines closed during the 1920's. The depression of the 30's shattered the rest, despite a brief stimulus that came when President Roosevelt raised the price of gold. What little ore was produced by desultory lease operations traveled the rough gravelled roads in trucks. Locomotives and freight cars gave way to a monstrous hybrid called the Galloping Goose, a Pierce Arrow automobile rebuilt to run on rails and painted a silver-gray. Six or seven passengers could ride up front with the driver; the awkward van behind them could haul six or seven tons of freight. Shipments of uranium during World War II staved off death for a time, but in 1951 the debt-boggled little giant finally expired. Even its tracks have disappeared.

That same year, curiously enough, San Miguel County, of which Telluride is the county seat, ranked second among the metal-producing regions of Colorado. In 1950 and again in 1953 it ranked first, thanks mostly to the Idarado mine, which bought the old Smuggler-Union properties, added more claims as far away as the other side of the range at Red Mountain, and ever since has been burrowing out the entire uplift from one side to the other, milling the ore at a modernized plant at Pandora. Idarado officials are annoyed when they hear old-timers wish that

HOMER E. REID

*Winter reigns on Wilson Peak as spring starts on the mountainside. The meadow, like many in Telluride, seems a sign of prosperity with sheep feeding where the town's horses and mules once grazed. But the sheep are transients from Utah adding only to the scenery.*

mining would come back. They say it is back. Idarado miners, most of whom live in Telluride, produce as much ore today and the mill at Pandora turns out as much concentrate as every mine in the region put together turned out in the so-called boom era of sixty years ago.

It does not seem the same, however. Gold and silver are by-products now; the primary values are copper, lead and zinc. Technology has lifted ton-output per man sixfold over what it was at the turn of the century. As a result the labor force has shrunk sixfold.

The tumultuous herds of draft oxen, horses, and mules have disappeared. Once they found hay and pasture land on numerous ranches scattered along the benchlands bordering the canyons below town, pastoral fairylands that looked out on vistas of heart-catching loveliness. Now, in the summer, huge flocks of sheep graze there and scatter dandelion seeds; most of the animals are "foreign," brought out of the deserts of Utah for a quick fattening in Colorado before they go to market. A more romantic industry is movie-making; Hollywood has discovered the photogenic qualities of the area and an occasional camera crew drops in to shoot spectacular background scenes.

Nevertheless the shrinkage continues. By the fall of 1963 Telluride's population had declined to 600, most of them supported in one way or another by the Idarado's million-dollar-a-year payroll. There is some precariousness in depending on a single industry that eventually is sure to exhaust its ore bodies. Even so, the town has not lost faith in the future. Those stubborn six hundred know they live in one of the nation's most beautiful spots. They are confident tourists soon will find them. They do what they can to lure travelers. A principal attraction, in addition to trout streams and deer and elk hunting, is the jeep. Given a minimum boost in the way of removing boulders and fallen trees, those sturdy little four-wheel-drive vehicles can all but climb cliffs. The local jeep club has reso-

lutely cleared roads that tiptoe hair-raisingly across the precipices to timberline and beyond, opening views which many old-timers, for all their boasting, never saw; fifty years ago those remote, dazzling spots could not have been reached in reasonable time on horseback.

Another growing lure is the fall color of September—frost comes early to Telluride—when masses of aspen lie pure yellow against the rolling meadows or lace the spruce with pink and orange-red. But what the people dream of mostly is an angel who will appear with money enough to build a towering ski lift up the steep hill south of town, where Nunn built his power line, and then fortify it with a luxury resort where sportsmen can gather to take advantage of one of the heaviest snowfalls in the state. As Aspen, Sun Valley, and other resort centers have learned, the magnetism of winter developments carries merrily over into the crystal blue days of mountain summers. But Telluride's last residents are not content just to dream. A strong town. During much of 1963 volunteer workers manning chain saws and bulldozers spent their Sundays slowly clearing ski runs where more volunteers built as large a tow as the town could afford. A humble start—but a confident one, as in the old days. They'll show the world what they have.

The effort just might succeed. Telluride's gigantic peaks brood over one of the last untapped recreational areas in the United States. And this year (1964) her isolation is less forbidding than it ever was before: the final link soon will be paved in a road connecting with the new Navajo Trail highway, which leads past Four Corners, past the proposed new Canyonland National Park and the spectacular water playgrounds at Glen Canyon, to Phoenix and Los Angeles. Today no other comparable Rocky Mountain area lies so close to those burgeoning centers of population. Soon, the townspeople say, talking like prospectors again, soon the new boom will start and Telluride once more will become the Rocky Mountain fantasy that she used to be.

*A bounty of elk, brought in by hunters in 1910, confirmed the hunch of the adventurers twenty-five years earlier that the area would be a lively place to live.*

# The End of Their Wanderings

—

## *Choteau, Montana*

—

### BY  A.  B.  GUTHRIE,  JR.

The little town of Choteau, Montana, where I spent most of the first two decades of my life, is a bead in the strand of American westering, or, rather, a bead at the edge of a pattern, for the ways to the West were many and the great threads wound south of Montana.

The early settlers—in the 1880's—were one-time seekers of gold, one-time workers for fur companies, one-time Indian traders, one-time wanderers come to the end of their wanderings.

Gold drew them to the Montana mining camps of Bannack and Virginia City. Beaver and buffalo brought them up the Missouri. Indians with their just-discovered de-

pendence on wrought metal and whiskey took them to outposts.

Then the gold was panned. The fur trade languished. The traffic with redmen pinched out or was pinched out. But there had come along a rich substitute, the substitute of grass, for men had discovered that cattle and sheep and horses throve on the high plains' costless forage. Even in winter, they said, even without grain or hay. They were misled about winter, but the substitute was nevertheless real and nevertheless rich.

So some of the miners settled in and near Choteau and turned into ranchers. So did some whose business had been fur. So did a trader, for reasons later stated. And after them came others, pursuers of the free gold that was grass, a multiplication in ratio to the Indians' diminishment.

Samples:

Sam Burd of New York, bound for Virginia City, came across the plains in 1864. Subsequent occupation: freighter and stock raiser.

Francois Truchot, born in France, traveled to Utah and reached Montana in 1859. First a trapper, he turned rancher.

Charles Chouquette of St. Louis came up the Missouri in 1844. For twenty-eight years he worked for the American Fur Company, then settled at Choteau.

John Wren of Pennsylvania also ascended the Missouri for the American Fur Company. Later occupations: miner and ranchman.

Different origins. Different names. Various routes and means of travel. Yet these and all the followers of the sun somehow seem alike. They push into the push of western winds. They ford the streams, climb the hills, pitch down the pitches and roll interminably across the interminable prairie. They buck that impossible river, the Missouri, sawyers here, planters there, sandbars everywhere and no channel anywhere.

Why? Gold? Furs? Profits? No.

There was adventure in their hearts.

And something else.

Out of my boyhood re-emerge the real old-timers of my town. James Gibson, first man to homestead in the upper Teton valley. Ed Garrett. Uncle Al Warner. Sterling McDonald. Others. Even my father, who came along later. It can't be mere imagination or my distance from their days that puts the look of distance in their faces.

Like many another high-plains town, Choteau is an accident of trail and geography—and in its case, government Indian policy—and of enduring resources that didn't exist or didn't endure for uncounted camps that gold or speculation or exuberant folly created and saw die. It is a spot embraced by blue distances. It is an island in shimmering space. It is a church-and-bar cluster with wheat elevators and stockyards. It is wind and dust and high sky and small talk. Its distinctions are close to absolute, as distinctions tend to be in Montana. You are either a Republican, which means you are pally with Birchites, or you're a Democrat and Farmers' Union man (which nearly equate), and hence sympathetic with Commies.

Nothing much there, a man might say and be partly right; yet that judgment, generally exercised, would debase and belittle western history and ignore many values. It is incidental but persuasive that a man like me belongs to his place somehow, to early circumstances and experiences and observations, to the community that shaped him and helped plot his course.

However alike towns may be, however related in history, no town is typical. Choteau may lay claim to four marks of distinction and call some of them unique.

My atlas lists but one town of that name.

Its weekly paper, the *Acantha*, has no nominal rival that I can find.

Some of the first white settlers planted trees to flank the broad main street. They're there yet, some of them, the grandfathers of cottonwoods; and the motorist drops down from the parched and treeless benches that shoulder the place and sighs at the prospect of shade. In other climates one might expect such foliage, though not along the main street, but on the high plains of Montana where little towns for the most part blister at the sun's touch, it comes as a welcome astonishment.

And surely Choteau (pronounced show-toe) is the only settlement to be founded by nomadic Indians, in this case the Blackfeet. They were allowed, these once proud claimers of thousands of square miles, to choose the site of the first agency on the restricted lands the white men had said were to be theirs, inviolably. They picked Choteau or a site so close as to give the place in later years the name of Old Agency. The Blackfeet, who earlier had killed four Cree Indians there, knew the immediate area as Four Persons.

The agency, the headquarters, that is, for government management of Blackfoot affairs, was to be situated on 640 acres of land, as it shortly was. A stockade with portholes went up, along with quarters for staff members and the white man's enforcers. Stores of food, arms, and the like were moved in. No pictures exist of the fortification insofar as I know, and none can be taken now. In later years, the government moved off or sold or destroyed the last stick of timber and sold, in pieces, the section of land—at a top price of $2.50 an acre. But recent interest has marked the site, and a couple or three small excavations attest the location. And if you look hard, as I have, you may spot a square nail.

The Blackfeet chose a good site. Two streams, Spring Creek and the Teton River, watered the valley. Close together to the north, they united a few miles to the south. Along them grew willow and black birch and cottonwood, as well as serviceberry, chokecherry, and bullberry. There were beaver in the streams, and fish, though the latter could hardly have been an inducement to folk who feared to offend the "Under-Water People" by eating their representatives. Up on the benches were buffalo in plenty.

Though written evidence is scanty, undoubtedly the mountain men, the fur hunters, the free trappers, the partners of old Jim Bridger and the adherents of the great American Fur Company, coming from Fort Union or Fort Benton, planted their traps in the clear and beavered streams, ever alert for Blackfeet, else surely dead. Echoes of those times sound when a man stumbles upon a piece of metal that might have been an arrowhead or finds in the remains of a buffalo wallow a disintegrating buffalo horn. The assumption that fur hunters hunted here finds support in the fact that numerous one-time employees of the fur company settled in and near Choteau.

Earlier times, times beyond the sure reach of history, float like a mist in a man's mind when, having journeyed a few miles from town, he picks up a stone arrowhead at the foot of a buffalo trap, or pishkun, for tribal remembrance embraces no tradition of fabrication from flint and obsidian. And westward, along the foot of the mountains, runs the Old North Trail, subject to no more than the surmise that in years erased from knowledge the Siberians who were to become our American Indians paced southward, having crossed a land bridge which connected their homeland with Alaska.

In effect the Indians of the sixties said, indicating their choice of an agency site: Here is the place. And so for a while it was, from 1869 to 1875, when, with the reduction of the reservation, the agency moved north to Badger Creek and eventually, in 1894, to Browning, the present headquarters, some seventy miles from the original site.

The Montana *Post*, published at Helena, was happy that the Indians had been allowed to choose the grounds for the first agency. It commented, in 1868, "This disposition on the part of Capt. [Nat.] Pope to consult the wishes of the Blackfeet in this manner is indicative of a new and more equitable Indian policy, which cannot fail to result in good to the people of this Territory."

The writer wrote a little too soon. Hardly more than a year later a doughty brevet colonel by the name of Eugene M. Baker led a column of cavalry and mounted infantry against the Piegan Blackfeet. The Indians were not on the warpath, but certain of them, members of Mountain Chief's band, had committed thefts and murders, and white settlers were demanding protection and retaliation. With the encouragement—and later the stubborn protection—of the highest officers of the war department, Colonel Baker led away from Fort Shaw and passed east of Choteau on his way to the Marias River, where the Indians were reported encamped. That was in January of 1870, and the weather was bitter; as cold, some said later, as forty below. The given target was Mountain Chief's band. Sure enough, there was a camp on the Marias. Baker and his men sur-

COURTESY OF LARRY BANKS

*Its main street a stretch of prairie, Choteau in 1890 was a town of hitching posts and saloons, shops with false fronts, and trees planted by the settlers.*

prised it one morning and trod the road to glory—temporarily. With the target practice over and the smoke cleared away, the colonel counted 173 dead Indians, more than 100 captive women and children and more than 100 spoils-of-war horses, all at the cost of one white life and one white leg broken in a fall from the saddle. Everything in the camp was destroyed, he reported. Word went out from the military that the expedition had been a complete success.

Success? The Indian agent, himself a military man though on special duty, made his investigation. Of the Indians killed, he reported, 90 were women and 55 children. Thirty-three men had been shot down, but only 15 could be called young or fighting men. The lives of 18 women and nineteen children had been spared.

Other facts transpired to diminish the colonel's proud victory. The camp was not Mountain Chief's but that of Bear Chief and Red Horn, whose people had not been accused of crime. The band was plagued with smallpox. On the grounds, first, that some children were found to be sick and, second, that the command lacked transportation for captives, the surviving women and children, scantily clad, without shelter or prospect of succor, were turned loose in the frosted miles.

I have not checked on the later career of Colonel Baker, fearing to find that he did not come to a bad end.

Montana generally approved this feat of arms; and, indeed, the mindless savagery of it did frighten the Indians into a closer compliance with piety. Choteau had no opinion: the town wasn't born yet.

But the first agency hadn't lived long before a white trader, A. B. Hamilton, established a post close by. I. N. Hazlett joined him a couple of years later, and the two are often referred to as the founders of Choteau, though the truth of the assignment is fractional. With the survey of the townsite in 1883 Hamilton gave the settlement its name, intending thus to recognize Pierre Chouteau, Jr., one of the principal members of the American Fur Company. Somewhere in the works the first "u" got dropped and never found its way back, although the misspelling didn't altogether please the kinsmen of the honoree.

The present Teton County, in which Choteau is located, was then part of Chouteau County, which kept and keeps that first "u." Chouteau County was impossibly big, embracing a large part of northern Montana. When Teton County was scissored off, three villages, if they could be called even that, immediately determined, each on its own, that by nature, by justice, and by God, it would be the seat of the county. One was Dupuyer, some thirty-five miles north of Choteau; Bynum, fourteen; and the other, naturally, Choteau, the temporary capital.

But the name of the county came first. No difficulty attended the matter, though people today disagree as to reasons. As impressive a volume as the *Montana Almanac*

states that the county got its name from the Teton Indians, a branch of the Sioux, with a heartland hundreds of miles to the east and south. One is inclined to suspect that the *Almanac's* source was propriety, for the French *teton* means the breast of a woman. It was from the bald and nippled buttes that stand out from its shores that the Teton River, in earlier times variously called the Tansy, the Rose, and the Breast, got its eventual name. It stands to reason the county drew, directly or indirectly, on the same symbol.

In these settled days one reads with amusement of the capital and county-seat fights so common in American history. But they were real, and they must have been fun if only because conflict fed the current of life; and they brought to newspaper pages, though in mannered language, a vigor and spirit and individuality now largely dead.

In its first issue the *Acantha*, rooting then for Dupuyer because that was its birthplace, announced:

"Today the *Acantha* is launched upon the journalistic world and the fight for the county seat begins in earnest. Dupuyer takes her place in the arena, and she will emerge wearing the laurel wreath of victory. . . . The young gladiator, whose appearance is hailed upon all sides with shouts of welcome and encouragement, whose claims are those of truth and justice, will overthrow all opponents and win the fight. . . ."

The writer added with fine condescension:

"The valley of the Teton is capable of supporting a nice little town. Choteau will be a good trading post after the county seat is moved to Dupuyer. No one will be injured by the change save a few town lot sharps."

The *Acantha* was contemptuous of Bynum, saying, "The little Bynum boomlet has come and gone." It added that people were beginning to wonder why they ever considered establishing the county seat on "an inhospitable prairie."

Choteau had an editorial defender in the *Montanian*, another county paper. The other choices would satisfy merely "the speculative disposition of certain persons and the jealousies and spites of others." It then reported with some editorial license:

"The Dupuyer *Acantha* is the significant name of the new "Helena-for-the-capital and Dupuyer-for-the-county-seat organ."

In my boyhood, rumors still whispered that the monstrous purses of those warring and wanton copper kings, Marcus Daly and Williams Andrews Clark, had determined this or that Teton-newspaper position in the capital-city fight between Anaconda and Helena; yet there's no open mention of bribery in the old papers I've read.

The *Acantha's* truth and justice did not prevail. In the election of November, 1894, the tally went: For Choteau, 517; Bynum, 198, and Dupuyer, just 5—a figure that must have gone to show that you couldn't believe what you saw in the newspapers.

Bynum is little more than a crossroads these days, and Dupuyer just a bit bigger. Yet the *Acantha* editor in Dupuyer had in his mix one pinch of prophet. The valley of the Teton was and is capable of supporting a nice little town. It was so nice that within a decade the *Acantha* forsook its stricken young gladiator and moved in with the victor.

The *Acantha* wasn't the first newspaper in what was, or what came to be, the original County of Teton. The Choteau *Calumet,* the *Montanian,* and the Teton *Times* antedated it; but it alone survived, and for that reason—and for its name—gets more attention here.

Outlanders bound north and south between Yellowstone and Glacier parks, if they happen to see a copy of the *Acantha,* wonder at its name, as do inquisitive local readers, too. You would think that the *Acantha* would have accounted for its name first thing. It didn't, perhaps preferring that its puzzled readers guess. Some of them are guessing still, but most don't care, familiarity having come to be acceptance, and not even the present ownership is able to explain. Yet evidence is there. The acanthus is a prickly plant, once widely imitated in ornamental architecture, and "acantha" means a prickle. Add that the editor signed his notes Quill Driver, and you have *Acantha.*

Just who Quill Driver was no one professes to know. The paper came out first as the publication of England and Wright. Almost at once the name of Wright was dropped from the masthead, which then listed Hardy F. England as publisher. Perhaps the writer was Charles E. Trescott, who purchased the paper in 1895, later moved it to Choteau and still later, in 1907, sold it to my father. He couldn't keep out of newspapermaking, though. Some years afterwards, after my father himself had sold out, Trescott founded the Choteau *Montanan.* He is in my eye yet, a portly, mustached man, gruff, educated and prickly and not unacquainted with the bottle. It would have been like him to hit upon *Acantha* and Quill Driver as descriptions and mates.

Whoever Quill Driver was, he calls to mind the old and usually wandering editor who went about with his prejudices, a shirtful of type, a headful of classical references, and probably a thirst. The disappearance of the tribe is unhappy. They brought courage and individuality, orneriness and life and fun to newspapermaking—qualities which nowadays the country press has so little of.

Flavorful as they could be, however, the newspapers didn't capture the full flavor of the Teton frontier. Stories unprinted but still told for their humor add a seasoning that lingers after the taste of laughter.

A sheepherder died in a blizzard outside Dupuyer. Once the body was brought into town, a problem confronted the winter-bound residents. Who would deliver the funeral oration? The one man deemed literate enough was the justice of the peace who, unhappily, happened to be an atheist. It took a lot of prodding to make him consent. At the services, such as they were, he dwelt at length on the good qualities of the dead man, those he could find at least, remarked soberly on the inevitability of death and concluded:

"And now, just in case there is a God, we'll all repeat the Lord's Prayer."

And near Choteau another sheepherder out with his flock froze to death in a storm. By the time it was found, his body was as hard as a plowshare. The town had just elected a coroner, a tailor by the name of Jake Schmidt, who presumably was as well qualified as anyone else. So now the town could have an inquest. It had to have one, said Jake's fellows, without pleading that it had been a long time between entertainments, if not between drinks. They arranged themselves along the sides of the Joseph Hirshberg and Company store. The body was brought in, still in its deep freeze, and deposited on a platform that rested on two sawhorses. Jake was late, probably because he had wanted to be suitably dressed. He came in wearing a swallowtail coat and striped choke-bore trousers. Fitting, indeed. But this was his first case, and that fact and the presence of so many onlookers flustered him. Uncertainly he walked to the body, put a finger on it at one place, then another. His verdict:

"Boys, this man is in a damn bad fix."

There are many stories involving the sheepherder, who was—and in a measure still is—a target of derision. He smelled bad, unless by rare chance you liked the smell of sheep. Acrawl on him were likely to be a couple of sheep ticks, those squat, white bugs that would gag a trout. Mostly he served his days afoot—in contrast to the dashing elevation of the cowpuncher—and his days were long and lonely. I know. I've herded sheep on occasion. The sun comes up and inches its sweep across the giant sky. With the sheep grazing peacefully, the herder scratches himself and asks his sheep dog what to do, and maybe he climbs a butte and, to pass the endless time, builds a cairn of rocks, a sheepherder's monument, many of which still crown the hills like assertions of personality against infinity. He talks to himself and to his dog, and at last the slow sun bids good night, and he beds down his band and goes to his wagon and heats his solitary meal.

Or the weather turns rough, and out of the north comes a wind of spiked hate and with it a sweeping, blind smother of snow. For the herder a commandment stands, an unwritten and unuttered first article: Stick with the sheep! He may die, but, low as his rank is, here is his honor, this sticking.

All sheepherders are crazy, they say, equating occupation with idiocy when not universalizing one case. But long solitude does make some herders queer, and a few it deranges. The stereotype gets etched deeper when the herder comes to town. The contrast, the company, is too much for him. Not all of them but all in my experience blow their money. They drink until prostrate. They shower coins for children to scramble for. They get bled by leeches. One or more, that's for them. And I am regretful but not overcritical, considering.

And I suppose it is the horse that makes the difference between old but enduring conceptions of cowpuncher and herder. The horse and the active as against passive hazard, and the relatively social as against lonely life, and the one-time scorn of sheep and the different smells of the animals, though cow manure itself is no bouquet.

I've seen the graveyard words in stone and wood, and what's the difference between "Drug to Death" and "Died in a Blizzard"?

Of political commentary the early papers had plenty, of social commentary virtually none. The editors were too busy fighting for community advantage, arguing over bond issues, promoting candidates and taking gleeful potshots at one another to report on the nature of their individual societies. Besides, what editor, boosting his town, wanted to take a hard look at it?

Here and there a small light shines, often cast by a contributor in one town to a paper in another. The Sun River *Times* told its readers: "The boom at Choteau still boometh, and the carpenters' hammers by day and the concussion of billiard balls, the music of violins and accordions, and the occasional shot in the suburbs by a stray cowboy, remind us that we are passing through the stages of a frontier town. A piano is expected soon and then we shall be utterly fixed."

It was still another sheepherder, of all people, who wrote of early Choteau as editors did not. His name, long since lost to the oldest old-timer, was Hance Mullien, and, though his writings lie dusty and unknown in foxed newspaper files, he tackled the social realities with fine spirit, sullied, however, by a hatred of Jews.

In 1892 the Teton *Times* reported that Mullien had written a thirty-eight-page book titled *Society out in Montana*. He must have done so, for the paper quoted passages, if reluctantly; but the people most likely to know of the booklet shake their heads blankly.

The Teton *Times* admitted that some of Mullien's observations had "sufficient veracity to make them interesting. . . . The publication seems to have been kept a profound secret and it was only this week that a few copies have found their way into the hands of our citizens."

Just to be fair, the paper impeached the witness before allowing his testimony. "Hance Mullien is a sheepherder, who when not engaged on the range, lives in a log cabin about 10 × 12 feet with a mud roof in the suburbs of

*Resting from the range, cowboys like these in 1889 came into Choteau to spend money freely in saloons and stores, but rarely fired guns and then only into the air.*

*The first elected officers of the county government, in an 1894 portrait at Choteau,*
*included three women, their role made possible by the egalitarian frontier.*

Choteau. To judge from the appearance of the man he is not one who would be thought competent to judge the merits of Montana society, with his ragged clothing, slouching gait and with the habits of a hermit. But these, if he continues as an author, will soon be reckoned eccentricities; but the fault evidenced throughout the whole book, that the mind of the writer grasps nothing but evil, is one not to be forgiven."

So to the evidence, presumably the least evil of it:

"Strung out on the sidewalk, waiting for the laboring men to come and 'blow themselves in,' the professionals of the town sit and figure out how much So-and-So has earned, how long he has been at work, how much they can fleece him for, and that his time is up for his regular spree.

"At the words 'Sheepherder in town,' there is a general scattering, and every place has a poker game in full blast when the innocent herder, with five or six hundred dollars tied up in his three months dirty garments, pokes his nose inside the door.

"The bright young man who comes to Montana with great expectations, whose childhood was carried in the arms of prayer, whose Sunday school days were the happiest of his life, sits now, ragged and dirty, behind a stack of poker chips. He has forgotten that the days of his youth are fast ebbing away. He is a disgrace to labor in his personal appearance, and arguments against the laboring men's demand for shorter hours in the use of his time and money. His intentions may be to make a stake in Montana and go home, but at present his whole life is concentrated on a jackpot, a hole card and the vanishing stack of chips; while his half-starved old mother, back in Wisconsin or Ohio, cries out in heart-rending anguish, 'Oh Lord, where is that boy of mine tonight?'"

The loyalty of old-timers, one to another, vexed Mr. Mullien. Witness:

"Tom So-and-So is an old-timer, and a candidate for official honors. Turning to the crowd in the bar-room, one of his supporters says: 'I don't like his politics, but me and Tom used to eat sowbelly out of the same frying pan, on the trail, in them early days. We chased the same deer through the same brush. We mavericked on the same range. Mobbed the same horse thieves. Cheated the government on the same hay contract, and hired the same man to do time in the penitentiary for us. I don't like his politics, but Tom is a good fellow, an old-timer and a prominent citizen, —and I will vote for him.'"

Hance Mullien disappears from my record in 1893— with a black eye, that was not-quite-full payment, the *Montanian* indicated, for a letter of his that the Great Falls *Leader* published. Said the *Montanian,* "Tuesday evening Hance had a new townsite put around his left eye and barely escaped a coat of tar and feathers and a ride out of town on a rail."

Organized religion, with a resolution in inverse proportion to its forces, God excluded, came to town after defeat on the Teton River a couple of miles to the south. There, in 1859, the Jesuits built a mission of three rude buildings, thinking to have among the Blackfeet as much success in saving souls as they'd had among the Flatheads. They learned better. A Blackfoot compared to a Flathead was as a grizzly is to a brown bear. One year was enough, or almost. The fathers decamped, taking the name, St. Peter's, with them, in favor of a presumably better location, which was no better. They kept moving—had to—and at last acknowledged virtual defeat. They labored with bravery and dedication and in the name of the Lord endured hardships difficult to believe; and they accomplished nothing except hunger and no doubt chilblains unless there be marked up to their local credit a name that still stands: Priest Butte, a pitch of rock close to the original mission, five miles from the present town.

The later town itself, however much in need of grace, was pretty well content to go its way to hell. A state—and Choteau must have upped the ratio—that in 1896 had but one church for every 866 people and a saloon for each 107 might be a challenge to evangels, but it hardly wore the face of ready opportunity. Yet the Methodists came in 1894, notably in the person of the Reverend George Logan, resident minister. I suppose he was a good man according to his lights. Certainly he was dedicated. I remember him,

for he didn't leave the place till 1909. I remember him as a big horn cocked to an ear: deafness forced him to resign.

He recalled his early days in a report: "In the county there were 5 Methodists. . . . Logs had been cut to build a parsonage. I went to find these logs, but hunting for ready made house logs in the Rocky Mountains was like hunting for the proverbial needle in the haystack. The facts are, the church had not a cent's worth of property, nor a cent of money it could call its own, and no organization. . . ."

With the brave and hopeful faith that even the faithless must admire, he added, ". . . yet handfuls of precious seed had been sown, scattered from 1873 to 1894 by God-fearing self-sacrificing men."

He was thinking of the Reverend William W. Van Orsdel, "Brother Van" to everyone, conference superintendent of the Methodist church, who has become something of a legend in Montana. In 1872 he preached the first Protestant sermon to be heard in Teton County. He lived a long time and preached many more, often in saloons. The place didn't matter to him. Just give him an audience. If he was guilty of a sin, aside from the simplicity that embraces dogma, it was the cardinal sin of gluttony. He used to come to our house and weep for Jesus, then wolf Mother's fare. No matter. He was a man, promoter of churches, schools, and hospitals. His earnest yet agreeable conviction won him the esteem of all manner of men, including rowdy cowpunchers and saloonkeepers whose business he interrupted.

COURTESY OF LARRY BANKS

*Sporting the graces of a national institution, the town drugstore in 1900 had a marble-top fountain, fancy iron chairs, a full cigar stand, and cases of patent medicines.*

During the ministry of Brother Logan, it is good to record here, the Methodists and the Catholics for a time used the Methodist-church building with apparent satisfaction to both. An author later commented, needlessly but truly, "Such co-operation was indeed rare not only in those days but even at the present time."

After the Methodists came the Catholics and after them others. Today the count of churches and bars gives the churches a majority of one.

History keeps returning to the Blackfeet because, so to speak, they just went out of Choteau's back door. And they had been there before, long before, there was a back door. No prouder Indians ever lived, and none braver or more belligerent. With their allies but not kinsmen, the Gros Ventres, who were lumped with them in early designation, they warred and hunted and held frolic from Green River far into Canada, from the lands of the Flatheads to those of the Sioux and Crow. Battles they might lose, but never a war. What defeated them was smallpox, brought up the Missouri by the white man in 1837. The Blackfeet died by scores, by hundreds, indeed by thousands, and, so decimated, never rose again to old-time rank. Yet they remained warriors, those who lived and their successors, and as individuals and groups remained an ever-present danger until at last the white man had his way.

You seldom see a full-blood in the town these days, though you do see men and women and boys and girls whose skins are copper-toned, not always from a touch of Blackfoot but often from a touch of luckless, landless Chippewa and Cree. "Breeds," we call them, in derogation or accepted fact, depending; and there are people in their superiority who refer to them as "warwhoops." But without the Piegans, Bloods, and Blackfeet—the nominal divisions of the Blackfoot tribe—there'd be little history of Choteau and perhaps no town at all.

Nine agents for the white civilizers labored with the Blackfeet between 1863 and 1885. Of the nine, one was "relieved" of duty, one "removed," and two "suspended." Some agents were crooked; some incompetent; one or more, perhaps, conscientious, but undone by politics and by the indifference, ineptitude, or cupidity of superiors. Often suppliers of Indian food and goods were corrupt. The Indians had either to undergo cold and hunger and sometimes starvation or to steal. The stealings were simply added proof of Blackfoot incorrigibility.

In 1907 my father, then publisher of the Choteau *Acantha*, put an exhibit in evidence, an occurrence at the county fair:

"The stock parade had been formed, and the horses and cattle were being led down Main Street when they met the usual Indian outfit of two or three lean pack ponies, a small and badly worn wagon with a tumble-down cover, the whole presided over by an Indian and two squaws and followed by three or four hungry dogs.

"Naturally the Indians made way for the parade, but they were not attracted by it, and the squaws soon were busy with the garbage heaps on vacant lots near by. It was a meeting of the old and nearly dead past with the latest of what is modern; it was aboriginal savagery somewhat enlightened and improved coming face to face with conditions of civilization and passing them by with indifference which forbade even momentary curiosity.

"The horses and cattle in the parade, of the most highly improved breeds as they were, made the Indians' cayuses look all the more wretched. The blanketed squaws presented almost a forbidding contrast with their fashionably dressed sisters on the street.

"The incident called sharply to mind the apparently utter unconcern which progress in its march has for individuals and races. It seems to be eternally ordered that the less fit must cease, must perish. There is also a sad side to the consideration. All of the decay of the old Indian domination and picturesqueness, the shameful greed and injustice too often exercised against a people who were once supreme, their rapidly approaching extinction—all of this appeared if one really noticed what the passing little occurrence symbolized. It was a long epoch in the history of our national development."

The white man's good intentions often worked badly. A considerate agent let the Blackfeet consume government rations during the summer, when they should have been hunting. Came winter and no rations, and the tribe suffered. Under the treaty of 1855, Major Alfred J. Vaughan saw to the establishment of a government farm for the Blackfeet on Sun River, thirty miles or so south of what came to be Choteau. The land was fertile, and, after a good season, he felt greatly encouraged. Forlorn hope and wasted work. The men of the tribe were warriors and nomads and hunters, undisposed, while buffalo roamed, to settle down as white homesteaders did later. Yet the effort to instruct the Indians in agriculture continued at Old Agency, alias Choteau Town—and with as little success.

For all his mistreatment, for all his disinclination to become a tame Indian, the vanishing Blackfoot didn't vanish. An 1885 history of Montana counted 7,200 full bloods and 220 mixed bloods in 1876. This unofficial census is open to doubt. A head count of nomads, often off the reservation, often for months across the Canadian line, exceeded the powers both of bureaucrats and historians.

What is known for sure is that the enrolled members of the Incorporated Blackfeet Tribe of the Blackfeet Indian Reservation in Montana now number just short of 10,000. The rate of growth presumably has slowed with a recent tribal decision that infants must be at least one-quarter Indian to be true Blackfeet. Of the nearly ten thousand enrolled members only about one thousand are full bloods.

If the Blackfeet are vanishing, it is not by mismanagement but miscegenation.

More important to a town's becoming than the legalism of incorporation, it seems to me, is the first Fourth of July celebration. The early settlers apparently thought so, too, for Choteau saluted independence in 1883 long before it filed its papers. As part of the program, one Baptiste Champaigne read the Declaration.

I like to think of that, like to imagine I can hear "When in the Course of human Events. . ." recited by a man of French and possibly Indian blood—the record doesn't state—whose probably Gallic accent probably had been coarsened by his trader's years among the tribes. Choteau, a tiny melting pot, typical of others where breeds of men, schooled or not, met in obedience to the high demand of independence.

Rank criminality, apart from that justice by which both Indian and white excused their coups, was rare in Teton County and hangings rarer still. I doubt that more than one can be authenticated, and reports are contradictory and vague on it. The gunslingers of Dodge and Tombstone and their kind never came to Teton County, or went unreported or kept their guns cased. In the days before my time spreeing cowpunchers sometimes did discharge their Colts in town, but just for fun. In 1885 the Choteau *Calumet* spoke a largely true defense. "A few tenderfeet from the river metropolis (Fort Benton, obviously) have been circulating blood-curdling reports about the cowboys of Choteau. We trust that no intelligent person will for a moment believe that Choteau is controlled by any but the law-abiding citizens of the town. The cowboys do frequently visit Choteau, spend their money freely, and occasionally amuse themselves by shooting off their revolvers in the street, but there is nothing dangerous or desperate about them, and there are few if any of them who would not size up well with the average citizen of Benton or any other town in Montana."

Guns were for rattlesnakes and coyotes. Neither, in all Montana, were there violent differences between the growers of cattle and sheep. At one time they were opposed, but they didn't reach for their hardware. And soon, to employ a present and overworked word, they came to an accommodation. Mullien observed, as early as 1892, "The days when the sheepherder was denied the privilege of standing up to the same bar and drinking the same kind of whisky as the cow-puncher has passed away."

Just one shoot-out, just one man-to-man death that the screen takes as typical, occurred in old Teton County. That was at Robare, which bequeathed posterity a cemetery and little else, where Charles Simons, first on the draw, killed Charles A. Buckley in 1889.

Choteau always was on the edge of great things. Didn't the county embrace prime grazing land for cattle and sheep? It did and does. Couldn't hundreds of acres be irrigated? They could and were and are still. "New settlers are daily arriving and all bear testimony that we have the prettiest valley in Montana." Business? "Hamilton and Hazlett are receiving more goods than they can stow away. They sold a $500 bill before breakfast this morning. . . . Mr. Armstrong has sold his cattle to Main and Dennis. Consideration $14,000." Schools to attract parents ambitious for their children? Why, the grade school was established as early as 1884, the high school in 1901. "Should favorable report be received from the prospectors who are now in the main range 40 miles northwest of here, this place will spring into prominence as a supply point."

Early in the present century the buoyant residents marked up to progress such items as a telephone system of sorts, a flour mill, an electric-light plant, cement sidewalks, a creamery, new school buildings, a water system and two branch railway lines, the Great Northern and the Milwaukee, which eliminated, not without loss of color, the old livestock drives to Fort Benton and farther, and yet gave the passenger, through the unhurried indulgence of the crew, an opportunity to shoot at jack rabbits along the way to Great Falls. Progress was on the march all right. "We are again in the market for fat hens. Don't feed them the night before you bring them in."

But Choteau wasn't destined to be big. One, maybe more, of the very improvements it celebrated, like the paved road to Great Falls, worked against it. From a population of 720 in 1911, it has grown to one of only 1,966. Yet it was destined to be stable. More successfully than most, it survived the plight and flight of the dry-land homesteaders and later the great depression. It gets along today on cattle and sheep and, more and more in recent years, on wheat, which new methods of tillage, improved varieties of seed and government support have encouraged. It gets a share of tourist money, too, from travelers between Yellowstone and Glacier parks. Some of them remark, in this pleasant, cheerful, shaded town, on the occasional presence of whiskered men, or women and children companions in dowdy, just-alike uniforms. They aren't Amish. They're Hutterites and live communally and won't bear arms and renounce education beyond the eighth grade— and most of Choteau doesn't like them, not a one of the three hundred of them who live in the county after having been pushed out of Canada.

If you except the log cabin, which is no mean adaptation to environment, and the gewgaws of sixty and seventy years ago, Choteau has no traditional architecture. A good many buildings are still false-fronted, screening original log and rough lumber. Recent additions, whether residences, schools or hospital, are, as we say, up to date.

Neither can the community boast much of Hepplewhite, Chippendale, or Sheraton, reproduced or original. The people know little and care less about antiques. There is a reason. The fine old pieces of furniture followed the

*A crown in the big-sky country, Rattlesnake Butte outside of Choteau is a ridge of stone and a mound, a break in the vastness, a beacon to the roaming eye.*

waterways. A flatboat could accommodate much and, gliding with the current, didn't get sore-footed as wagon-trail animals, transporting less, assuredly did.

One building merits special attention. That is the courthouse, erected in 1906 at the end of the principal street. Alone of the buildings still standing, it was built of native stone, quarried out of what was known at one time as Grindstone Butte. The name was appropriate, for men chiseled grinding wheels from its stone. So is its present name, Rattlesnake Butte. Or so it was when rattlesnakes were abundant.

Out of my boyhood I can remember the prediction that the building wouldn't stand long. Weren't the building blocks sandstone, soft to the hard hand of the wind, saturable almost as sugar? But the building stands as stout as ever it did.

Probably, a son of the architect told me, its stones were cut and shaped by Irish and Croatian masons, for there were quite a few about in those days. Architecture? The son hesitated and at last answered with the uncertainty that allows for exception that it was "a sort of modified Romanesque."

I wouldn't know. I do know that, like the butte from which it was hewn, it does not offend nature. It looks as if it belonged there.

My father, together with dependents, came to Montana in 1901 to assume his duties as first principal of the Teton County Free High School, and nearly all my boyhood memories are of Choteau and the country roundabout, for we seldom ventured far afield.

That restriction of movement was all right, for all around the town, within reach of a boy's legs, was adventure. There were the fields and the fringes of woods along streams clear as air where suckers and whitefish and trout lay and flood water had scoured swimming holes at the bends. Gophers inhabited the fields and could be snared and sometimes tamed and sometimes, for fun, forced down the throat after being half-roasted on a stick. Prairie chickens with their nervous laughter fluttered from the thickets and could be shot when a boy was old enough. So could the teals and mallards on the potholes, the cottontails that sat fluid-eyed and sunning at the edges of the brush, the jack rabbits that bounced over the flatlands, leaving puffs of dust in seasons when stockmen searched the sky for rain.

And the wild fruits. The chokecherries. The buffalo berries. The "sarvice berries" that my father insisted against all local tongues were properly serviceberries. We harvested them, we youngsters particularly, for employment in pies and jams and syrups.

Shooting small game, catching fish, gathering berries, a boy got the feeling of self-sufficiency, the cozy comfort of being one with Robinson Crusoe or the Swiss Family Robinson. Nature wasn't too much for him. By wit and skill he lived on it.

Even winter had rewards. Skating. Sledding. Trapping muskrats. Daring blizzards while the snow cried to the step. Seeing freight wagons and teams and the turns they made on streets made broad on purpose. Watching the stagecoach gallop in from thirty miles away, its runners streaming sparks from gravel half-cleared of snow by other traffic. Napping warm behind the big wood stove, the dog alongside. The good cries of voices sharpened by below zero. The appearance of the cultural nonentity on the lyceum program, the cultural event of most importance. And after frost the chinook would blow, the benevolent wind from the west; and it sighed or whistled the promise of spring and all the waiting glories of the resurrection.

It was all good, all grand. A boy—I use that noun not in reference to me alone—could look twenty miles to the west, to the blue or snow-mantled wall of the Rockies, and find assurance there. Or he could look east to where the benchland rose, or south or north and feel at home in distances beyond reach of the mind. He was a natural part of this world, friend and killer of animals, eater of wild flesh and wild fruits, dipper in the waters, braver of the blizzards, finder of the first Johnny-jump-up and the woodsy Indian moccasin, hound-smeller of the season, of the growth he trod on unseeing, his nose undulled by age and nicotine. A good place to grow up in, Choteau, repository of wonders in itself and on its fringes, and what more was there to life?

After twenty-seven years afield I came home again, yet not quite home. The persons who had personalized the town of Choteau, the names that had given identity to it, largely were gone, taken by death or better prospects afar. Few in the town had memories that would reach to Jimmie Gibson and Al Warner and Ed Garrett or Ed Ferris or John G. Bair or Mrs. Nat Collins, "The Cattle Queen of Mon-

MUSEUM OF THE PLAINS INDIAN

*A Blackfoot burial, this rite of the tribe that originally controlled the range raised the body to the trees. But the custom, maintained on reservations, was stopped by the government.*

tana," or the Dr. Henri Beaupres or even of old Soo Son, a Chinese for whom, in 1933, the town gave a farewell party because he had decided to go home to die after forty-four honorable years in the county. There were no Cowells any more. No Cowgills. No Burrells. No Longmuirs. No Coles. None of those whose Sunday-feast laughter still rang in my ears, rattling what china lay unused in the cabinet. Thinking of them and others, I felt like a stranger, like a person displaced. When I spoke from my boyhood, none knew my references except the few whose memories spanned decades in the life of the town. Though I had observed the change fractionally while on vacation, now the fractions came together in a total that burdened me.

A new breed had come in, and some of these were already at the point of thinking of themselves as old-timers, the upstarts. It came to me with a jolt, for the years seemed so short and I not old by my count, that I had come to belong in the true ranks of old-timers.

Even the place names were lost, or largely so. Where were the Daly Lakes, where I hunted? Where was the Cascade Lane, that terror of the Model T? Where Ralston Gap? Where the Bynum and Red bridges? Where were the Hodgskiss and Woodmen's halls where we danced to the music of Mrs. K. B. Cohoe and a jeweler named Holland and whatever drummer could beat time to "There's a Long, Long Trail A-Winding?" Did anyone hunt the Burrell Lakes any more? You remember the Burrells! Built what was then a palace yon side of the Teton. Cashman Coulee? Used to be good for a brace of teal every trip. The ranch called Sober Up? The slough called Ox Bow, where we skated or fished according to season? The old swimming holes, replaced by a town tank that bore the printed plea, "Patrons are requested not to urinate in the pool"?

Few of these places of remembrance had disappeared: The impertinence of change had changed the old names. And places were called old now that were old only by newcomers' reckonings.

What had seemed great seemed diminished. The fields were smaller, the lakes shrunken, the swimming holes shallow, the creeks narrowed. Where was the old excitement, the sense of high adventure? I looked for myself and saw a strange boy with his world's enlargement in his eyes. Only distance remained as of old, distance and wind and the great blue lift of the Rockies. Buttes still swam away, and the wind could make you bend into it like a fullback charging the line, and Ear Mountain, called because of a fancied resemblance Elephant Ear Butte in years so long gone as to leave but an echo of origin, still stood guardian at the gorge of the Teton, but, looking at it, I wasn't tempted to sing about springtime in the Rockies. No more would I go to the hazel wood because a fire was in my head and cut and peel a hazel wand and hook a berry to a thread and catch a silver trout.

Yet here I was. Some men escape and some renounce their origins. I didn't want to. Most of me was what I had been, and most of what I had been I would always be, son of a scholar, boy explorer of field and stream, part bookman, part aborigine, and the core of me Choteau, Montana.

But later boys are growing up and later boys exploring, finding first what I found first. Trout still rise to a Royal Coachman, and gophers and rabbits inhabit the land close around, and a boy tangled in the brush will fight through to a beaver dam and call it his own and maybe name it the Inner Shrine as I once named a pool. Adventure is still here, the old adventure made new by new eyes.

If I had the choice, I would choose Choteau for the years of my boyhood, unchilled, as I am chilled now, by the presence in Teton County of eighteen Minute Man bases, eight of them within fifteen miles of the town.

*An ornate landmark, the Cone & Kimball Building with its clock tower attracted parasoled ladies in the 1880's. It still stands on Main Street with the hotel at its left.*

# Victorian Shadows on Walnut and Main

---

## *Red Bluff, California*

---

### BY OSCAR LEWIS

Red Bluff is a river town near the upper end of California's Central Valley. Sacramento, the state capital, lies 120 miles to the south; the California-Oregon border is about the same distance north, and the Pacific Ocean is approximately 80 miles due west. Except on the south, the town is ringed with mountains. Less than an hour's drive across the valley are the lower reaches of three ranges: the rugged Sierras and Siskiyous to the east and north and, to the west, the gently rolling Coast Range. On clear days—which are the rule except during the three hot summer months—two famous mountains may be seen. To the

northeast looms Lassen Peak, 10,455 feet high and the only recently active volcano on the continent. Mount Shasta stands athwart the head of the valley, its 14,162-foot crest perpetually blanketed in snow, visible for hundreds of miles in every direction. Viewed from the south, where it rises abruptly from the valley floor, Shasta has a solitary grandeur that once seen is unlikely ever to be forgotten.

Tehama County, of which Red Bluff is the county seat, has an area of about 3,000 square miles—roughly half that of the state of Connecticut—and is devoted mainly to lumbering, the raising of cattle and sheep and, on the irrigated lands near the river, to a variety of orchard and dairy products. Three main highways and a number of lesser roads converge on the town. U.S. Highways 99W and 99E—one on the west side of the river and the other on the east—join there; together they carry virtually all the valley's heavy north-south traffic. There, too, is the western terminus of State Highway 36, a scenic route that serves the Mount Lassen recreational area and passes over the crest of the Sierra to Susanville, 105 miles distant. A fourth through road, this one much less crowded, slants off to the northwest, meanders over the wooded ridges of the Coast Range, and eventually reaches the ocean at Humboldt Bay.

During any day of the year it is possible to stand at the corner of Main and Oak streets, where the three main highways meet, and in less than an hour count the license plates of twenty or more states. The fact that in recent years the nation has taken to the highways in such numbers has brought about revolutionary changes in the town's economy. It was because of the need to provide that army of transient motorists with meals and beds and gasoline and a variety of other products and services that this once staid and conservative country town unexpectedly found itself in the tourist business. And having embarked on that unlikely enterprise—and having found it uncommonly remunerative—the townspeople have been following it ever since, and on a steadily more elaborate scale. It was the tourists who built the group of luxurious motels at the lower end of town, with their landscaped grounds and swimming pools and neon "Vacancy" signs blinking on and off to attract the eye of the traveling public. The tourists account, too, for the restaurants, shops, and cocktail bars sandwiched between these posh resorts, and for the filling stations, garages, lunchrooms, and motor courts that line Red Bluff's Main Street from one end to the other.

Today the newly arrived motorist, driving past a succession of signs urging him to stop and dine or sleep or replenish his supply of fuel, might be led to believe that here is a town exclusively concerned with catering to the needs of the traveling public. Anyone who reaches that conclusion would be doing the town an injustice. The truth of the matter is that the tourist trade, conspicuous as its manifestations are, is only a part, and not the most important part, of its business life. Red Bluff is now, and has been for more than a century, the financial, trading, and distributing center for a region of orchards, farms, cattle ranges, and timber lands that extends for many miles in all directions. The visitor who wishes to learn something of the background and traditions of the real town would be well advised to leave the crowded through highways and explore the quiet streets that lie on their left and right.

Should one follow that advice, one of the first things to claim his attention would be the names of the streets them-selves. For when the town was first laid out, the streets running north and south were named for American Presidents, and the east-west streets for varieties of trees indigenous to the valley. (The one exception to that rule was the main business street which, after the all but universal custom of the day, became—and has remained—Main Street.) Today the sound of these traditional names falls pleasantly on the ear. To learn, for example, that the City Hall is at Washington and Pine, the Post Office at Walnut and Jefferson, the Veterans' Memorial at Oak and Monroe, and the Municipal Swimming Pool at the end of Sycamore gives one the feeling that the town is as much a part of the American tradition as chicken and dumplings or a Fourth of July parade, and the thought is somehow a comforting one.

A walk through the older residential district a few blocks back from the river does much to strengthen that impression; it also makes clear that the town has been in existence long enough to develop an individuality and flavor all its own. One attractive feature of this area is its many fine trees. Soon after the town was founded, the sidewalks along Washington, Jefferson, Madison, and their intersecting streets were planted with sycamores, black walnuts, and other varieties of shade trees. Over the years these have grown and spread out until their branches meet overhead. This casts whole streets into shade and does much to mitigate the midsummer heat when the temperature frequently rises to one hundred degrees or more. Like the streets themselves, the lots here are of a generous width, with rarely more than two or three houses to the block. With few exceptions, the houses date from well before the turn of the century. All are set in spacious gardens, and many are separated from the sidewalks by old-fashioned iron or picket fences.

It was there, a generation or more ago, that the town's leading merchants, county officials, and other business and professional men built their homes. And, because changes come slowly to these Sacramento Valley towns, the houses in many instances are still occupied by the children or grandchildren of their original owners. In architectural style the older homes vary from austere New England-type farmhouses dating from the 1860's or earlier (a number of these, still occupied and in good repair, are to be seen near the southern edge of the town) to those reflecting the ornate tastes of the 70's, 80's, and 90's. To whatever school they belong, however, all but a few have one feature in common: wide front porches where in former years the families gathered on summer evenings.

Unlike towns in many other parts of California, which have a habit of doubling in size at least once every decade, Red Bluff's growth has been comparatively modest. It took a full fifty years for its population, which stood at 3,500 in 1910, to reach 7,100 in 1960. One consequence of this more leisurely rate of increase is that although many of the old landmarks have been demolished to make way for progress in the form of chain stores, motels, and parking lots, enough remain to make it possible to visualize the town as it was three-quarters of a century and more ago. Then as now, the three square blocks bounded by Main, Walnut, Washington, and Elm streets made up the central business section. There were located the leading retail stores, the town's two banks, two of its three newspapers, and all but a few of its numerous bars. There, too, were the second-floor offices of doctors, lawyers, wheat and wool brokers, and other business and professional men.

On the west side of Washington Street, occupying the block between Oak and Pine, is the parklike Court House Square, which has been the seat of government of Tehama County since 1857. In recent years the original wooden court building, put up in the late 1850's, and its brick annex, which dated from the 1870's, were torn down and replaced by a larger but undistinguished court house of modern design and fireproof materials. Another recent addition is the county jail, which stands on the southwest corner of the square.

The two blocks on Main Street between Oak and Walnut have seen far fewer changes than elsewhere in the downtown area. There both sides of the street are solidly lined with narrow, two-story brick buildings, with stores, restaurants, bars, and other businesses on the street level and offices or living quarters above. Nearly all these picturesque structures date from the 1870's or earlier. Although on the ground floors new store fronts and other modern features have been installed, in only a few instances have the upper stories been changed. Thus, their façades still have the ornamental cornices and the elaborate window treatment common to mid-nineteenth-century commercial architecture in all parts of the country. Another feature that was long characteristic of this and other valley towns has disappeared. These were the wooden awnings, or marquees, that projected out from the store fronts, completely covering the sidewalk and sheltering pedestrians from the winter rains or midsummer sun.

Easily the outstanding example of the early town's business architecture is the Cone & Kimball Building, at the corner of Main and Walnut streets. This, an unusually large and handsomely designed structure for its time and place, was put up in the early 1870's by Joseph S. Cone (of whom more later) and L. C. Kimball, two of the county's leading citizens, whose general-merchandise store long occupied the ground floor. The second story is reached by a stairway on the Walnut Street side. Opening off the upper corridor is a series of spacious rooms with tall, narrow doors and windows, and bronze gas fixtures depending from plaster medallions in the center of their high ceilings. This second floor is no longer in use; there was a time, however, when occupation of one of these elegant chambers by a doctor or lawyer was regarded by the townspeople as proof of his high professional standing.

The Cone & Kimball Building's predominant feature is its ornate clock tower, which rises high above its immediate surroundings and is visible from all over the nearby countryside. The tower is easily the town's most conspicuous landmark. If Red Bluff ever has need of an identifying device for use on its official seal, it could hardly find a more appropriate symbol than this. Four successive generations of residents have regulated their comings and goings by the position of the hands on its four faces and by the sound of its bell tolling off the hours of the day and night. Only recently, after nearly nine decades of faithful service, has its mechanism worn out beyond the possibility of repair. To many, the motionless hands and silent bell have seemed both a reproach and a challenge. As this is written, a local service club is conducting a campaign to raise funds to replace the outworn machinery. If all goes according to plan, the venerable clock will presently again be performing its traditional function.

Red Bluff is so named because of a peculiar feature of the landscape; that is, for a stratum of reddish sand and gravel near the top of a cliff facing the Sacramento River a short distance up from the town. During its first few years, however, a number of other names were applied to the spot. Historian Hubert H. Bancroft states that when the town was first laid out it was called Leodocia. But Leodocia must have failed to find favor with the untutored first settlers, for the place was several times rechristened. It was known briefly as Bulltown, after Alpheus Bull, a partner in the merchandising firm of Bull, Baker & Company at the then flourishing mining town of Shasta City. Then it became Reedstown, honoring an early settler named E. C. Reed, after whom Reeds Creek, which passes through the lower end of town, was named. A year or two later it was being referred to as Cavertsburg (or Cavertsborough) for a local merchant who, under the name of M. L. Cavert & Company, conducted a trading and freight-forwarding business at the mouth of Reeds Creek. None of these names lasted long; the early-day settlers persisted in calling the place Red Bluff—or, less formally, "the Bluffs"—and so it has remained ever since.

The series of events that led to the town's founding date back to the first quarter of the last century. It was in 1821 that a Spanish-Californian named Luis Arguello led the first party of white men up the Sacramento valley to a point near its northern end. Although there is no record of the precise route Arguello followed, the probabilities are that he and his men passed the site of the future town. They were soon followed by others. In 1828, Jedediah Smith, who was breaking trails over the West, opened up the route between California and Oregon. Then came numerous others: members of the Wilkes and Young exploring parties, Hudson's Bay Company trappers, and assorted unattached hunters, trappers, and traders. By 1840 the trail, which on its passage down the valley closely followed the course of the river, had become the standard route for travel between California and the Northwest.

Up to that time the entire upper valley was uninhabited save for roving bands of Indians, most of whom belonged to the peaceful but unenterprising Wintun and Yana tribes. The first white man to settle there was a Danish emigrant named Peter Lassen, a blacksmith by trade, who had reached California in 1840. Three years later, while working for John A. Sutter at the latter's fort farther down the valley, Lassen and two companions set off after a band of Indians who had stolen a herd of Sutter's horses. The chase ended at a point a few miles north of present-day Red Bluff, where they overtook the Indians and recovered the animals. Lassen was so impressed at what he had seen of the northern end of the valley that he applied to the Mexican authorities at Monterey for a grant of land there. Later that year, 1843, he was given title to the Rancho Bosquejo, a 26,000-acre tract of range and farmland which lay in what is now Tehama County and which included the site of Red Bluff.

Peter Lassen was a man of ambition and enterprise, and had his judgment been on a par with his other qualities, he would be better remembered today. When he had worked at Sutter's Fort, it had been in a flourishing condition, mainly because of trade with the emigrant parties who were arriving in considerable numbers from beyond the Rockies. There is evidence that Lassen hoped to gain a share of that lucrative trade and at the same time to attract settlers to his lands. This he planned to accomplish by persuading the emigrants to leave the main trail at a point east of the Sierras and enter California by a more northerly route that would end at his ranch. His first step, accordingly, was to lay out a town that would serve as headquarters of his projected colony. The town, which he named Benton City after the expansionist senator, Thomas Hart Benton, was on the east bank of the river about twenty miles below where Red Bluff now stands.

That done, Lassen went back to Missouri and recruited a party of settlers. On the return trip he induced his own group, plus several wagonloads of other emigrants, to turn off the main trail and take what he described as an easier and shorter route. This was a bold venture on his part. For

LEO A. MC COY

*A long haul past the clock tower (left), teams like this in 1900 gave the staid business center a flavor of its overland beginnings. The van carried machinery.*

# OVERLAND MAIL ROUTE
## TO CALIFORNIA.

## Through in Six Days to Sacramento!

### CONNECTING WITH THE DAILY STAGES

To all the Interior Mining Towns in Northern California and Southern Oregon.
Ticketed through from PORTLAND, by the

# OREGON LINE OF STAGE COACHES!

## And the Rail Road from Oroville to Sacramento,

Passing through Oregon City, Salem, Albany, Corvallis, Eugene City, Oakland,
Winchester, Roseburg, Canyonville, Jacksonville, and in California—
Yreka, Trinity Centre, Shasta, Red Bluff, Tehama, Chico,
Oroville, Marysville to SACRAMENTO.

## TRAVELERS AVOID RISK of OCEAN TRAVEL

Pass through the HEART OF OREGON—the Valleys of Rogue River, Umpqua and Willamette.

This portion of the Pacific Slope embraces the most BEAUTIFUL and attractive, as well as some of the most
BOLD, GRAND and PICTUERESQUE SCENERY on the Continent. The highest snow-capped mountains, (Mt. HOOD,
Mt. SHASTA and others,) deepest ravines and most beautiful valleys.

Stages stop over one night at JACKSONVILLE and YREKA, for passengers to rest.
Passengers will be permitted to lay over at any point, and resume their
seats at pleasure, any time within one month.

## FARE THROUGH, FIFTY DOLLARS.

*Ticket Office at Arrigoni's Hotel, Portland.*

### H. W. CORBETT & Co.,

PORTLAND, July 19, 1366.

Proprietors Oregon Stage Line.

W. D. Carter, Printer, Front St., Portland, Oregon.

*A mid-century stagecoach poster, conveying the burgeoning spirit of the coastal west before
rails were laid, offered passengers a stop at Red Bluff and a look at scenic Mt. Shasta
outside of the valley town, all in a swift and safe journey.*

*Steamboats in 1860 boasted of their services to the town at the head of the Sacramento,
then a link to the gold mines and a way station to the Northwest.*

not only did the "Lassen Cut-Off," as it came to be called, pass through an extremely rugged country, but it was many miles longer than the regular trail. Nonetheless, the party eventually got safely through, and by the end of 1847 the future of Benton City looked bright. The discovery of gold early the following year brought a temporary check to Lassen's plans, for the rush to the diggings quickly depopulated his town. Before many months had passed, however, it began to appear that this new development augured well for the future of his enterprise. For by the end of 1848 a number of gold camps had sprung up in the foothills to the north and west of his holdings, and he envisioned the day when Benton City would become the principal trading and distributing center for that entire district.

Lassen shrewdly foresaw that the way to bring that about would be use the river and make the town accessible to the sources of supplies farther south. No roads then existed in the upper valley, and virtually everything needed to

sustain the new camps had to be carried many miles on the backs of pack animals—a slow and expensive procedure. Lassen hastened downriver to Sacramento, bought a small stern-wheel steamer, the *Lady Washington,* loaded her with merchandise, and headed her upstream. But again his hopes went unrealized. The *Lady Washington* lacked sufficient power to cope successfully with the currents and bars of the upper river; the trip to Benton City took a full three weeks, whereas the pack trains were covering the distance in less than half that time. Admitting defeat at last, Lassen sold his holdings in the valley and moved to the mountains of present-day Plumas County; there he was killed by Indians some ten years later.

Benton City quickly faded from the picture in the early 1850's. Today a concrete monument beside U.S. Highway 99E and an excavation that was once a cellar are all that remain to mark its site. There is an element of irony in the fact that although the town Lassen sought to establish has long since been forgotten, his name looms large

*In less than an emergency, the volunteer fire department pulled out its hose in front
of a flag-draped town hall during an 1880's Fourth of July celebration.*

in the nomenclature of the region: in a famous mountain, a California county, a national forest and national park, and a still-remembered transmountain trail.

The development of the valley soon proved the soundness of Lassen's theory that the Sacramento River provided the most expeditious and least expensive means of supplying the northern mines. For as operations at Shasta City, Weaverville, and the other towns of the area continued to grow, so likewise did the traffic on the river. As larger, more powerful steamers were put on the run from Sacramento, several new settlements were founded on the upper reaches of the stream, each hopeful of becoming the point where the cargoes would be unloaded and transferred to wagons or pack mules for the final leg of the trip to the diggings. The names of three such towns have been preserved: Danville, Trinidad City, and Red Bluff. Of these, the first two quickly disappeared; Red Bluff alone survived.

Not a great deal is known about Red Bluff's beginnings, and such details as have come down to us are often contradictory. Nevertheless, most versions agree that it was first laid out by a surveyor named Thorn (or Stout) in May (or June) 1850, and that Thorn (or Stout) was hired for that purpose by two men, Sashel (or Sachell) Woods and Charles L. Wilson. Both Woods and Wilson had been associated with Lassen's Benton City venture, and both bore the honorary title of Colonel—a not unusual distinction in the California of the day. Colonel Wilson, who later became one of the state's pioneer railroad builders, had bought part of Lassen's Rancho Bosquejo, and Colonel Woods was a member of the group that reached California by way of the Lassen Cut-Off.

The diary of J. Goldsborough Bruff, who led a party across the plains in 1849, throws some further light on the town's origin. Bruff, who was making his way up the Sacramento Valley in the spring of 1850, reached Lassen's rancho toward the end of April, and because he had a knowledge of surveying, its owner engaged him to prepare the first map of Benton City, then still in existence. His diary entry for May 2 reads:

"Colonels Woods & Wilson . . . wish me to accompany them to the 'Red Bluffs,' about thirty miles up the valley, to lay off a town there. They offer me 2 ounces per day, and board, with a good riding horse. Having previously engaged to lay off a town here for Lassen, whenever he is ready, and being under obligations to him, I can only go above if he will wait till I return. But as I know he is not ready, I shall merely observe to him that I wish to start tomorrow . . ."

His employer, however, was in no mood to wait. "Lassen objects to my going to the Bluffs . . . ," wrote Bruff the following day. "[He] expects me to keep my previous engagement, and says he will be ready at once." Several weeks later, on May 23, the diarist reported that he had been "introduced by Col. Woods to Mr. Thorn, a surveyor, whom he has engaged to lay off the town of Red Bluffs. They mounted and rode off, for the Bluffs."

From the above, it seems clear that the town was first "laid off" in late May or early June, 1850. At any rate, there is ample evidence that once under way the little settlement's growth was rapid. One account states that by the summer of 1852 the place had two hotels, two boarding-houses, three merchandise stores, two blacksmith shops (one of which built and repaired wagons), two corrals, a physician (who doubled as the town's druggist), a barber, and a population of from 100 to 150. The growth continued. In its issue of January 31, 1853, a San Francisco paper, the *Alta California,* carried this dispatch, "per Adams & Co.'s Express," under the heading, "Trade on the Upper River":

"We have before spoken of a trading post that has been established near Red Bluffs called Cavertsburg. It . . . commands an eligible and convenient position for all trading purposes, and is nearer the Shasta mining district than any other point that can be reached by water. Boats leave daily from this place [San Francisco] loaded with freight and passengers, and the town is represented as being a thriving little settlement. We received from this new commercial depot the following letter, with a prices current and a list from the house of Cavert & Co.:

" 'Cavertsburg, Jan. 26, 1853. To-day, in addition to our many arrivals by steam during the last week, we had the pleasure of welcoming the new and splendid Steamer GAZELLE, with a full cargo of assorted merchandise. Consignees—P. B. Reading, Todd & Jones, Fox & Co., Church & Mix, Cavert & Co. These houses have established at this point, and . . . will be able to furnish traders with a general assortment; and judging from the appearance of business to-day, we cannot but come to the conclusion that a heavy trade is springing up at this place. We counted, on our walk from the landing to the Upper Bluffs, 140 pack mules and 15 teams, loaded, and making their way to the interior. Being not only surprised but interested with the excitement of the business, I am prompted to forward to you to-day's Prices Current and a list of the steamboat arrivals.' "

Among the steamers that had recently reached the town the *Alta's* correspondent named the *Orient, G. Winter, Fashion, Sutter, Express, Daniel Moore,* and *Gazelle.* The charge for transporting freight from Sacramento to Red Bluff, he stated, was then from 4¢ to 4½¢ per pound, and from Red Bluff to Shasta, 6¢; the combined total, hence, was about $200 per ton. Then followed a list of articles carried in stock by the local merchants and the prices charged for them. Here are a few examples: "Flour, per bbl. $70; corn meal, do. $40; potatoes, per 100 lbs. $15; pork, clear, per bbl. $70; sugar, crushed, per lb. 25¢; brandy, American, per gal. $2.25; whisky, Monongahela, per gal. $1.50; blue flannel shirts, $3; heavy boots, per case, $84; gunpowder, 1-lb. cans, $1.50."

When the above dispatch was written, Red Bluff had been the head of navigation on the Sacramento a little less than three years. One steamer also on the run in 1853, the *Orient* (Captain Albert Foster) is believed to have been the first to reach the town; it is known that on one trip—presumably her first—she tied up at the mouth of Reeds Creek in the spring of 1850. Once it was demonstrated that the stream was navigable to that point, other ship-owners entered into competition for a share of the profitable upriver trade. One of the first of these was P. B. Reading, a leading merchant of the Shasta area. Reading's ship, the *Comanche,* was built especially for service on the upper river; she drew so little water (some twenty-two inches when fully loaded) that she is said to have been able to navigate "wherever the ground was a bit damp." The *Comanche* reached Red Bluff on her maiden trip in January, 1851, bringing two hundred tons of freight at $60 per ton.

By 1853 so many ships were engaged in this lucrative trade as to bring about a sharp drop in freight rates and passenger fares. Faced by that emergency the operators joined forces, organized the California Steam Navigation Company, and restored rates to their former levels. Thereafter until the California & Oregon Railroad was built up the valley in the early 1870's, the steamship company enjoyed a virtual monopoly on river traffic from Sacramento north. By the early eighteen-sixties, however, both the Shasta and Trinity mines had passed their crest, and the number of steamers regularly plying the upper river had dwindled to two: The *Victor,* Captain J. Rogers, and the *Gem,* commanded by A. Forbes. In June, 1864, a California Steam Navigation Company advertisement in the Red Bluff *Semi-Weekly Independent* announced that one or another of its steamers would "leave for Sacramento every Monday and Friday on the arrival of the stages from Shasta," and that passengers from the south would "be met on arrival by Stages for Shasta, French Gulch, Trinity and Scott Valley, Callahan's Ranch, Yreka and Jacksonville." The charge for passage between Sacramento and Red Bluff was then $10.

In the summer of 1862, William H. Brewer, member of a scientific party that was making a geological survey of the state, reached Red Bluff after a seven-day trip by steamer from San Francisco. In a letter dated Sunday, August 17, Brewer noted that the town was three hundred miles from Sacramento by water but less than half that distance by land. "Our boat," he added, "was the *Gem*, and we towed a barge with two hundred tons of freight . . ." The passage from Sacramento had consumed four days, for the little steamer, with the heavily loaded barge in tow, had made slow progress during the daylight hours, and after dark was tied up beside the bank, "it being impossible to run in the night, owing to snags, bars and rapids."

The *Gem* docked at the Red Bluff landing on the afternoon of August 16. The next day Brewer described the place as "a stirring little town of a few hundred inhabitants —saloons, taverns ('hotels'), and corrals being the chief features, for here pack trains and teams start for the whole northern country, Oregon, etc. But oh, how hot it is! I am writing at eleven o'clock at night and it is 94 degrees in my room—it has been 100 and 102 most of the day. I went to church this morning—an audience of about twenty-five only—in the schoolhouse. . . ."

Not long after Brewer's brief—and uncomfortably warm —stay, the town found itself playing host to another unexpected guest; namely, Mary A. Brown, widow of the celebrated abolitionist, "John Brown of Osawatomie." With her were three daughters, Annie, Sarah and Ellen (age twenty-three, eighteen, and ten respectively), a son, Salmon, and the latter's wife and two daughters. The party had recently completed an arduous overland trip from the east, carrying all they possessed in ox-drawn wagons. When it became known that the newcomers were homeless and almost destitute, a meeting was held at which the townspeople undertook, in the words of one of the local papers, to raise funds to build a "neat little cottage where, during her declining years the widow might be made comfortable in a home of her own."

The fund-raising campaign got under way in mid-April, and was presently attracting attention throughout northern California. Sacramento contributed $350 and San Francisco about the same amount; the balance—which amounted to approximately $2,500—was raised locally. With it the committee in charge bought a lot on Main Street near the corner of Willow, had an attractive five-room cottage built and furnished, and presented it to the widow. During the next several years Mary Brown was a familiar figure about the town, where she served as nursemaid to a number of the local families. In 1870 she sold the Red Bluff cottage and moved to the town of Rohnerville, in Humboldt County, where her eldest daughter, Annie, who had meanwhile married, was then living. Later she made a second move, this time to Saratoga, on the lower San Francisco Peninsula. There she lived until her death in 1884 at the age of sixty-four. The son, Salmon, operated a sheep ranch in southern Tehama County for several years; then he, too, moved elsewhere. So far as is known, no descendants of the family now live in the Red Bluff area. The John Brown cottage still stands on lower Main Street, the only present-day reminder of that curious episode of the town's past.

The advantages Red Bluff had long enjoyed as the head of navigation on the Sacramento were seriously threatened by the coming of the railroad. At the time, however, few seem to have realized that fact. The townspeople had long been waiting impatiently for the coming of the iron horse, and when the first train arrived on December 6, 1871, it was welcomed by this jubilant headline in a local newspaper: "Red Bluff to San Francisco Only a Twelve Hour Ride—Our Fondest Hopes Realized!" The story that followed was in the same exuberant vein. "Thank God," the editor exalted, "that we are no longer separated by distance . . . from the busy hives of industry that we have hitherto been compelled to visit . . . by means of mudwagons or that other played-out means of locomotion yclept steamboats. . ."

The town's jubilation was short-lived. For as the road was extended up the valley and eventually over the Siskiyous into Oregon, traffic on the river declined sharply. Thereafter the bulk of the freight and virtually all the passenger traffic went by rail, and only such bulky products as lumber, hay, and wheat continued to be shipped by the less expensive water route. Nonetheless, the picturesque steamers continued to visit the town, though in fewer numbers, for half a century longer. It was not until after the close of World War I that this colorful period of its history came to a final end.

Steamboating on the Sacramento would have ended much sooner than it did but for the fact that from the 1870's on, large areas of valley land were planted to a single crop: wheat. For the next twenty years the growing of wheat was a large-scale operation all over California's Central Valley. One of the largest and most successful of such enterprises in the Red Bluff area was the Cone Ranch, which consisted of close to 100,000 acres of farming and range lands. Its owner and operator was Joseph S. Cone, a native of Ohio, who reached California in 1850. In the early 1870's he acquired the Rancho de los Berrendos ("Ranch of the Antelopes"), a 14,000-acre tract fronting on the river a short distance below Red Bluff. This he added to from time to time until by 1890 he was the largest landowner in the northern end of the valley. The fertile lowlands were laid out in a series of wheat fields, and numerous herds of sheep ranged over the foothills. Both were major operations. During its heyday the ranch annually produced an average of 125,000 bushels of wheat and

*A wonder of the 1880's, the flume carried lumber thirty miles from a camp in the hills to a factory in town. This loftiest stretch was put in appropriate scale by a woman at the top and a group at its base. Abandoned, the flume was later torn down.*

300,000 pounds of wool. Several hundred workers were employed during the planting and harvesting seasons— the standard wage was $30 per month and found—and the assemblage of corrals, stables, barns, and sheds for the storage of reapers, plows, and other equipment gave the headquarters farm the appearance of a sizable village. The sacked wheat was left in the fields until the harvest was over. Then it was hauled to landings beside the river and loaded on barges, which were towed downstream to deep water on the upper bay and there transferred to the holds of sailing ships for delivery to the markets of the world.

By the mid-1890's lower prices and a decreasing yield per acre—the latter caused by planting the fields to the same crop year after year—had made the growing of wheat no longer profitable. The Cone Ranch and other large holdings were accordingly broken up and the land put to a variety of other uses, thereby inaugurating a new era in the economy of the region. Over the years the peach and almond and walnut orchards, the vineyards and dairies, and sheep and cattle ranches, greatly increased the productivity of the land and so added measurably to the prosperity of this, the area's chief trading center.

Today as in the past, however, the mainstay of the town's economy are the forests of pine and fir that cover the mountains to the east and west. For close to a century Red Bluff has been a major shipping point for lumber and an important center for the manufacture of wood products of many sorts. The first large-scale lumbering operation in the region was the Blue Ridge Flume and Lumber Company which in the early 1870's established logging camps and sawmills in the mountains to the northeast, built a thirty-mile-long flume to float the timber down to the town, and, on the east bank of the river, put up a large mill for the manufacture of doors, sash, blinds, and other products. The company was several times reorganized, eventually becoming the Sierra Lumber Company, under which name it continued to operate for many years. The flume was abandoned in 1911, and shortly thereafter the planing mill, which had long been the town's leading industry, also shut down. Later, operations were resumed under other management and on a larger scale at a 400-acre plant a short distance below Red Bluff. This is one of several wood-processing plants now active in or near the town.

Over the years Red Bluff has shared the experiences common to a number of other river towns up and down California's interior valley. Like them, it is a product of the gold rush, although no gold was ever mined within miles of its site. During its first half-dozen years it knew the excitement and violence and hectic activity of the gold camps themselves. After the gold fever had subsided, it lost its appearance and attributes of a frontier boom town and became by degrees a conservative shopping center serving a sparsely settled region of lumber camps, sheep and cattle ranches, and mile-square wheat fields.

That transition was not accomplished rapidly or without growing pains. As late as 1873 an English traveler, Charles Nordhoff, found its main street "to consist mainly of barrooms, livery-stables, barber shops and hotels, with an occasional store of merchandise sandwiched between," and concluded that if one did not look farther one would form "but a poor opinion of its people." He went on to state that on the residential streets a number of "pleasant, shady cottages" were to be seen, and that the townspeople had recently completed a handsome new schoolhouse. "Such enterprises," he commented, ". . . astonish the traveler, who imagines, in driving over the great plain, that it is almost uninhabited, but sees in a $30,000 schoolhouse . . . that not only are there people, but that they have the courage to bear taxation for good objects, and the means to pay."

Nordhoff failed to mention one feature characteristic of this and all the other Sacramento Valley towns. At the time of his visit and for several decades thereafter, High Street—which overlooks the river from the top of the cliff and is by far the most attractive location in the town—was occupied by the ramshackle wooden cabins of the local Chinatown, and, at its northern end, by a row of cottages housing Red Bluff's *filles de joie*. Both cabins and cottages have long since disappeared; today the thoroughfare, renamed Rio Street, is lined with the homes of prosperous merchants, professional men, and other pillars of respectability.

There have been other changes. But, unlike many towns in this fastest-growing state of the union, the old has not been completely buried beneath the new. The population has not remained static; it has merely increased at a less headlong pace than elsewhere. While evidences of progress are to be seen on every hand, so too, if one but looks, are numerous reminders of what may have been a simpler, less stressful way of life.

This commingling of the present with the past is to many the town's most interesting feature. The place abounds in contrasts. On Main Street one sees not only several score of down-to-the-minute motels, service stations and drive-in restaurants but, sandwiched between them, the two blocks of quaint, false-front stores dating from the 1870's and earlier. About its perimeter, new subdivisions cover what only a generation ago were hayfields, cow pastures and almond orchards, yet long lines of Victorian homes still line the streets of the older residential district. The old iron "Centennial Bridge"—so named because it was completed in 1876—has been replaced by a modern, four-lane concrete structure. On the far side of town, however, the Southern Pacific depot, a prime example of late-nineteenth-century railroad architecture, is still standing, although passenger trains operating over the company's Shasta route between San Francisco and Portland no longer stop at Red Bluff.

In the business district livery stables have given way to garages, and hitching posts to parking meters. Along the railroad, the warehouses of the wheat and wool brokers are deserted and falling to ruin, and the big sash-and-door mill across the river has, as stated earlier, disappeared entirely. Gone, too, is the Kingley Glove Factory that during the seventies and eighties made a brand of buckskin gloves famous all over the West. But compensating for the loss of these early enterprises is the giant wood-processing factory of the Diamond National Corporation and half a dozen other industrial plants.

Today's resident enjoys a variety of conveniences and privileges unknown to his parents and grandparents. Air conditioning and swimming pools have mitigated the discomfort of the hot summers; radios, TV, and local and metropolitan newspapers keep him in touch with the serious and frivolous concerns of the outside world, and he has reason to believe himself as well informed and knowledgeable as his fellows elsewhere. But for all his new-found advantages, he has not entirely shunted off the habits and attitudes of his pioneering forebears. For he is only two or three generations removed from the time when his present sophisticated town, with its art association and musical society, its airfield and country club, was a raw frontier village—and it is not altogether unlikely that because of his awareness of how much has been accomplished in the past, he is better prepared to meet whatever the future might hold.

EDWARD G. ZELINSKY

*Colorful and loud, the local band of costumed youngsters paraded through town in a circus wagon in the 1890's offering music and driven by a bearded Uncle Sam.*

BERT KELLOGG

*Homesteaders of the 1890's, settlers like these prized their ownership of land, farmed their clearing in the woods, packed produce to and from distant ports.*

# The Last Frontier in a Dark Forest

—

## *Forks, Washington*

—

### BY WILLIAM O. DOUGLAS

Forks, Washington (population 1,155) was, until the 1930's, the prisoner of forests so dense and so filled with fallen logs as to be almost impenetrable by men who had only axes and saws as their levelers. This region, now known as the Olympic Peninsula, is famous for its rain forests. They receive 140 inches of rain a year and drip water day after day. Their understories never know direct sunshine. The trees are mostly western hemlock, Sitka spruce, and Douglas fir; but red alder and big-leaf maple occasionally dominate forest communities. The floor litter is damp and filled with all the wonders of mushrooms, mos-ses, and lichens. Down-logs, covered with moss, are seed-beds for seedlings that will in time send their roots down and around the nurse log and consume it. On bright days the rain forests are filled with a soft emerald light. When the rains start, there is no dry spot and man is soon soaked to the skin.

The rivers of the Peninsula—including the Bogachiel and Calawah at whose junction Forks lies—were ample to float logs; but the Hoh and Quillayute, the main arteries leading to the ocean, had no ports at their mouths. So while other portions of the Pacific Northwest heard the

176

singing of saws well before 1850, the region of Forks, Washington was largely isolated and underdeveloped until shortly before World War II.

While the advent of industrialization made ghosts of some towns, it created Forks. Only the arrival of roads and trucks and the change in logging techniques which they entailed brought Forks to the front. Prior to then it was a lonely frontier town with few facilities; it was isolated, remote, and stagnant. All that has changed. But many old characteristics remain. The original Forks had warm-hearted God-fearing people; self-help was the norm; good neighborliness brought everyone together in an emergency. A recent episode eloquently illustrates that community co-operation still flourishes. Moreover, Forks—settled by white people—was the historic area of the Quillayute, Ozette, and Makah Indian tribes. When the whites first explored these coasts, the races were pitted against each other in bloody conflicts. But their differences were largely resolved as a result of negotiations conducted by Isaac I. Stevens who in 1853 became the first governor of the newly created Washington Territory. Reservations were created for each of the three Indian tribes—Quillayutes, Ozettes, and Makahs; and each tribe acquired valuable treaty rights including the use of nets in the rivers. By the time settlers reached the interior of the West End, peace had settled over the area. Not once in its long history did racism lead to violence. White settlers and Reds lived peacefully together as they do today. While the Ozettes have died out, the Quillayutes and Makahs flourish.

The schools at Forks have long been integrated and no compulsion was required; 70 Quillayute school children now attend the Forks public schools. Fred Woodruff, head of the Quillayutes, and affectionately known as Woodie, is a member of the Forks school board; and Roy Black, another outstanding Quillayute, is janitor at the Forks High School. The new Forks perpetuates the best traditions of the old.

Fred Woodruff sets an example by which the peoples of all nations must in time live. Most of the Quillayutes are members of the Indian Shaker church, the institution that perpetuates the original Indian religion that teaches the existence of one Supreme Being dominating the spirit world. Fred Woodruff is a member of the Assembly of God, which has an active church at La Push headed by a young, outstanding Finn by the name of Esko Rentola who markets exquisite black and white line drawings as a hobby. Religious differences among men are to Fred Woodruff as irrelevant as racial differences; all men are in one circle of brotherhood, a circle which can be formed anywhere, any time, provided men understand one another.

"The moral" he says, "can be found in the history of the Quillayutes. To the north of us were the Makahs whose language we could not speak. To the south were the Chinooks. We could not speak their language either and neither they nor the Makahs could speak ours. That is why we were always fighting. But when we could talk to each other about our differences, peace settled over us."

One who searches can find in modern Forks the anatomy of peace the world over.

The story of Forks is the story of the West End, the farthest reach of the State of Washington—the land that lies between Lake Crescent on the east, Cape Flattery on the west, and the Hoh River on the south. This is a land that grows the biggest trees on this continent except for California's *sequoias.* It is sometimes referred to as the "long-log country," for here the Douglas fir grows 300 feet high and up to 15 feet or more in diameter. Sitka spruce and western hemlock have as great a girth and reach almost as high. The rain forests are prodigious producers of these gigantic trees. Trails are winding, tortuous affairs that search hard for ways around gargantuan debris.

Sawing through one huge log took two young and strong men one whole day. The felling of a tree was only the start. Once a tree was down, the arduous task began. It took months to turn cedar and fir by hand into rough lumber for farm buildings, and more months to clear the land of stumps. Stumps twelve feet or more in width were burned. One augur hole was drilled as a flue, another below it as a firebox. Cedar bark was used as fuel to start with; then as the burned-out area enlarged, other fuel was added until the stump could be pulled out, root by root, with oxen or horses.

Sometimes an entire tree was felled by burning rather than cutting. The procedure of drilling augur holes was also used then; and the burning continued until the massive tree stood on such a slender stem it fell or could be pushed down. It took weeks to burn one tree and months or even years to make a small clearing known as a "chipmunk" farm.

"We got tired of doing it the slow way," John Fletcher, veteran of the Hoh says. "At times we took kerosene torches and started forest fires to level the wilderness."

Burning forests was indeed an ancient practice. The West End has a half-dozen or more prairies created by burning. The Indians burned to create meadows which in turn would attract game. They burned the prairies annually in the fall to keep the brush down. The Forks, Quillayute, and Ozette Prairies were the largest. White settlers burned forests not only to open up land for farming but also to encourage the growth of berries.

In the year 1592, a Greek, Apostolos Valenanos, who served in the Spanish Navy under the name of Juan de Fuca, claimed to have found the Strait that bears his name; but no formal possession of the Olympic Peninsula was taken for Spain until 1775. Spain in 1792 built at Neah Bay the first white settlement in the State of Washington but the settlers stayed only one summer. Moreover, the

British and Americans were close on their heels; and Spain finally relinquished her claims in 1819.

Captain George Vancouver in 1792 wrote eloquently of the land he saw from the sloop-of-war, *Discovery,* as he entered the Straits and named peaks of the Cascades that loomed against the eastern sky for officers of the British Admiralty. Captain Robert Gray, the American fur trader, had preceded him in the *Columbia* in 1789. But none of the Spanish, British, or Americans who first came this way penetrated the interior.

The first white men into the West End were probably agents of the Hudson Bay Company who landed at Pysht in 1850, traversing the area and collecting large amounts of furs. One, Peter Fisher, settled in the West End in 1860 and trapped and hunted there for twenty years. The first to settle as farmers in the interior at Forks were Ely Peterson and Ole Nelson. They arrived in 1874 and laid claim to part of the Forks Prairie as a homestead. Luther and Esther Ford, who arrived in 1878, did the same.

Though there were some Indian trails from the coast to the interior, the earliest settlers often came by sailing canoes from Seattle, landing at La Push and working their way inland up one of the waterways. In time, the settlers cut additional trails, foot and horse passage over some of the huge down-logs being arranged by piling logs and brush on either side. Later, puncheon (corduroy) roads were built, settlers often paying their "poll" tax (which in the 1880's and 1890's was $2.00 per man) by working on them. Before those links were made with the outside world, cattle were driven to market along the beach to Neah Bay and then east. Later, trails were made to drive both cattle and turkeys to market. Once a family on the Hoh drove 200 turkeys over 40 miles along a dark colonnade of a trail without losing a single one. It took days to drive turkeys that distance, and weeks to drive cattle across the West End by trail. The venture with both turkeys and cattle was a hazardous one, for this is cougar country; camps had to be made at night and raiding by cougars was notorious. It was so common that Mrs. Nance Anderson recalls walking furtively to school through a dense forest thinking that perhaps, if she threw her lunch away, the cougars might be less apt to attack her. At an Old Timer's picnic one will hear a legend about a cougar eating a ten-year-old boy, overalls and all. It, however, is unverified. Seldom if ever did cougars attack people in the West End. But they were a menace to man's livelihood that as the years passed depended more and more on cattle.

While today only 4 per cent of the West End and only 6 per cent of the people are engaged in farming, it was the prime concern of the settlers. By national standards the soil is "fair," not "excellent." Almost any crop will grow, the season being 180 days long and the weather mild. Before the turn of the century, hops were raised in abundance. But they could be sent to market only by ship. They were carted to the mouth of the Quillayute or floated down, then loaded on scows launched in a heavy surf, and rowed to a ship anchored off shore. The cargo losses were so great that hop growing was discontinued by the turn of the century when cattle became the leading agricultural article. A cattle buyer (Harvey Liesure in the early days) was the regular outlet for beef.

Before the advent of roads, records were set by men packing supplies into their homesteads. From the Hoh River to Forks it was a distance of 42 miles; and the trail was not passable by horses. For nearly twenty years men packed in their supplies on their backs. A six months' supply meant nine or ten barrels of flour, several hundred pounds of sugar, 100 pounds or more of coffee, 200 pounds of salt, many yards of cloth, dozens of cases of canned vegetables, 25 pounds of chewing tobacco and as much smoking tobacco. Charles Lewis walked the 42 miles to market in one day and walked back the next with a 67-pound pack. That was customary, not unusual; and many trips were made in the fair-weather months to bring in the six months' supply for winter. The record packing was by John Huelsdonk who homesteaded on the Hoh with his wife Dora in the 1890's, raising four daughters in the rain forests; and many Huelsdonks still live there, including three married daughters—Mrs. Marie Lewis, Mrs. Elizabeth Fletcher, and Mrs. Dora Richmond —who have their father's sturdiness and independence. John was known as the Iron Man of the Hoh. He packed in food for his family; and when lumbering started, he packed in food for the camps. A man carrying 80 pounds got regular rates; one carrying twice that weight got two men's pay. John Huelsdonk did the latter. His feats have some of the flavor of a Paul Bunyan tale. Once he packed a cook stove 42 miles into the Hoh, a long camp stove with legs about 18 inches high. He encountered a friend who asked him how it was. "It isn't so bad," said John Huelsdonk, "except for the sack of flour in the oven that keeps shifting around and unsettling the load."

Mail came to Forks either by trail from Pysht, Sekui, or Ozette and from Neah Bay to La Push *via* the beach. Ben Oium who brought it for years from Ozette usually traveled by horseback every Monday and Friday. Wesley Smith carried the mail from Neah Bay to La Push on foot down the beach. He carried an ocarina with him and with its music he could get the seals to follow him. Once he had an encounter with a bear; and when he retrieved the mail sack, the animal's teeth marks appeared on some of the letters. Parcel-post packages were limited to four pounds. Ben Oium tells of one man who ordered shoes and got them in two packages several weeks apart.

Martin Konapaski, an enterprising Pole who settled at Beaver, twenty miles from Forks, ran pack trains over the mountains from Clallam Bay to Beaver to Forks—two cents a pound to Beaver, three cents to Forks. When a puncheon road was built, he hauled commercially by an ox team; and that ox team continued in operation until 1925. Some supplies were brought from Seattle by boat. Ernest Fletcher of the Hoh country had a launch which he brought, loaded with "everything from baled hay to buttons," to the mouth of the Hoh. There the people came with pack boards or pack horses to purchase provisions. Other boats besides Fletcher's brought provisions but they made infrequent voyages and some were lost in the treacherous waters of the Pacific where tides run high and fast, headlands mark rocky shoals, and a string of nearshore islands makes navigation difficult and dangerous.

From Forks, in the early years, butter and cheese were back-packed to markets in Pysht or Port Townsend. So was cream. Mrs. Albin Wahlgren and Mrs. Oliver King recall how the cash proceeds from these back-packing trips sent some children of the settlers through school at Bellingham or Seattle. Barter in these early days was common, as cash was scarce. Some of the liveliest bartering took place between the Indians and the white settlers. The Indians

hunted and traded furs, hides, and fish for blankets and utensils at trading posts along the Straits of Juan de Fuca or at La Push. White settlers had an abundance of cabbages, potatoes and other vegetables; and so they traded them for articles the Indians had. This systematic commerce between Indians and settlers was one reason for amicable relations along this, our latest frontier. The other was that the settlers were few in number; they occupied the prairies or chopped out clearings up the rivers to make their "chipmunk" farms, while the Indians were coastal residents. Moreover, an Indian Agency was established at Neah Bay in 1865 and the Indians from that date on obtained vocal spokesmen for their complaints.

The Federal Government was a unifying force in the West End in other ways. It built a telegraph line from Neah Bay to Clallam Bay. In 1908 the Peninsula Telephone Company built a line from Clallam Bay to Mora, *via* Forks. It ran at a loss from the very beginning, the line blowing down in 1921. But between then and 1930 the line

BERT KELLOGG

*A beachhead on the Pacific, the supply base at La Push brought in goods essential to the inland community. Run by Indians, it encouraged Indian-white accord.*

*An American Gothic of 1905, a son and his mother with an ox team and a sled of
hay were characteristic of the sturdy family settlers in pre-logging days.*

was temporarily restored by the forest service and the lumber companies. Thanks to them the telephone line was a link with the outside world; and in 1930 Boyd Schlaefer acquired all its stock and put the company on a paying basis.

There was no doctor in Forks until 1925 when Dr. E. W. Myers, still in residence, settled there. Dr. Myers, short, slight, and wiry, finished medical school in 1905, practiced briefly in the Midwest and then went with his wife to Sierra Leone, West Africa, as a medical missionary for the Seventh Day Adventist Church. On his return to this country, he headed for the Pacific Northwest looking for a town that had no doctor. He stopped at Vancouver and Mt. Vernon, but found other doctors there. Soon he heard of Forks, and to his delight discovered that it had no doctor and that it needed one badly. So he and his wife moved there, where they have remained to this day. Mrs. Myers, a talented trained nurse, shared the burden of medical practice with her husband. They converted their home into a small hospital, having met the state's require-

ments, and ran it until the present small Forks hospital was built after World War II. Mrs. Grace Fletcher, who arrived in 1909 as a temporary schoolteacher (but who married and never left), tells how a doctor was summoned prior to the arrival of Dr. Myers. A call over the noisy line to Clallam Bay resulted in a telegram being sent to Neah Bay. Within twenty-four hours the doctor from the Indian Agency arrived in Forks on horseback.

"We sent for him only in emergencies," Mrs. Fletcher states. "And as near as I can recall, no life was ever lost because the doctor did not arrive in time."

If a house burned, neighbors had a "house raising bee" and helped build a new one. Road building was a community affair. Every Fourth of July a barrel was put into the Calawah River at a point about 15 miles above the point on the outskirts of Forks where Route 101 crosses the river. Bets were made as to the time it would take in hours, minutes, or seconds for the barrel to reach the bridge. Tickets, on which the contestant wrote the estimated time, could be purchased for $1.00; and one could purchase as many as he desired, writing a different time on each one. The lottery flourished for years until someone got away with the large deposits.

Social occasions in the West End were rare. One social center for men was the huge, round stove in the country store, where the crackle of tobacco juice against hot iron punctuated gossip and discourse on news of the world. Before the turn of the century, when hops were still grown at Forks, a huge barnlike hop house was used for dances on Saturday night. A fiddle, guitar, and accordion supplied the music; and the dancing continued until dawn. Twenty miles away at Beaver there was Saturday-night competition. Konapaski put on dances on the second floor of a large store he owned; and to enliven things he brought in five-gallon casks of whiskey by pack horse or oxen team. While the Beaver dances also continued until dawn, they were not, according to Mrs. Albin Wahlgren, President of the Old Timers Society, "too uproarish." A wandering minstrel occasionally showed up and would perform for a fee. But contacts with the outside world were very few.

Missionaries seldom penetrated the West End. There was no regular minister in Forks until 1902. The Reverend Rufus Fletcher came there in 1885 for his health and ministered part time to the people. But he soon left for Seattle, only to return and organize the first church (Congregational) at Forks. He built a church for the congregation in 1903. Konapaski at Beaver was a Catholic with a large family. There was no place of worship for them nor any priest to administer to their needs. Every spring he bundled them all in a wagon, traveled the puncheon and graveled road to Lake Crescent, traversed that lake in a side-wheel gasoline-propelled ferry, and went on to Port Angeles. He kept the family there several weeks, attending Easter Masses and catching up with confessions.

The early settlers in the West End were ravenous for land. They did not think in terms of "timber rights," as lumbering had hardly started. They thought of homesteads in terms of farming and homes. Many were Norwegians, Swedes, and Finns. Ole Boe, whose girl, Brit, waited twelve years for him in Norway and finally, in 1894, came out to Ozette and married him, wrote of the development of the Norwegian and Swedish community there. They even had a church at Ozette before Grover Cleveland was President and a young Norwegian minister to occupy the pulpit.

"Those countries were crowded even then," Ben Oium recalls. "You can't imagine what the prospect of owning 160 acres meant to a Swede in the Old Country. Land ownership was a passion with them."

John Fletcher paints a picture of deeper perspective. "Why did our people push west across the Appalachia?" he asks. "They were restless. Why did they cross Ohio, the Missouri, the Great Plains, the Cascades, Puget Sound?" Pausing for emphasis he adds, "Restless people. Restless people." And then he asks, "Restless people. Did they not make America?"

By the 1890's some settlers had their eyes on "timber rights." But when President Cleveland caused the Olympic National Forest to be set aside, word spread that the woods would be locked up and "timber rights" would become valueless. Ole Boe wrote in his memoirs, "It is like after the black death in Norway in 1300 when there remained only an isolated human here and there after the pestilence." Most of the early settlers evacuated the Ozette area. Later McKinley opened National Forest lands for settlement. Then, as Ole Boe recorded, a "different sort" of person came to the West End. "They did not come to till the soil and build homes, no—just to keep the land until it was proved up, then sell it out to the timber companies."

Down on the Hoh they tell somewhat the same story. Some homesteaders were only agents of the lumber companies. Many were indeed on their payrolls, tilling enough land and growing enough produce to satisfy the homestead laws. A homestead, once proved up and patented, was transferred to the lumber interests.

There were logging camps at Discovery Bay and Dungeness in 1860; and one was established at Crescent Bay in 1870. The rough, unfinished lumber found a large export market in Australia and New Zealand. Clipper ships came down the Straits, where tides run strong, to pick up their overseas cargoes. And the coast towns prospered until the importing countries put prohibitive tariffs on the lumber. In 1889 a factory was established in the West End to reduce hemlock bark for tanning, an industry that had flourished for years in New England. But new chemicals soon displaced it; and no logging or lumber-products industry was established inside the West End until pretty close to World War I, when spruce came into great demand for airplane construction. The Federal Government built a railroad from Port Angeles, along the northern edge of Lake Crescent, and on to Lake Pleasant about ten miles from Forks. It sent out so-called "falling experts." People in the West End still talk about them. They were supposed to mark selected spruce with an "X" cut in the bark. But not knowing the difference between the species, they soon marked hundreds of fine straight hemlock instead. The road actually was not finished until after World War I; and little spruce from the West End reached the war plants. Some, however, did. Nance Anderson and Ernest Fletcher went to work cutting it on the Hoh. A tree once down was trimmed of boughs and dragged on skids to the river where it was floated down to the ocean. There the huge logs were loaded on scows and towed to Seattle or Port Angeles. Thus some West End spruce, but precious little of it, got into war production.

*Dwarfed by a huge spruce, two husky loggers at either end of their cut in the early 1920's symbolized the supremacy of manpower over forest that changed the Forks economy.*

After World War I, logging penetrated the West End more and more, the most active company being Bloedel, Donovan (later succeeded by Rayonier). A railroad was built from Quillayute to Sekiu (and it still operates). Logging camps were established in the interior after lumber cruisers had made a count of the type, quality, and size of the timber. Those timber cruisers were a hardy lot, carrying packs of forty to seventy-five pounds in waterproof, heavy-duty canvas. They traveled in groups of four or more. A cook went along; one gun was in every unit so that game "for the pot" could be obtained. These cruisers worked for weeks on end in rain-soaked forests, climbing over huge down-logs. They wormed their way through stands of the thick salal bush that become almost impenetrable; they were scratched and clawed by the sharp thorns of the ever-present devil's-club; they were wet through by night and by day. One timber cruiser who wrote history in the West End was Edward R. Murrow, famous journalist and broadcaster. Ed Murrow had spent one year (1925–1926) between high school and college working as axman and then as head chainman for a survey team of Bloedel,

Donovan doing topographic mapping and locating logging railroads in the West End. Each summer during four years of college he worked as timber cruiser, finally becoming a compassman. "I still regard" he says, "as one of my major accomplishments the ability to pace a mile through rough country, blow-down, devil's-club, and vine maple, and hit a section corner within 50 feet."

In the early days logs were felled by axes and two-man cross-cut saws. The girth of the trees at times made it necessary to weld two cross-cut saws together. Skid roads of logs were made and teams of twelve or more oxen (or horses) dragged the Paul Bunyan logs to loading stations. Three-hundred-foot trees were topped and converted into spars to which cables were attached; and winches, operated by donkey engines, were used in the lifting of logs first to wagons and later to freight cars. The history of logging operations from then to now is a book in itself, for many technological improvements were made. The ox and the horse were displaced by machinery. While the lumber cruiser still exists, he has been largely displaced by

BERT KELLOGG

*A joint enterprise and a family outing, farmers and lumbermen posed with a log ridden by women and children and dragged by a farm team on a skid road.*

the aerial photographer. The locomotives alone made up a distinguished array.

In the late 1930's paved roads were built; and these black surfaced roads marked a change in logging techniques that helped transform Forks from a remote village to a bustling, modern community. The logging truck appeared; most of the rails were pulled up; huge trailer trucks brought the gigantic trees to market.

The transformation in logging techniques had several parallel developments. Prior to World War II, the lumber interests in the West End had different attitudes than they have today. Then they commonly cut an area clean and left it, ravished and denuded.

In the beginning, as Hult says in *The Untamed Olympics,* logging methods were"relatively gentle."

"Line horses side-stepped small trees . . . Taking only the best of the Douglas fir forests, loggers usually left seed trees behind; or, even where they denuded long stretches of land, their operations lay in low river valleys where seeds drifted down from the forested hills above to start a new crop growing on the land.

"Then came high-lead logging, together with the 'high-ball' or speed-up. Cables from high overhead spar trees yanked huge logs so roughly and rapidly from the woods that they came out like battering rams, knocking everything down before them. Not a stick of green timber was left standing; and when the logging crews moved on, the debris was many feet thick upon the ground . . .

"The 1930's—that low ebb for everything in the timber industry—saw the worst of the unlimited clear-cut logging. And as loggers left behind them mute, ugly hillsides crisscrossed with the waste of these once beautiful forests, conservationists rose up to point accusing fingers and demand that something be done."

By World War II the lumber companies planned differently. The cut-and-run tactics were largely abandoned. With the advent of professional foresters in private companies, owners became convinced they could grow trees on land which had grown trees before—and make it pay. Private holdings were consolidated, disciplined tree farms established, contracts with state and federal forestry units were made for selective cutting. In short, plans were made for the forest products company to become a permanent (and therefore a more responsible) member of the community. Today, three large companies, Crown Zellerbach, Rayonier, and Merrill & Ring have several hundred thousand acres of Clallam County forest lands in tree farms.

In the early days the plight of the lumberjack was severe. He was recruited from skid-row employment agencies in Seattle and shipped to the West End for low wages and to miserable working conditions. He carried his own bedroll and slept in three-tiered, hard, round metal beds. He paid high prices for miserable food. While some companies brought large herds of beef cattle into the country for logging-camp tables, loggers' complaints piled high. The story was that the tired, old, tough oxen that used to haul logs were eventually butchered and fed to the loggers. "The meat is so tough you can't stick a fork in the gravy," was a common saying. The old time West End logger was virtually locked into a logging camp (or company town) for months on end with no reading room or other recreational facilities. The first to espouse his cause were the IWW's (International Workers of the World) commonly known as "the wobblies." They were active in the Pacific Northwest; they had a hall in Port Angeles; but they did not deeply penetrate the West End. They were neither anarchists nor Communists. Their tactics were, however, often violent. They drove spikes into logs to ruin saws; they showed their dislike for World War I by insulting soldiers and sailors on the streets of Port Angeles. The tactics of the government and of the vigilantes who opposed the IWW's were also violent. Some were forcibly loaded onto a passenger steamer in Port Angeles and "exported." But their advocacy in time worked wonders. Logging-camp conditions greatly improved. The variety and quality of the food on the tables today are evidence enough. The wage scale, too, has vastly improved; the lowest paid logger in the West End getting $2.505 an hour. By reason of the "crummy wagon" (bus) that hauls men thirty or more miles to work, home life is possible for many.

The loggers of the 1910's and 1920's, who were mostly Swedes, Norwegians, and Finns, wore stagged pants, a small round hat, galluses, a colorful shirt outside heavy blanket-like trousers, and shoes with one-half-inch calks. Forks never had a saloon; but there were some in the West End where lumberjacks under the influence of liquor delighted in tearing out an entire floor board by driving the calks in deep and making a quick twist with the foot. After pay day many of them would pour into the nearest town and spend all their money on drink and cards. Not all of them, for men like Huelsdonk of the Hoh sent four daughters to school in Seattle on lumberjack's wages. But dissipation of wages through liquor and gambling was common.

J. M. Goodwin of Sappho (named for the heroine of Daudet's novel *Sapho,* but spelled differently), who has run a beer and card parlor for a quarter century, has been witness to most of the excesses of the loggers. Thousands of dollars went the way of beer on Saturday night.

"After three beers, every logger wanted to wrestle me," Goodwin says. "Sometimes they preferred to fight. But I soon got too old for athletics."

Those days are passing, for the logger himself is changing. The old-time swaggering, hard-drinking, quarrelsome logger is being replaced. Young men just out of high school or college are taking his place, living at home, husbanding their earnings.

*A going concern, this hophouse near Forks in 1900 dried a fresh harvest (in bins) on second-story nets and shipped bales like that in the foreground to Seattle brewers.*

"Some of the professionalism of the logger is also disappearing," an executive says. "The old-timer was very strong physically, having come to manhood through hard physical labor. Today's worker is softer. Moreover, he doesn't have the same interest in the woods—that animal-like love for them that the old-timer showed. Today's worker is more interested in the pay check than in the work."

Ed Murrow puts somewhat the same idea into different words. Explaining the abiding affection he developed for the Swedes, Norwegians, and Finns of the West End, he says it was because "they worked, played, and fought hard and were experts at their jobs."

Today people of the West End say that the woods are growing faster than they are being cut. In a limited sense there is truth in the statement. The first trees cut were four or five hundred years old. They produced fabulous spars for sailing ships and fabulous boards for building purposes. But with technological advances, timber uses have greatly changed. Today about 50 per cent of the timber logged in the West End on private lands goes into cellulose, pulp, and allied forms, though the vast proportion of trees cut in the Olympic National Forest is for lumber and plywood. Today a whole tree—branches and twigs as well as trunk—is usable for chemical purposes and is considered mature when it is fifty years old. Government-owned forestry land far exceeds lumber-company-owned land, the average annual cut on federal land being about 300 million board feet. Both are important contributors to the forestry industry.

In Hult, *The Untamed Olympics,* it is said that the fleet of logging trucks based at Forks is "the largest in the state" of Washington. "Loggers in tin helmets (to keep off 'widowmakers'—falling branches) stride about, striking sparks from the pavement with their caulked boots." While it is "a lusty place, with a real logging-town flavor," it also experiences tourism in increasingly large dimensions. Forestry is still the mainstay of the West End with fishing and tourism next.

Forks was only a village with no more than a dozen homes, three stores, and two hotels well into the 1920's. The roads of the West End were dirt, many of them puncheon. People crossed Lake Crescent by ferry on one of two side-wheelers, named *Storm King* and *Marjorie,* and were met by a Stanley Steamer, the stage that carried

*Isolated in a clearing, one-room schoolhouses like this in 1900 served neighboring farms before transportation and roads made a central school possible in Forks.*

them beyond the lake. The boats operated until 1922 when a road was built along Lake Crescent's south shore. The first automobile in Forks was the Metz, soon displaced by the Model-T Ford. By the late 1920's roads were numerous; but they were still difficult of passage.

Until the Olympic National Park was established in 1938, tourism was pratically nil. The ocean, of course, attracted salmon fishermen; and many penetrated the vastness of the Hoh and Quillayute for the steelhead trout. But in the totality they were not numerous. Before World War I, a resort was built at Mora near the mouth of the Quillayute, now the site of a large National Park camp grounds, primarily for fishermen. But fire destroyed it in 1916 and no trace of it remains. Another resort had been built at Sol Duc Hot Springs by a lumberman, Michael Earles. Mineral waters made it "the best spa in the Pacific Northwest," though experience showed that the waters lost their good qualities when bottled. Earles built a four-storied hotel there and a three-storied sanitarium, spending half a million dollars on the project. His brother, a doctor, ran the sanitarium and the undertaking showed promise. But it, too, was entirely destroyed by fire in 1916.

As a result of the Mora and Sol Duc disasters, some of the West End knew once more the silence of the forests, received few of the profits of tourism, and experienced little of its inconveniences. Yet the Lake Crescent area did a fine tourist business even then. East Beach, Log Cabin, Piedmont, Sunger's Tavern, Qui Si Sana, Ovington's, Rosemary, and Storm King attracted many tourists who came by launch or ferry and remained for longer periods than is customary today. And when the Park Service was created, tourism grew by leaps and bounds.

There was much sentiment in favor of the Park, the Chamber of Commerce of Port Angeles being an active promoter of it. The lumber companies, however, created powerful propaganda against it. Opposition was directed at its size and at the inclusion of certain areas. Franklin D. Roosevelt came to Lake Crescent, conferred with the leading federal and local officials, and obtained a consensus for a large rather than a small park. William D. Welsh of the Port Angeles *Evening News* wrote of that meeting, "You can bet your shirt, your marbles, your oiuja board, and your father-in-law's store teeth that there will be a major park on the Peninsula." The Park as originally created included 680,000 acres with a proviso authorizing the President to expand the area to 892,000 acres. In 1940, Roosevelt did enlarge it by 187,411 acres, including areas on the Hoh and Bogachiel and along the coast that brought a storm of protests.

The lumber companies were not alone in their opposition. Those who had homesteaded, as Lars K. Ahlstrom did in the Ozette area, denounced the absorption of their homes into the Park. Ahlstrom was compensated for his property; but he ignored the superior claim of the Federal Government and continued to live on his homestead until his death. Those on the Hoh were more vociferous and aggressive; and there are, indeed, sparks of that opposition left today. John Huelsdonk led the Hoh protest. He went to Olympia, the state capital, carrying a placard, "Stalin took Finland, and Hitler took Czechoslovakia. Don't let it happen here, too."

The Park (which encompasses the central core of the Olympic Mountains including the famous rain forests and a three-mile coastal belt some miles to the west) becomes more and more popular with the passing years. It preserves an elk herd, once in jeopardy but now totaling about 6,000 head. It also preserves a sanctuary of unique natural wonders, letting each succeeding generation see the magnitude of the trees and the density of the forests, and thus understand the skill and fortitude of the men and women who first established homes there. The people of Forks are proud of this tradition and of the manner in which the Park perpetuates it. Already the Park has spent nearly fourteen million dollars in roads, trails, camp grounds, picnic areas, water systems, sewer systems, buildings, etc. Moreover, the annual payroll of the Park is not a small item in the economy of the West End. The Park is also tourism;

BERT KELLOGG

*A weekly newspaper, serving scattered farms, operated out of this frame house from 1897 to 1905. It had also been a print shop before this 1910 picture.*

and tourism is an increasing factor in the livelihood of the people. Tourism means people who come in cars and trailers to camp in the environs of the Park. It means hikers and pack trains that follow the trails to the high basins. Tourism includes the hundreds who come by car or put down in small planes at the Forks airport, to fish for salmon in the ocean, to follow the cutthroat trout up the streams in the summer or the steelhead in the winter. Tourism means automobiles and motels, roadside stands and picnic areas.

Tourism brought more than two million people to the Park in 1962, and is not now lower than fourth place in the economy of the West End and probably closer to second. While it has lifted the standard of living appreciably, it still has a seasonal impact that makes for difficult adjustment. A period of feverish activity, as in the summer, is followed by a letdown; some must make a few months' earnings cover twelve months of living. Water must be drawn, wood hewed, and groceries bought even after the tourists have left. After the tourists, fishermen, and elk hunters have left, after the clam diggers and the driftwood and Japanese glass fish float ball gatherers have gone home, "Somebody's gotta hoe the corn," as one old logger puts it. That is why William D. Welsh calls the forest industry "the all-year-around soupbone" of the West End.

The growth in the economy of the West End is illustrated by electric power. In 1941, the private utility that served Forks had 267 customers. In 1944, a public power authority (PUD), distributing power from Bonneville Dam on the Columbia, acquired that distribution system and greatly expanded it to cover the entire West End. In 1963, it had over 6,000 electric customers. One cent per kilowatt is the basic rate; and of 5,340 residential users over half were "all electric," using the current for heating and cooking as well as for lighting. This growth has been so phenomenal that the PUD serving the area reached in 1963 the goals which the Bonneville Authority had set for 1972.

Ernest Fletcher was talking about the difference between today and sixty or more years ago when Forks was a frontier town, locked in a deep forest. It is now only five hours by car to Seattle, when once it was two long days by horseback to Port Angeles, fifty-eight miles from Forks. Travel is now quick and cheap; restaurants and motels are excellent; hospital and medical services are at hand; all the comforts of modern life have reached Forks. Ernest Fletcher mentioned these things in contrast to the arduous backpacking of the old days, the lack of luxury items, the scarcity of the comforts of life.

"But life in the old days was not so dangerous as it is today," he says. "Nowadays, look at the highway deaths and injuries. I can't think of any serious harm coming to any backpacker in the old days."

Highways, automobiles, and a more mobile population have affected Forks in collateral ways as they have other communities. A group was discussing the matter at a recent Old Timers Picnic.

"Up to five years ago," Mrs. Albin Wahlgren says, "no one had to lock their doors. We never did lock them. Nowadays there is thievery." Vandalism, almost unheard of prior to the 1960's, is rampant. The feeling of respect for property that dominated the old days has more and more disappeared. Neighbors do not plunder one another now any more than they did before; but speeding cars bring in lawless elements and take them out before their vandalism is disclosed.

The growth in population has caused the loss of some of the "togetherness" that once dominated the West End. The feeling of dependence on each other, prominent in the frontier community, has been gradually displaced by dependence on the services now available. Moreover, people nowadays do not move in as intimate circles as they once did. Back in the early 1930's when the telephone company had less than 300 subscribers, a person putting in a call would tell the operator "Get me John Fletcher." In 1935 the telephone company had to educate its subscribers to give the operator the number being called, rather than the name.

Another element of separateness has entered the scene. The treaty rights accorded the Indians in the last century are the source of some friction between the races and cause conservationists concern. The Indians can and do place nets at the mouth of the Quillayute River that from September to March capture most fish ascending the stream for spawning. This is the Indian's right; it is also ruination for others because fishing upstream is depleted. A law was passed by Congress banning interstate transportation by common carrier of steelhead that were netted. But the law was evaded by Indians using their own trucks to take the steelhead to market. Nowadays the talk in the West End is for condemnation of those treaty rights, the Indians being compensated for the taking.

The Indians of the West End are today *rentiers*. They seldom engage in business, but instead are landlords who rent reservation property to the whites. Thus at La Push the fleet of boats that puts out for salmon and tuna pays wharfage to the Indians. And a white who lives there or does business there must likewise rent from the Indians. Unequal treatment when it comes to liquor has been ended and Indians, though peculiarly susceptible to alcohol, can purchase it at the state liquor stores on the same footing as the whites.

In the old days people mingled with Indians and whites without compunction. Today a class line sometimes enters. A few—very few, it is true—accuse a person who consorts with Indians of being a "Communist." Forks has a small corps of "vigilantes" who on occasion try to fill the role of Hitler's storm troopers. But these are in the minority in Forks, as they are in America. The people of Forks—warmhearted, tolerant, and friendly—have inherited the tradi-

*Forks in 1916 was a crude village in the wilderness with a garage, hotel, and stores. Visited by loggers and farmers, it was the home of only a few families.*

tions of the frontier; and those traditions are still lively influences in their lives. The recent episode that eloquently illustrates their continued presence in the community is the forest fire that swept part of the West End on September 20, and 21, 1951, and almost wiped out the town of Forks.

The fire, a historic one that burned over 100 million board feet of lumber, started from embers of a small fire that a lumber company had thought was extinguished. A fresh northwest wind whipped the embers into a roaring crown fire that traveled over 30 miles an hour and whose scars are visible today from the main street of Forks.

Mrs. Elizabeth Klahn, one of the three telephone operators at Forks, was up that morning at two o'clock because her husband was on the "hoot owl" shift (3:00 A.M.–11:00 A.M.) of the lumber company. She says that "It was dark and stuffy that morning." By sunrise the sky was filled with smoke and soon the wire services would carry the story to the nation. By mid morning the state police ordered Forks evacuated. The three telephone operators called all city and rural subscribers to break the news. Farmers turned all their stock loose and opened all gates so that the animals could run ahead of the fire. Some people loaded their prized personal possessions in cars and trucks and headed east to safety, Route 101 being open. Others fled to La Push and prepared to evacuate by boat if necessary. One colorful citizen dug a deep hole in his back yard, burying in it his refrigerator (filled with food), his kitchen stove, and his washing machine.

The state police recruited fire fighters, and two hundred men fought the roaring blaze. Bulldozers kept ahead of it, clearing land and trying to make a "fire brake" that the flames could not jump. But that did little good; the fire cleared every barrier, moving closer and closer to Forks.

The three telephone operators—Elizabeth Klahn, Minnetta Edwards, and Velma Langfelt—were ordered to evacuate, but they refused. They took all incoming calls and informed worried distant relatives of local residents and the press what the state of affairs in Forks was. The fire soon burned the poles carrying the electric power lines; so the town had no electricity. The phones had to be rung by hand, which meant that two of the three operators took turns answering calls while the third rang the phones. Maury Hull, owner of the telephone system, set up in his office a coffee, doughnut, and first-aid station to which fire fighters could come. One doctor, who during the years he served there had become known for the fees he extracted from the people rather than for the service rendered them, quit the town even ahead of the evacuees and did not return until things were safe; another, Dr. E. W. Myers, in the best of the medical tradition, stayed to administer to those needing help.

The fire kept galloping closer and closer to the town of Forks. It entered the town, consuming twelve houses; and on the second day it came within a block of the telephone office. The state police again ordered the three telephone operators to evacuate. They refused as the switchboards were still ablaze with lights. They—and Forks—were saved providentially. The wind changed from northeast to southwest, and the fire fighters finally were able to make "fire brakes" that worked.

While twelve homes were burned, no one was killed and no livestock was lost. In a few days the evacuees returned, some to find their homes in ashes.

"The entire town went to work, helping them build new homes," Elizabeth Klahn says. "House raising bees were indeed organized and the homeless were built new homes."

The spirit of the old Forks was rekindled by the emergency. The three undecorated telephone operators—the heroines of the 1951 fire—seemed to be reincarnations of the first settlers. They served beyond the line of duty and put the needs of their fellow men ahead of their own convenience and safety. Thus does the spirit of the Forks of the frontier survive in a modern town.

BERT KELLOGG

*A modern town with a frontier heritage, Forks today is a springboard*
*for tourists visiting the forest, a base for lumber companies, a*
*co-operative community of well-acquainted residents.*

# Notes on the Authors

Hodding Carter, the Pulitzer-Prize-winning editor and publisher of the *Delta Democrat-Times* in Greenville, Mississippi, is the author of many books on the South, including *The Angry Scar* and *Southern Legacy*.

Thomas D. Clark is a Professor of History at the University of Kentucky, author of a history of the state, of *The Kentucky* in the Rivers of America Series, of *The Southern Country Editor*, and of *Frontier America*.

William O. Douglas, Associate Justice of the United States Supreme Court, is noted for his books and articles on the Northwest and on the world scene.

James Gray, journalist and critic for the St. Louis *Post-Dispatch* before teaching at the University of Minnesota, is the author of *The Illinois* in the Rivers of America Series and of several novels set in the Midwest.

A. B. Guthrie, Jr., reared in Choteau, Montana, about which he writes here, is the author of *The Big Sky* and *The Way West*, for which he won the Pulitzer Prize in 1950. He has also written other books and many articles concerning the region's life and history.

David Lavender, who grew up in Telluride, Colorado, the town he writes on in this book, wrote *Bent's Fort* about the fur-trading empire of the southern Rockies, *Westward Vision: The Story of the Oregon Trail*, and *The Fist in the Wilderness*.

W. Storrs Lee, once a resident of Middlebury, Vermont, is the author of several books on that state, including *The Green Mountains of Vermont*, and of many others on different regions, among them *The Sierra* and a forthcoming book on Hawaii.

Oscar Lewis, who makes his headquarters in San Francisco, has written many books on the West, including *The Big Four*, *The Town That Died Laughing*, *High Sierra Country*, *Fabulous San Simeon*, and *Silver Kings*.

Conrad Richter, who has written about rural life in many novels, won the Pulitzer Prize in 1951 for *The Town*, the National Book Award in 1961 for *The Waters of Kronos*, and has recently published *The Grandfathers*. He is a native and resident of Pine Grove, Pennsylvania, about which he writes in this book.

Winfield Townley Scott, a prize-winning American poet whose *Collected Poems* appeared in 1962 and whose most recent volume is *Change of Weather*, is now a resident of Santa Fe after many years in the Northeast as literary editor of *The Providence Journal*.

Wallace Stegner, who has written widely on natural resources and the West, is a prize-winning novelist and short-story writer and Professor of English at Stanford University. His latest book, *Wolf Willow*, is an evocation of a small town on the plains frontier.

John Edward Weems, who lives in Austin, Texas, is the author of *A Weekend in September*, the story of the Galveston floods; also of *Race for the Pole* and *The Face of the Maine*.

William E. Wilson, novelist and regional historian, has recently published the definitive history of New Harmony, Indiana, *The Angel and the Serpent*, the town about which he writes in this volume.